D1452373

THE YEAR THEY THREW
THE RASCALS OUT

THE YEAR THEY THREW THE RASCALS OUT

CHARLES DEATON

Shoal Creek Publishers, Inc.

Austin, Texas

Library of Congress Catalog Card No. 73-84553
I.S.B.N. 0-88319-013-3

Lithographed and bound in the United States of America
by Steck-Warlick, Austin, Texas

To Suzan,

and

to all those who helped throw the rascals out.
(Keep watching, for yours is a job that's never finished.)

ACKNOWLEDGMENTS

I would like to thank a number of individuals for help they gave me before and during the writing of this book.

A very big "thank-you" must go to the members of the working press in Texas, from the members of the Capitol Press Corps, whose names are widely known in Texas political circles, to the lesser-known reporters and newscasters for newspapers and radio and television stations all over the state. The job they do of recording utterances and chronicling events provides an invaluable tool to anyone writing about Texas politics. I would not even attempt to list them all here; I did try, however, to give credit in the book to reporters who wrote especially valuable articles. A special "thank-you," though, must go to Felton West, chief of the *Houston Post*'s Capitol Bureau, whose critical reading of the manuscript of this book provided some much needed suggestions for improvement. The *Houston Post* must be thanked, also, for granting permission to reprint lengthy excerpts from Lynn Ashby's columns of March 7 and May 17, 1972, and Henry Holcomb's article in the June 11, 1972, issue (all three pieces are Copyright 1972 The Houston Post).

Thanks must also go to a former colleague of mine at Del Mar College in Corpus Christi, Madelin Olds, for her encouragement when this book was only an idea. Del Mar College also provided a faculty research grant which helped defray the necessary traveling and research expenses.

A debt of gratitude is also owed to Dr. Joe Ericson, Chairman of the Department of Political Science at Stephen F. Austin State University, a memorable teacher whose gentle and knowledgeable guidance helped awaken and develop my interest in things political. To my parents must go the credit for my habit of looking for both sides of an issue before making judgments. At times it's an inconvenient (and infuriating) habit, but I have tried to exercise it in the political judgments I have made in this book.

I must also give thanks here to the hundreds of students from all over the state that I have taught in my classes. More than anything, they helped me realize that if the people only knew, they really would want to throw the rascals out.

A.J. Lerager, Margaret Davis and Helen Rugeley at Shoal Creek Publishers earned a note of thanks for their help in making the transition from a very rough manuscript into a book a relatively painless one.

And to my wife Suzan, of course, must go the biggest thanks of all, for putting up with all the inconveniences a writer's wife must face: the days, the nights, and the weekends when *the book* steals her husband away.

C.D.

CONTENTS

PART ONE:
THE YEAR OF FRANK SHARP

Chapter 1

ELECTION YEARS AND POLITICAL CHANGE

Texas election years rarely have specific beginning and ending dates. They are not at all like calendar years, which begin with football games, black-eyed peas, and hangovers, and end with parties, gifts, and Christmas trees. The election year never really begins and never really ends. Part of the problem is the calendar dates for such things as primaries, legislative sessions, and filing deadlines; another part of the problem is the reluctance and indecision on the part of some people faced with those calendar dates.

Most Texas politicians are elected to two-year terms of office. So, for example, a freshman representative travels to Austin in January of the odd-numbered calendar years, still drunk with the heady brew of victory over the devil himself, takes the oath of office, and thus subjects himself to about five months of the most tremendous pressures he has ever encountered. He emerges reeling from the strains of those unbelievable last two weeks of the session, and stumbles home to rest for awhile and wait for a call to a special session. He then finds himself later in the year trying to do his Christmas shopping at the same time he is trying to decide about a re-election race, for the deadline for getting his name on the ballot in his party's primary election is only a little over a month away from the carols of Christmas-time.

Once he disposes of the Christmas season and the filing deadline, he faces the familiar grind of campaigning, a never-ending series of meetings with supporters, prominent citizens, moneyed men, volunteer workers, civic groups, and friends and neighbors. He travels over his district day and night for weeks, wearing out shoe leather and automobile tires, shaking hands with the people and asking for their vote, weeks at a time, driving, shaking, meeting, shaking, driving, all the time wondering when (or if) he'll ever be able to spend a night at home again with his wife and kids.

If he's lucky, his battle is over in May, if he's not, he must crank his machine up again for the runoff in June. And if he's really having a streak of bad luck, he'll have an opponent in the general election in November, and will have to get a tune-up and perhaps a grease job for his political machine to keep it ready for the last part of the year. Then, if he's made all the right decisions, said all the right things, and shaken all of the right hands, he will have a moment or two to get intoxicated once again on victory brew, perhaps emerging from his hangover only when he finds himself in Austin, with his hand upraised, repeating all those words, and muttering under his breath, "Wait a minute, isn't this where I came in?"

By this time the representative is likely to be a person who gets dates and seasons of the year all mixed up. To him New Year's Day may no longer be January 1, it might become that day in early February when filing fees are due. But he'll probably remember it's winter when the cold breath of a norther blows his hat off as he talks to a constituent on a coffee-shop parking lot. And he'll probably know it's summertime when his shirt becomes soaked with perspiration early in a long day of campaigning and handshaking.

The 1972 election year differed from normal election years in several respects. One of the most unusual and most significant differences is that it does have a specific beginning, although it is a date not related too closely to calendar year 1972. For election year 1972 began building inexorably to its climax on January 18, 1971, the day the story of the "Sharpstown Scandal" hit the newspapers, and the day before the inauguration of Preston Smith and Ben Barnes to their second terms as governor and lieutenant-governor. That date will probably become as infamous to Texas politicians as November 22 has become to Dallas civic leaders, and the trail of events that began that winter day culminated some eighteen months later with the biggest housecleaning ever put on by Texas voters. Election year 1972 would see Texas get a new governor, a new lieutenant-governor, a new attorney-general, not the first but the second new speaker of the House, new faces in over one-half the chairs in the House of Representatives, and new faces in over one-half the chairs in the Texas Senate.

While this might have been the Year of Our Lord One Thousand Nine Hundred and Seventy-two, it was also the Year of Frank Sharp Number One, the Year of Sharpstown. It was the year when voters went to the polls asking election judges just to tell them who the incumbents were, a year when letter-to-the-editor columns in newspapers around the state were full of complaints about the deeds and misdeeds of office-holders ("Gus Mutscher's had his trial," said one letter-writer, "and the rest of them will get theirs on election day").

It was a year in which one big scandal and any number of small scandals enraged voters almost daily. The *Houston Post* printed a day-by-day summary of events surrounding the Sharpstown affair for the entire year of 1971 on Dec. 27, 1971, and there were listed no less than *fifty* separate days during the year in which a substantive piece of news about the case developed. It was a tough time to be an incumbent, all the incumbents said, because even the incumbents who had fought the scandals the loudest and hardest were tainted in the minds of many voters simply because they had been there. It was a year when one conservative voter, faced with voting for either a conservative incumbent or his liberal challenger, mumbled to a reporter that he was trying to decide whether to vote for the liberal or the crook.

"The people are mad and afraid," remarked one observer, "mad that those people in Austin have gotten all that money, and afraid that now they're stealing everything in the Capitol that's not nailed down, typewriters, chairs, stamps, and all."

The only thing constant about politics is the fact of change, the fact that nothing is constant about politics. History, both Texas and American, is full of men, ideas, and movements which at one time had immense popular support and were the movers and shakers throughout the land, while a later time finds them remaining as only shells of their original selves, the men broken and bitter, the ideas forgotten and ignored, and the movements without leaders or followers.

To most Texans, the ones whose political knowledge comes in one- or two-minute doses as read by a television newscaster or from the headline and first paragraph of a newspaper article, change is a surface thing and occurs beyond a doubt when one politician is voted out of office and another is voted in. And, by any surface measurement chosen, there was great change in 1972. Some political careers were ended, some sidetracked, and some invigorated.

A career which had carried one office-holder at blinding speed from a peanut farm to the House of Representatives to the speaker's chair to the lieutenant-governor's position had its meteoric rise sidetracked. Even though that peanut farmer had been touted by a former President and by U.S. Senators as the next Texan to occupy the White House, even though the pundits declared him to be unbeatable and to be the saving, moderating grace for the national Democratic Party, the common voter threw him rudely out of office.

Another career rose meteorically because of the events of the Year of Sharpstown. From a legal-aid office in bi-cultural South Texas to the House of Representatives to the leader of a small group of outraged legislators who called almost daily for an investigation of the stained affairs of state to a run-off for the Democratic gubernatorial nomination, the patrician daughter of a respected pioneer family provided class to the election year, and added a degree of honesty and candor rarely seen in Texas politicians. From passing out her own campaign cards on a lonely shopping-center parking lot only four years earlier, she vaulted into national prominence by her campaign, gathering over 400 votes for the vice-presidential nomination at the Democratic National Convention, and perhaps amassing more respect and support in the national

Democratic Party in a few short months than most Texas politicians could attain in a lifetime.

Change such as the effect on these two careers was easily discernible, even for the headline-reading Texan. He might even have understood that the name Connally would no longer appear on the muster-roll of the state's office-holders. But true change goes deeper than that. And our headline-reading Texan might not have understood that. "That may be one of our greatest failures," a leader of that small group of outraged legislators lamented one afternoon in the state Capitol: "I don't know if we made the people realize that true reform is more than just a change of personnel."

That leader was right, of course, as anyone who has delved beyond the television report or newspaper headlines into the workings of the political process would know. Rascals can always be thrown out, but unless the voters pay attention, their replacements may soon become rascals in their own right. If voters really want reform, then their responsibility goes far deeper than merely asking an election judge who the incumbents are . . . . This responsibility, however, is the most difficult one that a voter has, for change sometimes pays no attention to election days. For example, the Texas House of Representatives was greatly influenced in its 63rd session by a device called a single-member district, a term the average voter may not even understand. But there were representatives from Houston, Dallas, and San Antonio showing up in Austin who were so far removed from their predecessors from those towns, that the walls of the Chamber of Commerce buildings in their hometowns cracked a little as they took the oath of office. This bit of change came through the judicial process and was hugely ignored by the Texas newspaper-reading pubic. Texans living in those districts, though, had their voting favors courted as never before, many of them meeting a legislative candidate (or a legislator) for the first time.

Change was truly apparent, also, when the leader of the Texas delegation to the Democratic National Convention stood up on national television and cast the votes for the presidential nomination not for one man, as they had for eons of unit-rule years, but for *three* different candidates. Surely Sam Rayburn is still moaning in his grave about that. That bit of change was so startling, so important, and so significant that it slipped away with too few people grasping its meaning. At last, at long last, a precious bit of democracy had crept into the Democratic Party, and the party was never to be the same for it.

Although this change and the single-member districts went largely unnoticed, all the surface changes, those of personnel only, did not go unnoticed. The job of the voter gets harder and more complicated. And therein we approach the purpose of this work, for it is the hope of the author to tell in these pages the story of the Year of Frank Sharp, from the effect Sharpstown had on the elections to the fight for reform in the

63rd Legislature, and thereby to help determine the difference between true reform and surface change. The last part of the purpose is, of course, the most ticklish, for one man's reform may be another man's corruption. It is a task to be approached with a deep sense of duty, and, in a day when political advertising has become a contest to see who can say the least with the most glorious phrases, a task to be considered an obligation to the good people who would really like to do something about it all, but just don't know where to begin.

Chapter 2

SETTING THE STAGE

The third Tuesday in January of odd-numbered years is usually an occasion for gaiety and merrymaking in Austin as the brand-new governor and lieutenant-governor are formally inaugurated into their offices. Their friends and neighbors, their faithful campaign workers, their political hangers on, and the state's self-appointed politicos flock to Austin by the thousands to savor the election victories, meet old friends, drink good booze, and talk politics.

Tuesday, January 19, 1971 promised to be no different from many other Inauguration Days as the week began. Both Governor Preston Smith and Lieutenant-Governor Ben Barnes had been returned for second terms by the 1970 elections. In a rather dull election year both Barnes and Smith had escaped battle in the Democratic primary and then Smith had disposed of Republican Paul Eggers for the second time in the November general election, while Barnes had trounced Byron Fullerton.

Both Smith and Barnes came from the long-dominant conservative wing of the Texas Democratic Party, a business-oriented faction concerned with preserving a favorable climate for the state's large industries, and, while they had their own political differences and would shed no tears for one another's troubles, harmony and unity was the order of the day.

The Sixty-second Legislature was already underway, having commenced on January 12, but their attention was focused on the inaugural ceremonies, and on the legislative proposals Governor Smith was to present to them on Wednesday. Just beginning his second term as speaker of the House was 38-year-old Gus F. Mutscher, another conservative Democrat. He was a product of the Brenham area of Central Texas and had been elected unanimously, as expected, at the first of a session that many writers were predicting would be extremely stormy since it faced such items as raising an additional $600-800 million in new revenue, and passing a redistricting bill. Thirty-two freshman representatives and four freshman senators were present, and both legislative bodies were moving into newly redecorated and expanded offices. But, at the moment, all was quiet in Austin, and more Texans were probably aware that the Dallas Cowboys had lost another big one, this time in the last five seconds by a

16-13 score to the Baltimore Colts in the Super Bowl on Sunday, than were aware that Texas was about to inaugurate a governor.

The festivities surrounding the occasion of state were designed to please almost any philosophy and pocketbook. The Democratic Party was sponsoring a $30-a-plate victory dinner on Monday night with the entertainment to be provided by singer Wayne Newton. Early risers could attend the Governor's Prayer Breakfast on Tuesday morning (at $3 a plate); people hunting free activities could find receptions Tuesday morning being held by state officials; lovers of ceremony might witness the noon swearing-in ceremonies at the state capitol; parades with marching bands and floats were scheduled in the afternoon; and the day of merrymaking could be climaxed by attending the Grand March Tuesday night at the Austin Municipal Auditorium ($15 a couple) and any of the five free balls being held around the city, including square-dancing for the older generation, country and western music for the kickers, and three rock concerts for younger listeners.

This Inauguration, though, was destined to be unlike any other Inauguration in recent Texas history, for a lawsuit filed Monday afternoon in a Dallas federal court would turn the gala affair into a funeral-like occasion, and, although no one could possible know it at the moment, the careers of all the three leaders (Smith, Barnes, and Mutscher) would soon lose their glitter and turn to dust.

The lawsuit, filed by the federal government's Securities and Exchange Commission, provided the first glimpse for the public into what was to become infamous as the Sharpstown Scandal. (The purpose of this chapter is not to provide a detailed analysis of the Sharpstown Banking Bills and their trip through the Legislature, but, rather, to help the reader determine the effect that news surrounding this scandal and other smaller scandals might have had on a voter going to the polls fifteen months later. I refer readers interested in the bills and their legislative journey to two excellent chronicles of the affair, *Texas Under a Cloud*, by Sam Kinch, Jr., of *The Dallas Morning News*'s Capitol Bureau, and Ben Procter, a Texas Christian University history professor, and *Shadow On the Alamo*, by Harvey Katz, an investigative reporter who covered the affair under a grant from the Fund for Investigative Journalism.) The SEC's suit alleged that a number of prominent Texas businessmen and corporations had taken part in an extremely complicated web of financial transactions that artificially manipulated the price of stock in the National Bankers Life Insurance Company. With two or three exceptions, the names of the people and corporations listed were not well known and would not have caused many raised eyebrows outside a select circle of Texas businessmen. The best-known name was that of Waggoner Carr, a Lubbock product who had served two terms as speaker of the Texas House of Representatives, two terms as attorney-general, and had retired with a large campaign debt after trying twice unsuccessfully for higher office,

once for the U.S. Senate in 1966, and once for the Democratic
gubernatorial nomination in 1968. Carr was now a partner of an Austin
law firm that had as another partner John Osorio who was also named as
a defendant in the lawsuit. Osorio had been an aide to Governor Allan
Shivers, and had later served as president of National Bankers Life, the
insurance company whose stock was allegedly being manipulated.
Osorio's name would hardly ring a bell in the mind of the
headline-reading Texan, but he was better known among the inside
observers of Texas government. The only other name likely to be
recognized was that of Frank W. Sharp, an East Texas country boy who
had gone to Houston and struck it rich in the booming Gulf Coast
metropolis. Sharp's empire included banks, real estate developments,
investment companies and, since 1968, National Bankers Life. Any
Houstonian, or Southeast Texan, was aware of a large shopping-center
development called Sharpstown out on the southwestern edge of the city.
This development seemed to reflect the spirit of Southwest Houston in the
1960s: new, shiny, bold, expensive, made of glass and concrete, and
located on a freeway. Among the businesses located there was Sharp's
own bank, the Sharpstown State Bank.

Some of the dignitaries in Austin had been aware that this story was
about to break, and the ones not in the know learned about the suit
Monday night or Tuesday morning. Rumors were thicker than the
carpets in the legislative chambers of the Capitol, and many of the
assembled politicians were breathing huge sighs of relief because they had
not bought any of the stock involved. As complicated as the case was, only
its bare outlines were clear at first, and most of the state's newspapers
carried the story on Tuesday under a headline that typically read "Carr,
Others Named . . . ."

Although an encompassing cloud of gloom had settled over the
Capitol dome at this point, Smith and Barnes went gamely on with the
swearing-in ceremonies on Tuesday. Against the background of a
nineteen-gun salute fired by Texas National Guardsmen and the flashing
sabers of Texas A&M's Ross Volunteers, Governor Smith told the crowd,
"The turbulent seas we sailed throughout the 1960s are quieting."
Speaking of the glowing future, as inaugural speakers often do, he warned
the assembled politicians that "While we dream of, and labor for that
tomorrow, . . . We must live in the midst of yesterday's mistakes," a line
as ironic as any ever uttered by a Texas politician.

Representative Neal Solomon, chairman of the House Banking
Committee, said later that he heard someone mention during the
swearing-in ceremonies that a tremendous scandal was about to break,
and, within five minutes after the ceremony was over, a newsman
accosted him with the question of the day, "How much stock did you get
. . . .?"

As the day drew on, the crowds of spectators grew more unfriendly, often yelling threats and curses at the participants. The parade that afternoon was almost disrupted at one point by onlookers. By the time of the Grand March that night, it was becoming apparent that a number of the state's highest office-holders were going to be involved in the scandal, and at least one state official taking part in the Grand March compared his duties that night with those of a pallbearer: "We are at what is supposed to be a victory and yet what in many ways might also be a funeral. I've been in this business a long, long time, and one piece of advice I'll offer you is that if you want to stay in this business, then always be a pallbearer. All the guys in that category stay alive a long time. But once you start reaching up and get up, there's nothing to do but get killed off."

By this time the rumors and denials were multiplying in geometric progression, and Wednesday morning's headlines read "Smith, Mutscher, Baum Named . . . ." As more and more details became known, reporters and newspaper readers began speculating on the depth of involvement of specific politicians. It soon appeared that Frank Sharp's stock manipulation scheme was used to allow certain people an opportunity to buy NBL stock at a low price and sell it a short time later for a sizable profit. Among those who had been involved in the buying and selling were Smith, Mutscher, Dr. Elmer Baum, an Austin osteopath who had been named by Smith as chairman of the State Democratic Executive Committee, Representative W. S. "Bill" Heatly, a Paducah legislator who had ruled the House Appropriations Committee vindictively for years, Representative Tommy Shannon, a Fort Worth insurance man who was a key member of Mutscher's House "team," and two of Mutscher's aides, S. Rush McGinty and F. C. "Sonny" Schulte. Some legislators began calling for a full investigation of the dealings, and a few even began to suggest that Speaker Gus Mutscher step down from his position until all of the facts were in.

On Sunday, January 24, Waggoner Carr took the offensive in a *Dallas Morning News* interview. "I've done nothing wrong," he said. "If anybody's done wrong in this I don't want to be put in the same boat with them." His detractors, he said, "are trying to convince everybody I have committed some illegal act even before I have a chance to set the record straight in court. They can go to hell." The bills which Sharp had tried to get passed were good bills then, and he still thought they were good, according to the article.

The next week produced more developments, more complications, and much more newsprint for the now-awakened public.

On Monday, the doors of the Sharpstown State Bank closed forever after the bank had suffered a run of some $15 million in the few days since the story broke. If it had once represented the Spirit of Southwest Houston, it now resembled nothing so much as a dirty, tarnished jewel in which some flaws had just been discovered. Stunned Houstonians watched in disbelief as their city's first bank failure in history was recorded. Agents of the Federal Deposit Insurance Corporation came in later and paid out over $50 million to its depositors, the largest payout in FDIC history.

In Austin on Monday, the State Insurance Commissioner announced he was taking over two of the insurance companies named in the SEC suit, National Bankers Life and Olympic Life Insurance Co. Also in Austin on Monday, Representative James Nugent of Kerrville introduced an ethics bill which he had sponsored for the last several sessions, and there was a veritable stampede of publicity-conscious legislators seeking to sign their names as co-sponsors. Two years earlier the bill had never even been brought up for a vote in the then-apathetic House, but on this day over 100 of the 150 members crowded around to add their signatures. "There couldn't have been more activity if free beer were distributed in the rear of the house," noted Republican Representative Jim Earthman of Houston. (What finally happened to the bill is one of the saddest stories of the legislative session, but, let's not get ahead of ourselves.)

On Tuesday, Representative Curtis Graves from Houston, one of the two black members of the House, announced that he had a resolution ready which should unseat Gus Mutscher as speaker, and that he might call for a vote on the matter. On Wednesday the El Paso County Democratic Executive Committee passed a resolution urging Dr. Elmer Baum to resign his position as state party chairman. And on Thursday, Representative Neil Caldwell of Alvin introduced a resolution asking for the persons involved to appear before a joint session of the legislature to explain their actions. On Friday, a troubled Gus Mutscher journeyed to a long-scheduled $25-a-head reception in Fort Worth, an affair which had almost been cancelled in light of the revelations of the last two weeks. Newsmen there questioned him as to why Representative Graves had not asked for a vote on his resolution during the week, and found a confident Mutscher saying that Graves must not have done it because he didn't have the votes, "and he wanted to make sure I didn't receive a vote of confidence from his colleagues."

By this time the editorial heat for some answers had reached the white-hot level, as almost all of the state's newspapers were expressing the anger and frustrations felt by much of the citizenry. Editorial writers were calling for strong ethics bills, special investigations, and anything else they could think of. And they were being joined in increasing numbers by political, civic, student, and religious organizations, as well as by many individual citizens.

Action in the Legislature

As the month of February began, it was becoming clear that the white-hot editorial heat was searing only the sensibilities of the voters.

Mutscher's team began to clamp down even tighter on the House members. Neil Caldwell's resolution had been referred to Representative Tommy Shannon's House Administration Committee, and was languishing in a hostile subcommittee. Governor Smith mustered his resources and appeared at a Headliners Club luncheon on February 6, taking some of the wind out of his critics' sails momentarily by making fun of himself ("Let him who is without stock cast the first rock"). But the critics were not satisfied. Public opinion kept rising, kept asking for answers, and, while the public might not have known what to do if those answers were not forthcoming, it certainly knew that something was fouling up its Capitol. It was indeed a time of crisis in Texas government.

On February 16, Neil Caldwell lost an attempt to get his resolution out of the subcommittee by a 110-35 vote on the floor of the House. Speaker Mutscher interpreted that as a vote of confidence in himself, and exclaimed that the resolution was "politically motivated," while Caldwell blamed Mutscher's intimidation of the members for the defeat. It was "a vote of fear," said Caldwell.

As the Legislature began turning its attention to more mundane affairs of state such as taxes, utility regulation, and liquor-by-the-drink, some began to think that perhaps nothing substantial in the way of an investigation was going to come from within the Legislature. February turned into late February, and then into March, and the House calendar was filled with committee meetings, those important but almost invisible tools of government.

Early in March, Governor Preston Smith was to celebrate his fifty-ninth birthday. As was the tradition, a congratulatory resolution was introduced (by Phil Cates, a representative from Lefors) to honor this event. As was *not* the tradition, two House members, Caldwell and Mrs. Frances Farenthold of Corpus Christi, requested that their names be kept off the resolution. The only woman in the House, Mrs. Farenthold had already been one of the most outspoken critics of Mutscher's regime. On March 10, she introduced a resolution calling for a full-scale investigation of the Sharpstown Scandal. The inquiry would be conducted by a joint House-Senate committee, with each body responsible for appointing five members to the committee. This would take away the power of the presiding officer in each house to choose the members of the investigating committee. It was much stronger than Caldwell's resolution, and, if left alone, would probably wind up the same place his resolution had—in a hostile subcommittee. But Mrs. Farenthold, known to her friends by the nickname "Sissy," had no intentions of leaving it alone. Driven by a deep devotion to government in the public interest, on March 15, she rose and moved to immediately consider her resolution, HCR 87. When Mutscher refused to allow this, Lane Denton, a freshman representative from Waco, appealed the ruling of the chair to the floor of the House. A startled Mutscher turned the gavel over to Representative DeWitt Hale and left the chamber while Denton's appeal was debated and voted on. In a vote heralded by many as the birth of the Dirty Thirty, Mutscher's forces won, 118-30. An unknown Mutscher-man's growling remarks about those "thirty dirty bastards" was overheard by a sympathetic ear and repeated to the group later, thus coining a name for a group that was to become an important force in Election Year 1972.

Troubles continued to mount for members of the Austin establishment. Stories from members of the Capitol press corps began touching on Mutscher's troubles, saying that he was not at all enjoying his position of power, and predicting that his support would soon crumble.

Then on Sunday, March 21, the same day that Jon Ford of the Harte-Hanks Newspaper chain predicted that Mutscher's supporters might find him a "heavy load" to bear in next year's elections, Governor Smith, appearing on "Capitol Eye," a public events television and radio program, blamed it all on the press. "I've never subscribed to the theory that the people have lost any confidence," he said. "I think this is just the figment of the imagination of generally those who report the news."

Later that month, hearings held on the Farenthold resolution produced a stream of witnesses testifying that the public had lost what faith it had had in the Legislature, and then, on March 29, a watered-down resolution allowing Mutscher to hand-pick five members of a House General Investigating Committee passed. When five staunch Mutscher supporters were named to the committee, even some of the team members blanched.

As the session ground on toward its 140-day constitutional limit, the Dirty Thirty became better organized, nipping at Mutscher's heels as a pack of small animals might nip at a much larger animal. Twenty-one of them refused to sign the resolution honoring him for the customary Speaker's Day celebration. They pointedly attended their own party, hosted by Sissy Farenthold, instead of journeying to Washington-on-the-Brazos State Park with the rest of the House members to hear Smith call Mutscher "one of the true leaders in Texas history," and Barnes praise him as a "great leader . . . in a trying time in Texas history."

The Dirty Thirty members realized that Mutscher would get them if he could, and he got his chance with a redistricting bill which passed close to the end of the session. Blatantly ignoring all legal and common-sense rules of legislative apportionment, Mutscher-man Delwin Jones of Lubbock had carved out districts designed to kill off as many of the Dirty Thirtians as possible.

Some of them were paired against each other in new "Mutscher-mandered" districts; others found their original districts sliced up in politically damaging ways. When it came up late in the session, strong indications of cracks in the team were evident. The cracks were not strong enough to keep the bill from passing, but over twenty members joined with the Dirty Thirty to vote against its final passage. (A state judge careful to point out that he was no "judicial activist" later declared the whole thing unconstitutional.)

Action in the Courts

The embattled Legislature finally adjourned on June 4, having maneuvered through both the 140-day regular session and a short-lived special session. It had been one of the most turbulent sessions in recent years, and, while it had created that House General Investigating Committee, it had produced absolutely no answers of any significance to the questions in the minds of many voters. The cries of corruption were just as strong and the replies of those charged just as meaningless as they had been back on the first day the sickening news flashing over the state. Fighting long odds and vindictive retaliation, the members of the Dirty Thirty had tried every tactic they could imagine to get some meaningful answers to those questions. They would soon turn their attention to the ultimate hope of a democracy, the ballot box, where their success would be very satisying. And while they were plotting their electoral victories, the attention of reform-minded voters turned from the legislative halls to the judicial branch of the government, and there they settled in for a long wait.

Actually, the attention of the judicial branch of the government had already focused on the Sharpstown Scandal. For, in February, the SEC lawyers had gone to the court of U.S. District Judge Sarah T. Hughes, the strong-willed woman who had sworn in Lyndon Johnson as the nation's new President back in that blur that was November 22, 1963. The lawyers were asking for a temporary restraining order from Judge Hughes to keep all of the individuals and companies charged with the illegal financial schemes from trading in the stock of the involved companies and from tampering with the corporate records or wasting corporate assets. A number of the original defendants had already accepted the injunction, but several of them, including Waggoner Carr, were fighting it. After a two-day hearing, Judge Hughes announced, on February 10, a number of varied injunctions applying against all of the defendants except Carr. She could find "no conclusive evidence" that Carr was involved in a "scheme to manipulate the various stocks involved." It was a personal victory for Carr and he announced that he was "very happy" and was impressed with the Judge's fairness. No one, including Carr, was dismissed from the case, however, and August 30 was set as the date for a trial of the suit.

Frank Sharp, meanwhile, a man far-removed from the East Texas country boy he had once been, had begun trying to pull off the biggest deal of his lifetime. He quietly had his lawyers begin probing to find out whether the United States Department of Justice would be willing to trade with him. He was offering his information, his testimony as a government witness, and his price was his freedom. The deal took almost two months to consummate, and it had to climb the Justice Department's hierarchy all the way to Deputy Attorney-General Richard Kleindienst for final approval. As Harvey Katz pointed out in his book *Shadow On the Alamo*, "Kleindienst undoubtedly viewed Sharp as a vehicle for wreaking havoc among the big Texas Democrats."

So, the deal was approved, the final arrangements were worked out by U.S. Attorney Anthony J.P. Farris in Houston, and, on June 14, in the court of U.S. Judge John Singleton, Frank Sharp pleaded guilty to a relatively minor violation of federal banking and securities laws. The good judge assessed a fine of $5,000 and a three-year probated sentence against Sharp and granted him immunity from any other charges in exchange for his information. And let it be known that in the summer of 1971, the Frank Sharp Travelling Testimony Company did put on quite a road show. Almost daily, it seemed, Sharp would turn up in Houston, Austin, or Dallas to entertain a federal or state grand jury investigating the mess. Several grand juries were in operation, investigating different aspects of the case, and these, plus some travelling SEC hearings, plus the House General Investigating Committee, kept Sharp on the front pages of the state's newspapers all summer long.

But when all was said and done, most observers were disappointed in Sharp's revelations. Possibly the most damaging blow he landed all summer was a cheap shot to the political career of Ben Barnes. Testifying late one afternoon in Houston, Sharp recalled a conversation wherein John Osorio had told him that "Ben [Barnes] delivered for us . . . he's smarter than the others, he wants his in cash." The hearing abruptly ended there, and word of the amazing story quickly leaked to several different persons.

The astonished newsmen who got wind of the story took after it with true zeal, but most of their first reports were squelched by top management in their organizations. The big wheels recoiled from a story that murderous, and the next day, Sharp's testimony threw an entirely different light on the matter. The cash he spoke of on Wednesday turned out to be in the form of a $60,000 loan made to Barnes at Dallas Bank and Trust, a Sharp-controlled bank. Sharp's indications that he really knew nothing about what Barnes had done to help the banking bills get through, plus the fact that that particular loan was already known about by the public both served to temper the harshness of Sharp's allegations. Barnes vehemently denied the story of course, and he said that Osorio denied the story also. Speaking to the state AFL-CIO convention the next day, the lieutenant-governor told them: "I never borrowed any money from the Sharpstown State Bank . . . I never met Frank Sharp." (Barnes would repeat these lines all over the state in the next nine months.)

A week later Sharp told the House General Investigating Committee in Austin (yep, for the first time since it had been created back on March 29, it decided the affairs of state warranted a meeting . . . for two days) that he and Mutscher had had a "tacit understanding" on the passage of the banking bills. "He knew he needed help and I knew he needed help," squealed Sharp. The next day, August 19, the diligent committee members listened as Waggoner Carr called the suit a "calloused, colossal, political hatchet job directed by the Republican Administration in Washington."

As that historic two-day session of the House General Investigating Committee came to an end (and it was to be their last session for over a year), it appeared that its members were more alarmed at what Carr had said than what Sharp had said. The chairman let it be known that he wanted to get Will Wilson down from Washington to testify. Wilson was a Democrat-turned-Republican who had once been the state's attorney-general, and had been appointed by Richard Nixon as an assistant U.S. attorney-general in January of 1969. Wilson, so one story went, was the man really behind the suit, and was just using his exalted position to torment his past enemies in the Texas Democratic Party.

But, at this point, those Washington Republicans were not especially happy either, for they had thought Frank Sharp's testimony was going to be much more of a bombshell than it had been. They were, what you might say, disappointed, and Kleindienst later admitted that he felt Sharp had tricked them on the deal. If nothing else, though, Sharp did keep the voters stirred up, for it was almost impossible to find a newspaper that summer that didn't have some mention of the Sharpstown Scandal.

The Autumn Developments

The early fall brought no letup in publicity either; September was destined to be the most turbulent month since the end of the legislative session. It roared in with a bang when the Associated Press reported on September 2 that Speaker Mutscher, Representative Shannon, and Speaker's aide Rush McGinty would all be indicted by a Travis County [Austin] grand jury on criminal charges coming out of a summer investigation. Though the indictments were not yet public, the story, quoting reliable sources, stole the spotlight from the civil trial going on in Dallas. Judge Sarah T. Hughes started the trial of the SEC lawsuit without any further delay on August 30, and the best estimate was that it would last approximately six weeks.

But the Judge admonished the attorneys to speed up the proceedings as much as possible and the testimony was completed in a little over two weeks. On September 16, Judge Hughes issued her findings, holding the nine businessmen and four corporations still fighting the SEC allegations guilty of illegal stock manipulating. They were all placed under a permanent injunction enjoining them from any further fraudulent stock dealings. Carr came away from this trial "deeply shocked and disappointed," and vowing to appeal the decision. Judge Hughes'

decision stuck very strictly to the financial aspects of the case, ignoring the
political aspects of all the loans to the prominent politicians.

Then, Thursday, September 23 brought the biggest bombshell since
January 18. The Travis County Grand Jury's indictments were officially
filed, fulfilling the Associated Press's three-week-old predictions. Gus
Mutscher became the highest state official to be charged with a felony
since Governor James E. "Pa" Ferguson was impeached in 1917. He and
McGinty went down to the Travis County Courthouse and were
photographed, fingerprinted, and released on $10,000 bond (they were
treated "just like everyone else," said one deputy sheriff). The Speaker,
who said he was "tired and a little disappointed," was charged with
accepting a bribe, and conspiracy to accept a bribe. He told reporters that
it was an action "politically motivated," and "designed to destroy me."
Indicating the role he thought the press had played in the affair, he
responded to a reporter's question (about what political motivations the
twelve grand jurors could have had) with the statement: "I don't want to
go into it. You could even read your stories and other comments and see
there has been a lot of lobbying in that direction."

And he made one other statement that will be enshrined in the Hall of
Fame (or Infamy) of Texas political folklore: "The big fish are still
swimming." Shannon and McGinty were both indicted on the conspiracy
charges, and John Osorio was indicted for filing a false statement with the
State Board of Insurance. The grand jury's statement read in part: "It is
the opinion of the July session of the Travis County Grand Jury that some
Texas lawmakers, who have been elected by the voters of Texas to these
high positions of trust, were too busy granting political favors and being
influenced in exchange for turning 'a fast buck' to be concerned about
good government for the people. There is dire need for reform so that
good laws for the protection and well-being of our citizens might be
passed."

Mutscher's office resembled a battle zone Friday as House members
and lobbyists poured in to offer their sympathy and plot the next move.
Over forty of the House "team" members got together in Dallas that night
to try to decide what to do. A couple of them had stopped by Austin to
speak to Mutscher and brought with them his assurances that he would
step down or at least appoint an interim speaker to fill his shoes until the
charges were resolved. There was a decidedly troubled air about the
meeting and many of the participants were openly nervous about the
political damage that might come from their past association with
Mutscher. Some were even leery of accepting interim appointments to
study committees from the once-powerful Speaker. He had become "too
great a burden" for them to carry, thus fulfilling Jon Ford's earlier
prophecy. Little came from the meeting except a list of names from which
Mutscher supposedly would choose an interim speaker.

Meanwhile, back in Austin, at least two representatives who had earlier declared themselves to be candidates for Speaker of the Sixty-third Legislature set up command posts and began furiously seeking pledges of support from other members. Rayford Price of Palestine, once a Mutscher lieutenant but now an outsider, and Dean Cobb of Dumas, a Mutscher-man all the way in the Sixty-second Legislature, were vying for the position.

Through the weekend and into the following week, Mutscher mulled over his mess behind closed doors. He first let it be known that he would go along with the recommendation of the Dallas meeting and name a temporary successor. But, on September 30, he announced that he would set politics aside and remain in his position. The decision was not made lightly, he said, and "I have never, nor will I now, walk out on my colleagues in the House." Besides, he said, the Legislative Redistricting Board was about to meet in the wake of the wrecking job done by that state judge on his redistricting bill, and he could not legally delegate his position on that board to anyone else.

The following Monday, October 4, four members of the Dirty Thirty, outraged because Mutscher would not voluntarily step down, told an Austin press conference that they were meeting with Governor Smith to urge him to call a special session of the Legislature so that Mutscher could be impeached. If he refused, the four representatives (Frances Farenthold, Tom Moore, Lane Denton, and Walter Mengden) said they would look into the lawbooks to see if a majority of the members of the House could, by proclamation, call themselves into a special impeachment session. Smith listened to the four, but refused to call the session, possibly afraid that the legislators might become so zealous with the impeaching power that his own name would wind up on the impeached list.

Smith's use of his special session power throughout the whole Year of Frank Sharp deserves a huge black blot from history. He screamed his innocence in the affair from almost any pulpit the state would give him. Yet, while he was repeatedly urged to call a special session for the passage of workable reform and ethics legislation, he refused to do so. A session called in the crucible that was Texas in the fall of 1971 would have been watched more closely than any other session in Texas history, and would have been under great pressure to pass some laws with strong enforcement teeth. Yet, Smith refused. And even when he had to call a special session the following year, he refused to open it up for the consideration of such legislation. Smith has always been something of an enigma to political observers in Texas, but his refusal to allow the Legislature to clear the air when it was fouled with cries of corruption has to rank as one of the worst disservices to the people ever done by a Texas governor.

Later in October, the heat generated by Frank Sharp's Traveling Road Show produced another casualty, as Will Wilson tendered his resignation from the U.S. Department of Justice in a personal letter to

President Nixon. "Events... in Texas have through no fault of mine created difficulties and embarrassments which your organization should not be taxed with," said Wilson in his letter to the President. Wilson had been Sharp's chief attorney in the two-year period before he was appointed to office by Nixon, and it became apparent that he knew quite a bit about Sharp's financial empire. Although Wilson denied it, Sharp testified that Wilson had advised him on how to get around the state banking laws. Wilson had also okayed the payment of a $2500 bill for "some construction work," as he recalled it, but that construction work turned out to be work done in "bugging" a room that bank examiners were using during their examination of a Sharp bank.

Henry B. Gonzalez, a U.S. Representative from San Antonio, had been yelling for Wilson's scalp for some time now, even turning the U.S. Congress into a setting for the "Sharpstown Follies," as Gonzalez termed his speech-making efforts against Wilson. Wilson admitted making $230,000 in unsecured loans with the Sharp banking empire, including one for $30,000 eighteen months after he began his work at the Justice Department. As Mutscher had become for the Democrats, he was now too heavy a burden for the Republicans, and he was forced to resign.

The month of October was brought to its climax with the release, on October 24, of the results of a poll among the House members taken by the United Press International's Capitol Bureau. Roland Lindsey of UPI reported that a majority of the 150 representatives thought Speaker Gus Mutscher should resign his position immediately because of his bribery indictment. Replies to the survey were sent in by 86 of the House members, and 77 of them wanted Mutscher to resign. The same night there was another meeting of the Speaker's former supporters, this time in San Antonio, evidently for the same purpose as the Dallas meeting. Mutscher made no public response to either the poll or the meeting, continuing his public posture of silence as he had most of the time since the end of the session.

November brought a few days of welcome relief from the lofty pressures of state affairs. There were no major developments, and the entire state had a chance to relax and think about the turbulence of September and October. The lazy days came to an end in December, however, and a chain of events involving the Sharpstown affair and a number of other smaller scandals began to be seen. These events brought the collective conscience of the Texas public to a screaming, seething fever-pitch by the Day of the First Chance To Throw the Rascals Out, the May 6th first primary election.

December began with more front-page developments in the scandal that was by now as familiar to most Texans as their most unwelcome in-laws. On the second day of the month, the trial of Gus Mutscher, Tommy Shannon, and Rush McGinty was moved from Austin to Abilene. Both sides had sought the change of venue, Mutscher because of the publicity the affair had been given in Austin, and Travis County District Attorney Robert Smith because of the possible influence the Speaker might have had on a juror who worked for a state agency. Judge J. Neil Daniel of the 104th District Court in Abilene received the case and set February 28, 1972, as the starting date.

A few days later, Art Wiese, a young political reporter for the *Houston Post*, revealed that Mutscher was sending out almost 12,000 personal letters to his constituents--all printed and mailed at state expense. The letter charged that the Speaker's enemies were attempting "to destroy my future and kill me politically."

"The magnitude [of these attempts] has been so unjust that it has been unreal, but I can honestly say that I am innocent of the charges," wrote Mutscher.

Postage costs alone came to almost $1,000, and, not unexpectedly, the Speaker's critics jumped him for this use of state funds. Rush McGinty defended his boss by saying that the letters were nonpolitical, and the Speaker was only keeping in touch with his people, something that any House member could legitimately do.

More serious charges were made against Mutscher and McGinty in December by the same newspaper. Felton West and Henry Holcomb of the *Post*'s Capitol Bureau, had been digging for some time into the relations of Mutscher and McGinty with that mysterious morass of money in Galveston, the Moody interests.

Presenting their findings in a series of copyrighted articles, the two reporters at first charged Shearn Moody, Jr., of Galveston, a part heir to the immense financial empire of his grandfather, W.L. Moody, Jr., with using "a branch of Texas state government as a mighty platoon in his war with majority trustees of the giant Moody foundation," a war reportedly designed to obtain for Moody and other Moody heirs a larger share of the profits earned by businesses controlled by the trust. The October 31 article accused Mutscher of aiding Moody by setting up a one-sided legislative inquiry to help Moody, while at the same time being a "party to a loan" of approximately $90,000 from Moody's private Galveston bank, W.L. Moody and Co., Bankers (Unincorporated).

Articles in December presented further findings of the investigative team. On December 12, they reported learning from reliable sources that an executive of Moody's bank had testified that the bank had loaned $90,000 to Mutscher and McGinty, but that Moody himself had paid the loans off in November and then had ordered the loan records "cleared from his bank." Their investigation also revealed that some bills backed by James C. Day of Brookshire and Houston, a lobbyist for Moody, had passed the House after discussions began on one of the loans, a $60,000 loan to McGinty. One of these bills authorized the deposit of additional state funds in Moody's private bank and other private banks. Another of the bills created a "water utility district with unique powers apparently designed to permit issuance and sale of water district bonds to Moody's bank, which could buy and pledge them as security for its state and local government deposits." (The entire water district situation in Texas, one in which many abuses have been discovered, is discussed in Chapter 9 of Katz's book *Shadow On the Alamo*.)

A third bill had created the Texas Vending Machine Commission, a body which had become pretty controversial recently, and clouds of the intrigue which had already permeated the industry that the commission regulated now settled over the passage of the bill itself.

On the eighth of December, Joseph Novotny, the former president of the Sharpstown State Bank, was indicted on charges stemming from a Houston federal grand jury's probings of the mess. Two other bank officers and two bank examiners were also named in the indictments.

Then, four days before Christmas, Waggoner Carr sent Frank Sharp a present—hoping to collect the bill from him later. Carr filed a lawsuit in Austin seeking $100 million in damages from Sharp. The suit charged that Sharp had either "deceitfully" concealed the stock fraud irregularities or had "negligently"failed to reveal them to Carr. Asking for $25 million in actual damages and triple that amount in punitive damages, Carr said he had "suffered excruciating ridicule and widespread suspicion of personal wrong-doing from those neighbors, friends, and acquaintances among whom he must live."

Finding the Christmas spirit contagious, *Fortune* magazine presented a gift to the entire state in its December issue: a long feature article entitled "The Texas Banker Who Bought Politicians," by A. James Reichley. This was not the first national publication to become interested in the plight of honesty in the Texas Capitol. Several of the country's leading daily newspapers had run feature articles on the Sharp affair already.

The weekly newsmagazines had covered it; indeed, an article in *Time* about the Wilson-Sharp involvement appeared shortly before Wilson's resignation, and may have been the proverbial straw on the Republican elephant's back. But Reichley's article went deeper and struck more sensitive nerves than any article yet to appear in a national publication, and as word spread about the article, that issue of *Fortune* quickly became a collector's item throughout Texas. Although the magazine's limited circulation and its rapid disappearance from newsstands kept it from influencing as many Texans as it could have, the arguments Reichley espoused were not original, and had been shouted by serious-minded reformists for years. Exposing Frank Sharp as only the latest in a long line of establishment-type con men (remember Bascom, Ben Jack, and Billie Sol?), he suggested that the cause of the corruption lay as much in the basic attitude toward government in Texas as it did in the greed of the corrupt. The psychology of "frontier individualism" is what he called it, a philosophy that usually has as one of its tenets a belief in as little government as possible. Some of the governmental institutions and practices arising from that belief create a climate in which the seeds of corruption can easily sprout into poisonous vines clinging to the Capitol dome.

Short legislative sessions, low pay and inadequate research facilities for individual legislators, multimember legislative districts in most cities, and a governor whose powers are severely limited by an outdated constitution, were all factors that made the Texas governmental structure a serving of choice prime rib for the establishment's lobbyists. These gourmets had rewarded their employers by providing a structure of taxes and economic regulations highly favorable to the economic interests. Indeed, Reichley thought that the chances for true reform might depend as much on the establishment as on any other group: "Much will depend on the attitude of the leaders of the Texas business establishment, who have fueled the campaigns of the conservative Democrats and hold ultimate authority over the business lobbyists in Austin. Up until now, Texas business in general has felt that weak and ineffective state government served its economic interests. In order to preserve its privileges and power, it has been willing to tolerate an occasional Frank Sharp. If the establishment leaders continue in this view, they can still steer the Democratic organization away from reform, and back into the arms of men like Osorio and Carr. But the result might well be that the voters would at last turn the conservative Democrats out of office—and business would find itself, for the first time in many years, on the outside politically in Texas."

Toward the end of December, the first of the many smaller scandals that would arise by election day jumped to the front page headlines. On December 30, a federal jury in Baltimore, Maryland, found Congressman John Dowdy guilty of taking a $25,000 bribe in connection with his legislative duties. Dowdy was a ten-term veteran from Athens whose Second Congressional District went into the heartland of Deep East Texas. As a congressman he was never rated much higher than mediocre, but as a political gut-fighter, he was of championship calibre, defeating a long line of top quality opponents over the years. His indictment had come at a lucky time, from his standpoint, with the charges being filed shortly after the 1970 filing deadline had left him only token opposition. Dowdy's health, both physical and mental, had put the trial off for over a year, but what was to be an eight-week ordeal began on November 8, 1971. Several factors combined to keep the trial relatively isolated from the public spotlight as it progressed. For one thing, it was being held a long way off, and also, Dowdy himself had always maintained a low profile in Washington and was relatively unknown outside his rural, back-woodsy district. He was a champion of the far right during his twenty years in Washington and one ultra-conservative political action group, the Liberty Lobby, had raised over $20,000 to contribute to his defense fund, claiming that he was being prosecuted because of his conservative voting record. He had once remarked, after hearing that thousands of students were involved in a protest at the White House against the Vietnam War, that "the schools from whence they came are failing in their duty to teach cleanliness, manners, morals, and decency." He called the protesters "a convention of the unwashed."

John Dowdy's personal problem and eventual demise would shake hardly any public pillars anywhere, for he had never been a part of an establishment, either in Washington or Austin. But with the loss of public confidence that the Texas voters had suffered over the past year, his conviction came into the spotlight and was multiplied many times over, adding stains to the image of politicians in general. As one of his constituents told the Associated Press's Clayton Hickerson, "I'm of the opinion most of the fellows have their hands out."

The Most Unconstitutional Month

New Years are a boon to most people, bringing new hopes, promises of fresh starts, and commitments to exchange good habits for bad. But the New Year of 1972 crept on the Texas political scene, bringing with it only nervousness and announcements of opposing candidates for the incumbent Texas politicians. Oh, there would be a few brief diversions for the Texas public. The Dallas Cowboys, for example, would finally win the Big One, defeating Miami in the Super Bowl 24-3. But it was not really a time of celebration for most Texas politicians, since the filing deadline was just around the corner, and persons eager to run for office were pouring out of the woodwork in the wake of Sharpstown. The incumbents got more blotches on their records before the month of January was over. As the New Year began, only the politicians' honesty was in question; as the first month ended, their competency was under severe attack also.

The month of January brought with it an extraordinary number of actions declaring some Texas law unconstitutional. Amid the confusion, the rules of the political game underwent a big change, as the following laws lay mortally stricken: the 1971 Ethics Bill, the law setting up a filing fee system to pay costs of party primaries, the Congressional Redistricting Act of the last legislature, and the Legislative Redistricting Board's new apportionment of the Texas House districts. Toward the end of the month it was possible to pick up a newspaper with stories about the decision of the day, the status of the appeal on a second case, and the possibility of a judicial stay on a third case. A story about a three-judge federal court declaring the entire state of Texas unconstitutional might not have even raised many eyebrows. One legislator, surveying the confusion, remarked that he had no idea where his district was, how many opponents he would have, how much his filing fee would be, or even when it was due. And more than one person suggested that a "Texas" wing be built on the U.S.

Supreme Court's building in Washington, in light of the large caseload she was sending them.

Actually many of these decisions had been foreseeable, and the only great surprise was that so many of them had come in such a short time. The Texas business-conservative establishment had long ago figured out that the easiest way to control the elected officials was to control the types of people able to participate in the electoral process, and had consequently drawn up one of the most restrictive electoral codes of any state in the nation. The rules of the political game were weighted in their favor, making it difficult for anti-establishment voters or candidates to be very successful, and an anti-establishment politician who momentarily got the upper hand might find the rules of the game being blatantly changed in the middle of the fourth quarter. Attempts to democratize these rules were fought vigorously, and changes came slowly and grudgingly—and at the hands of the federal government. The entire history of the expansion of suffrage in Texas is a story of federal court decisions and constitutional amendments.

Many of the most insidious devices had been removed years ago. "White-only" political primaries had been outlawed in 1944, restrictions on voting privileges of servicemen in Texas had been removed in 1965, and the poll tax was stopped as a qualification for voting in any election in 1966, all by decisions of the U.S. Supreme Court. But many restrictions still existed. Texans had to register every year by January 31 to vote the rest of the year, for example, and the cost of getting your name on the ballot for county and district offices could go up into the thousands of dollars. Primary election dates were months away from the general election, increasing the costs of running for office. Legislators from urban areas ran for office in city-wide multi-member districts, allowing slates of candidates selected and backed by financially powerful groups to easily defeat independent-minded candidates and then revel in anonymity in the legislative session.

Some of these devices had been under attack for years, in both the judicial and the legislative arenas, and history just happened to catch up with many of them all at once.

Actually, the string of rulings began in December, with a ruling early in the month that the state could no longer enforce a law prohibiting aid to illiterate voters. This case had been in the federal court system over a year, and the judges had postponed action before in hopes that the Legislature would change the law, but when that august body took no action, the judges issued their order. On Christmas Eve, in a case not so much related to elections as to economic rules of the game, a three-judge federal court in San Antonio declared Texas's method of financing public schools unconstitutional. That the property tax system favored the richer school districts could not be denied by anyone, but only a few persons had expected a broadside of the magnitude fired by these judges. There had been warnings, to be sure. A similar decision had come earlier from the judicial trend-setter, the California Supreme Court, and similar cases had been filed around the country in other states. Texans had even been warned of the problems back in 1968 by Governor John Connally's Committee on Public School Education, but later sessions of the Legislature peered ostrich-like into the sand as the problems mounted. This decision gave the Legislature two years in which to act, though, putting a time limit on the ostrich act. Charges and countercharges spread across the newsprint as politicians hunted someone to blame. Since it had been a *federal* court ruling, some persons tried to place the horns and forked tails on that old nemesis, the federal judge. Government by crisis again became the order of the day, and calls for special sessions, states' rights, and even interposition were heard.

The January madness began on the seventh day when Texas's Attorney-General Crawford Martin ruled the 1971 ethics law unconstitutional. Sired by a House-Senate conference committee, the bill was a bastard version of Jim Nugent's House bill, and the Senate bill on ethics. The conferees had had almost insurmountable problems in agreeing on a final bill, and their report, which Nugent thought to be unconstitutional, passed the House on the last day of the session at five minutes before midnight on a clock that had been turned back one hour.

Martin found the bill's financial disclosure section to be overly broad, requiring upwards of 200,000 financial reports to be filed annually. He also noted that the Ethics Commission created by the bill would be so restricted that it would be almost impossible to punish any wayward legislator. After the bill's death, fingers of guilt were pointed at almost everyone who had a hand in passing the legislation. Barnes and Smith, by now involved in the governor's race, tried to pin the blame on each other. The Governor claimed his staff was working on a "tough, workable" ethics bill to be presented to a special session of the Legislature, but if they were, then he conveniently forgot to tell the legislators the next time they got together. This action left the state with only one ethics law on the books, a 1957 statute which itself was passed in reaction to a number of scandals. This law is ignored more often than not, and is generally considered useless for most regulatory purposes.

In Dallas, on January 20, a three-judge federal court declared unconstitutional the filing fee system used to pay primary election costs. This ruling was no surprise to persons aware of earlier developments. In 1970, the same three federal judges struck down the then-existing filing fee system which had required payments as high as $8900 from district judge candidates. At that time, the judges took no action, hoping the next session of the Legislature would remedy the situation. And they did, but, not wanting a flood of candidates, the new filing fee system set fees of over $3,000 for some offices.

For example, Rich Johnston of Dallas, who wanted to run for justice of the peace, found that his fee even under the new law would be $3,456. Thinking this a bit steep, he filed suit against the new law, thus setting the stage for the January 20 decision. After Texas had exhausted all of its appeal avenues, the court directed Bob Bullock, the secretary of state, to help clear the confusion, and Bullock promptly announced a schedule of filing fees ranging from $25 for some county offices to $400 for statewide offices. Johnston, under Bullock's new schedule, had to pay only $50 to get his name on the ballot. These fees, levied in order to regulate the ballot, were deemed acceptable in place of the old fees, which were levied as a revenue-raising device for each party. A candidate willing to take the status of a pauper could even get his name on the ballot by simply turning in nominating petitions with signatures from 10% of the area voters. For the first time, the State of Texas found itself paying the costs of each party's primary, although a special legislative session still had to make the final arrangements. Texas thus became the very last state in the union to begin paying primary expenses with tax money.

Two days after the filing fee decision, another Dallas three-judge federal court declared the past legislature's efforts at congressional redistricting to be null and void. The court substituted a plan of its own, based solely on population, but said it would reconsider its plan if the Legislature wanted another shot at the job. The court's plan, which had no more than 3/10 of 1% population variance, jarred more nerves among Texans on the Potomac than anything since the last vote on the oil depletion allowance. No less than six veteran Texas congressmen would be paired against each other in the May primaries through the decision. Graham Purcell of Wichita Falls and Omar Burleson of Anson would face each other, as would Clark Fisher of San Angelo and Abraham Kazen of Laredo, and Ray Roberts of McKinney and Jim Wright of Fort Worth.

The House plan had only one pairing of note, that of Democrat Purcell and Republican Bob Price of Pampa. John Dowdy had also been paired with Wright Patman of Texarkana, but Dowdy's health and legal problems left most people convinced he wouldn't run again.

The Texans in Washington held some frantic conferences, persuaded Senator Lloyd Bentsen to try to go to bat for them with the court, and began pressing Governor Smith to call a special session so the Legislature could guarantee their tenure once again. Smith took a swipe at Barnes by blaming the mess on the lack of legislative leadership and said he figured it would be "fruitless" to call a session for another redistricting bill. Then, for once in their lives, the U.S. Supreme Court came thundering to the rescue of the embattled congressmen by ordering a temporary stay of the lower court's decision, thus causing the Legislature's plan to be used for the May primaries. "Eminently proper, ..." "restores my faith," came the praises for the Supreme Court from the Potomac troglodytes. This was the only one of these January decisions to be delayed by any level of the court system.

On January 28, the same day the Supreme Court stay came in the congressional redistricting case, a three-judge federal court in Austin struck down the Legislative Redistricting Board's plan for apportioning the Texas House of Representatives. This was the second plan for the Texas House to be declared unconstitutional in six months, Gus Mutscher's political retribution plan having fallen to the axe of a state judge in August. Following that ruling, the Board's handiwork was subsequently challenged in a federal court. The main complaint was the use of multi-member legislative districts in every metropolitan area except Houston. A parade of witnesses told the judges that such devices made legislative races much more expensive, that it made slates put up by financially powerful backers more likely to win, and that they were used on purpose to dilute the voting strength of Blacks, Mexican-Americans, and Republicans.

These witnesses impressed the judges more than the State's lawyers, and the court ordered Dallas and Bexar counties to be split into single-member districts for the entire state by July 1, 1973. The task of drawing up the new districts fell to the County Commissioners' Courts in Dallas and Bexar counties, and a worried group of legislators watched as the lines were drawn.

Residency requirements were temporarily lifted so incumbents could run for election in a district in which they didn't live, and the race was on. This may have been the most far-reaching of all January decisions, and its impact will be discussed in a later chapter.

Surely some record in reverse must have been set in January, "the most unconstitutional month." It seems likely that the Sixty-second Legislature holds the dubious distinction of losing more legislation to the judges in one month than any previous legislature in Texas history. And this made an impression on the mind of the voter. The voter who had already decided that there were only crooks in Austin might now be snorting, "Hell, they're not even *good* crooks! They can't even pass bills when they want to." These decisions cast enough light on failures of the government's leadership that the Governor, the Lieutenant-Governor, the Speaker of the House, and many individual senators and representatives could each take his share of the blame. Since many of them were in campaigns now, finger-pointing and criticism became the Capitol's leading sports.

Ben Barnes and Preston Smith were trading barbs almost daily. Jon Ford reported on January 30 that the two men had taken on a "kind of Laurel and Hardy image. There they are: Caught in a revolving door, swatting each other with rolled up copies of the *Senate Journal* and the latest court order."

One other change in the rules of the game is worth a mention here. Until 1972, January 31 was the voter registration deadline. One who wished to cast a ballot in May or November had to register back in the wintertime, a period when people's minds were hardly on politics. Liberals had long groused about this setup, arguing that potential liberal voters were less inclined to register than were conservatives. This change came through the legislative process, however, instead of the judicial process. Termed by Sissy Farenthold later as the "Miracle of the Sixty-second Legislature," a bill was passed allowing year-round registration with a cut-off date thirty days before any election. Once registered, the voter renewed his registration automatically for an additional three years beyond the date of his vote every time he voted. Ironically, it appeared that this law might hurt some liberal-voting areas, because no big January voter registration drives were held. Persons and organizations who usually sponsored them became complacent after the easier registration law was passed, and only some hurried last-minute drives helped get the total number of voters up beyond the totals of past years in these areas.

January's confusion turned into February, but the political situation remained muddled. Politicians and potential politicians had until the seventh to decide what office they should seek, and file their intentions. This cleared the air in many races, but since the filing fees were not due until February 28, and the paupers' petitions not due until March 6, a bit of uncertainty still existed in some races.

The Trial in Abilene

Shortly after the seventh, though, the people's attention turned away from the Legislature's competency back to their honesty. The Abilene trial of Mutscher, Shannon, and McGinty (Free the Abilene Three!, said the bumper stickers) was set to begin on the last day of February. Perhaps the people's attention had never been too far off the honesty bit, considering that January had seen one trial of an elected official. State Senator Jim Bates of Edinburg was acquitted in a Corpus Christi District Court on January 29 on charges of receiving a stolen diamond from one of his legal clients. The case had never been connected to any of the better-known scandals, and had not attracted much attention outside Bates's South Texas area.

Another bit of February news about corrupt politicians was the ruling of Judge Roszel C. Thompson, the Baltimore, Maryland, federal judge who had presided over John Dowdy's trial. On February 24, he turned down Dowdy's plea for a new trial and slapped him with a $25,000 fine and an eighteen-month prison sentence. But, though the Dowdy decision made headlines, the attention of Texans was beginning to focus on Abilene.

The trial of the Abilene Three would become one of *the* political events of the decade. Its influence, like a Damoclean sword, would hang heavy over legislative halls, polling places, and political conversations for

years. What was on trial in that tiny Abilene courtroom was no less than
the structure of Texas society, or at least the way that society made its
rules.

Mutscher, Shannon and McGinty, no matter how great their
influence might have been or how shattering their falls to earth might be,
were only tools of that society, peons in the long-range scheme of history
that was the way the society called Texas made its rules. The trial became
a microcosm of the Texas way of life. Caught in its web were such diverse
groups as the state's beautiful people, and the sons and daughters of the
earth; some of the state's most expensive and successful criminal lawyers,
and a judge who had never been to law school; "good ol' boys" who had
received every honor their towns, school, and peers could place on them,
and men whose honors were measured in the gallons of gasoline they
pumped daily; women who were winners of beauty contests, wearers of
Neiman-Marcus's latest styles, and wed to the "good ol' boy" politicians,
and women who taught Sunday School, teased their own hair, and took
care of their farmer husbands. The trial shook the lives of college
presidents, telephone operators, professional golfers, college students,
stock brokers, and clerks, as well as the voters in the state.

Abilene itself was possibly a bad place for Texas's way of making its
rules to be placed on trial, at least from the standpoint of the three on
trial. It was just a small county town that had gotten big. Its people made
no pretense about big-city sophistication, preferring their own small-town
friendliness, their church-going atmosphere, and the morality that
country people usually expected from their elected officials. The town had
three colleges, one Baptist, one Methodist, and one Church of Christ, and
it was the largest dry town in the state (although local-option had
provided a waterhole for the evil beer drinkers). Read the wedding notices
in the Sunday Houston papers and you'll find the bride and groom's
college degrees and professional honors listed and see that they are going
off to graduate school or an establishment job; read the wedding notices
in the Sunday *Abilene Reporter-News* and you'll find many of the couples
are high-school graduates and the groom is employed by the telephone
company in Merkel and the bride is a secretary at a local finance
company.

This collision of life-styles, of attitudes about morality, was chronicled
by some of the state's top political reporters. Both wire services and most
of the metropolitan newspapers had their political experts present. Many
of these writers had observed the scandal at close range from its inception,
and their stories had helped keep the affair in the public's mind over the
months. Many of them had already been criticized for this by the
participants, and they all had more abuse heaped on their heads after it
was over.

Judge Daniel began the proceedings on the announced day, and
lawyers for both sides started the slow task of selecting the twelve good

men and true who would make the ultimate decision. In addition to the traditional local lawyers, the defendants had amassed an impressive stable of attorneys. Mutscher was represented by Frank Maloney, a bald legal scholar from Austin who had successfully defended Senator Bates in the Corpus Christi trial, and Richard "Racehorse" Haynes, a Houston criminal lawyer known for his eloquence and penchant for courtroom dramatics. Tommy Shannon had retained Joe Shannon of Fort Worth (the two were not related), and McGinty was defended by A. L. "Dusty" Rhodes of Abilene, who ran afoul of the judge's wrath on more than one occasion. The jury selection process consumed the first three days of the trial, and the major headlines in this period were made by the defense lawyers' announcements of witnesses they were subpoenaing. On Monday, subpoenas for Governor Preston Smith and Lieutenant-Governor Ben Barnes were issued.

On Tuesday several high-society Houstonians were added to the list: Mayor Louie Welch, Dr. W.H. Hinton, president of Houston Baptist College, golf pro Doug Sanders, Rev. Charles L. Allen, pastor of Houston's First United Methodist Church, George W. Conrad, an automobile dealer, and Robert Cruikshank, an auditor. The better-prepared reporters quickly listed for their readers the connection that these people had with Frank Sharp. Welch, Hinton, Conrad, and Sanders had all borrowed large amounts of money from Sharp's banking empire, mostly for the purchase of National Bankers Life stock. Hinton, whose college lay in the midst of Sharpstown, had even been on the Sharpstown Bank's board of directors. Allen, Sharp's pastor, had gone with him to Rome in 1969 when Sharp had received a high award from the Roman Catholic Jesuit order, and had accompanied him to a private audience with Pope Paul VI. Cruikshank had performed an audit on the books of the Jesuit Fathers of Houston, Inc., and organization involved in Sharp's wheeling and dealing.

When the jury selection process ended Wednesday, the lawyers had not settled on twelve good men and true, but four men and eight women, whom they hoped to be good and true. Of the men, three were workingmen and one was a student at McMurry College. The women selected included four housewives, one teacher, one clerk, one telephone operator, and one employee of a local manufacturing concern. Religiously, there were six Baptists, five Methodists, and one member of the Christian Church. After the twelve were empaneled Thursday morning, the state began presenting its case.

Travis County District Attorney Robert O. Smith, in charge of the prosecution, told the jurors the State's case would be based largely on circumstantial evidence.

"Conspirators generally work in secret and under cover, so in this case we will look to circumstances," said Smith, informing the jurors that the State's case had four points:

1. The communicated need and desire of Sharp for legislation.
2. The solicitation of money by Mutscher and the making of the loan.
3. The passage of Sharp's bills through the Legislature.
4. Immediate profit-taking by the defendants on their stock in National Bankers Life.

Then, the rest of Thursday and all of Friday was laboriously spent by detailing the circumstances. As Gayle McNutt of the *Houston Chronicle* noted in his Sunday story about the week's events, "a stack of letters, banking and hotel and telephone records are being amassed here: to prove the State's case."

Frank Sharp spent several hours on the witness stand Thursday and Friday, repeating the same story he had been telling all over the state since he had received his grant of immunity. He furnished some fuel for speculation when he did not use the same phrase that he had given the House General Investigating Committee. Testifying before that body he had referred to his agreement with Mutscher as a "tacit understanding," but he told the Abilene jury only that "he [Mutscher] smiled and I smiled and I left."

The third day of testimony, Monday, February 6, ignited a statewide explosion that took the trial far beyond the Abilene courtroom and sent shock waves reverberating down the halls of the State Capitol.

The fire was set off by an angry exchange between Bob Smith and Frank Maloney. A disagreement arose while Smith was questioning Eugene Palmer, a partner in John Osorio's law firm, who had drafted the banking bills at Frank Sharp's request.

The jury was removed from the courtroom while the dispute was settled, and did not hear Smith reply to a sharp Maloney question with, "I think it is going to become quite clear that the Governor is a co-conspirator in this case, and that he accepted the loans and that his call was necessary to keep this legislation going." Though the jury didn't hear the remark, the couple of dozen newsmen did, and the word "co-conspirator" flashed into the headlines all over the state Tuesday morning. Smith, who was now campaigning for a third term, angrily denied the charge, and sent his political ally Secretary of State Bob Bullock charging into the fray like a wounded water buffalo. Bullock held a press conference at the Capitol on about forty-five minutes' notice, charging that District Attorney Smith had exceeded "the bounds of good taste and the ethical limits of his office to defend and promote the candidacy of Ben Barnes," who was also running for governor. Then Bullock tried to drag Barnes into the mudhole by charging that District Attorney Smith was in possession of "significant evidence regarding Ben Barnes's personal involvement in the National Bankers Life-Sharpstown Affairs, which he apparently has no intention of pursuing." This evidence, indicated Bullock, was Mrs. Ruth Shockley, a former secretary in the Carr-Osorio law firm, who could testify that Barnes had visited the firm's office just before the banking bills were passed in the Senate. Mrs. Shockley was, however, not called to testify before the Abilene jury. Bullock also told the press conference that he hoped the district attorney would repeat his remark outside the courtroom "so a slander action could be filed against him immediately."

Bullock's blast, of course, brought a bombastic reply from the Barnes camp. Robert Spellings, Barnes's assistant, told newsmen, "As far as I am concerned, a drowning man [Governor Smith] going down for the third time sent his hatchet man [Bullock] to try to take Barnes with him."

The publicity surrounding Bob Smith's remark, and replies, charges and countercharges of Preston Smith, Bob Bullock, Robert Spellings and Ben Barnes completely overshadowed the Abilene scene for the better part of the week. In perhaps one of the most poignant newspaper columns in Texas history, the *Houston Post*'s popular Lynn Ashby told the story of the Alamo on March 7, the day after the "conspirator" statement had stunned Texans, and asked the rhetorical question, "What is the distance from the Alamo to Abilene? in Men?":

Imagine for a moment facing the jury box where the men in coonskin hats and leather jackets sit—holding their rifles and powder horns—explaining for them that they died for the glory of unsecured loans and bank stock. Invite Davy Crockett over some evening to watch the campaign speeches on the tube—the televised cop-outs. Sit on a siding with Jim Bowie and watch the campaign train roar by, and note his expression. Tell Travis all about the last session of the legislature—then duck. Duck.

Ah, the last letter from the Alamo—as drawn up by the House Investigations Committee: "We find no wrongdoing on the part of Mr. Santa Anna, a freely elected and highly responsible leader. His demand for a surrender has been answered with appreciation and the master key to the front door. If our call for support is neglected, we shall do something, or other. Maybe. If at all. Then again we may bug out the back."

And finally, imagine Sam Houston—a bit tipsy, perhaps, with scowl on face, hand on cane, floppy hat low over sunburned forehead—walking into the voting booth with you. Watch his face closely as you explain the list of candidates, their histories, their deeds, their headlines.

We need enough good men—150 in the House who once more are joined by 31 men from across the way—in the Senate. Add to them governor, lieutenant-governor, and so on. Alas, it appears that once again we need about 185 men who will stand up and be counted.

But where are you, Travis, now that we really need you? For we no longer answer the surrender demand with a cannon shot, we are no

*longer determined to sustain ourselves as long as possible & die like a
soldier who never forgets what is due to his own honor & that of his
country.*

Perhaps it is time once again to remember the Alamo.

While the public's indignation was growing, the twelve jurors were
seeing the State's case being built plank-by-plank. Joseph Novotny,
former president of Sharpstown State Bank, took the stand to testify that
Sharp himself had personally ordered the large unsecured loans made to
the politicians involved.

All three of the defendants had submitted financial statements, but
the statements alone would not have justified making the loans, Novotny
said. His former boss Sharp's banking acumen took some serious blows
from Novotny. "Mr. Sharp," he said, "is probably a genius in many areas
but in banking terminology he doesn't know the difference between an
overdraft and a cash asset." The former president stated that the
Sharpstown State Bank had kept an average of 85% of its assets loaned
out instead of the level of 60% which most banks shoot for, but "I was
never able to convince Mr. Sharp that a bank should have reserves. He
always said all the money should be put to work."

The jurors also heard a member of the House Committee on Banks
and Banking testify that there was a lot of confusion, and that the bills
were reported out of the committee after a thirty-minute meeting. That
legislator also said he didn't know the bills were introduced until just
before the meeting.

The state also presented Father Michael Kennelly, former president
of the Jesuit Fathers of Houston, Inc., a religious order which the SEC
claimed had lost $6 million in dealings with Frank Sharp. Kennelly said
Sharp had arranged for the Jesuits to buy the National Bankers Life stock
owned by the politicians at a $20-a-share price. He had always relied on
Sharp's financial advice, testified the Father, and did this time, too,
completely unaware as he signed the necessary papers that the stock was
selling on the open market for about $14.75 a share. "Why did you buy at
the inflated price?" asked prosecutor Smith. Kennelly answered in a
wavering voice, "Mr. Sharp advised me it would be a good investment to
buy NBL stock . . . that's the reason. Mr. Sharp advised me to."

A few more witnesses nailed the final plank on the State's case, and
they presented the last of their evidence on Friday, March 10. There was
much speculation over the weekend about what type of defense the three
men would employ. They had subpoenaed almost four dozen witnesses,
including the officials previously named, and twenty-eight members of the
House. Most observers were expecting a long defense with much political
fireworks, but in a complete surprise, the lawyers for the three stood up in
court Monday and rested their case without calling a single defense
witness.

"The State has not made a case," Joe Shannon told newsmen. "I don't think we are in a position where we need to be helped," he added. Richard "Racehorse" Haynes was of the same opinion, telling reporters that the prosecutors "just don't have one piddling iota of evidence" to prove their charges. Judge Daniel set the final arguments for Tuesday and then recessed the court overnight.

It was a day of oratory, that day of the final arguments, some good, some bad, some mediocre. By all accounts the most eloquent of the speakers was Mutscher's man, Richard "Racehorse" Haynes. He was the last defense speaker, reminding the jurors that we have a system of law and not of men: "It doesn't matter whether you personally approve of Gus Mutscher or Tommy Shannon or Rush McGinty. But when this trial is over, I want you to be able to look each one of them in the eye and say 'I followed the law.'"

Frank Maloney's summation made fun of the State's case. "All during this trial I have wondered where the State's evidence was," he told the jurors. "Are you going to let the State tell you that 'he smiled and I smiled' constituted an agreement?"

But if Haynes was the most eloquent, District Attorney Bob Smith was clearly the man of the day to the jurors, playing them "like a violin," according to one reporter. As many public men in Texas do, he relied on rural pronunciations and popular, if grammatically incorrect, phraseology to convince the jury that he was one of them. In a thundering "Mess in Austin" speech, he reminded the jurors of that old question "Why don't they do something about the mess in Austin?" "You are now 'they'. If you think what is going on in Austin is O.K., then you can put your Good Housekeeping Seal of Approval on it by saying 'not guilty' in this case," he told them. "If we can't convict a high public official on the evidence we've got here, then we might as well turn our State Capitol over to the money changers. And from what we've heard here, that's about where it is now."

Smith also reminded the jurors that "Those loans were collateralized by the Office of the Speaker of the House and that office doesn't belong to Gus Mutscher. It belongs to you and me and the people of Texas."

The next morning, on the "Ides of March," the jury began deliberating, and after two hours and twenty minutes they told the judge they had reached a verdict.

The jury foreman was Larry Yerger, the 28-year-old McMurry College sudent. He rose, dressed in cowboy boots and blue jeans, looked at expensively-suited Gus Mutscher and exclaimed "Guilty!" He repeated the sentence for the other two defendants and a state hung its head in shame. A few minutes after the decision, Mutscher, Speaker of the House, and his wife, a former Miss America, sat down on a courtroom bench and began helplessly sobbing. His old white-haired father stood ramrod-straight behind him, hand on his son's shoulder, tears running out of eyes that were peering straight ahead in the silent courtroom. After regaining their composure, a teary-eyed Speaker and his teary-eyed Miss America strolled out of the old red-brick courthouse onto the front page of every newspaper in the state.

It had been exactly one year before to the day that Mutscher's powerful team in the Sixty-second Legislature had defeated the Farenthold resolution and given birth to the Dirty Thirty.

After the defense requested that the jury be dismissed on Thursday, Judge Daniel sentenced the three men to five-year probated sentences. Then the three held a brief news conference to repeat their claims of innocence and announce plans to appeal the decision. "God knows I am innocent," said Gus Mutscher. "I have lived my life dedicated to the proposition that ours is a system of laws instead of men. I am disappointed and distressed at the verdict, but I have not lost faith with our system. I understand how the jury was persuaded that its verdict was right. They, like many good citizens of our state, have been subjected to an incessant deluge of publicity, for the most part adverse and critical." As he left the courthouse, he told reporters that "Donna and I leave you as church people," and referred them to a Bible verse, Matthew 5:44—"Pray for them which despitefully use you and persecute you."

Shannon and McGinty both maintained their innocence before the press conference, Shannon stating, "I hold no hatred or malice in my heart" . . . and "I will be vindicated" by the appeal.

Mutscher's lawyer Haynes maintained his eloquence outside the courtroom, trying as Mutscher did to place some of the blame for the decision on newsmen: "When you put the focus of every lens in the land on a single topic you create a pressure that jurors have a hard time overcoming. You prevent a fair and impartial trial . . . . Let's put an end to this system where we pillory people in public office who have no real opportunity to defend themselves and who are subjected to the criticism of citizens of this state because of what is written or said . . . . These people have been hurt. They are great Americans."

The courthouse was jammed with over 100 prominent Texans who had come in to testify as character witnesses if needed. State senators, representatives, judges, government officials, and ministers were present, some of them having driven all night to get there. One of them, Henry Boehm, Dean of Mutscher's alma mater Blinn College in Brenham and a former Bible school teacher of Mutscher's, described his former pupil as a "wonderful Christian man . . . the finest gentleman on the face of the earth." (Later the college hired Mrs. Mutscher to teach speech, and quit using as a text in its government classes a book of readings on Texas politics that had a long article about the Sharpstown Scandal.)

Some Texas politicians were quick to react to the shock wave. "The unsavory smell of corruption hangs like a rancid blanket over Texas," said Sissy Farenthold in Austin. Several members of the Dirty Thirty said they felt vindicated. Gubernatorial candidate Dolph Briscoe called it a "terrible disgrace to Texas," and said, "We must make sure this never happens again." Preston Smith put out an inane statement saying "All of us in State government must now put our shoulders to the wheel and push harder to find solutions to the pressing problems facing our state . . ."

Political analysts all over the state proclaimed the voters to be angrily waiting for May 6 so *they* could cast a verdict or two. Brenham was appearing to rally slightly to the side of its fallen hero. Radio station KWHI in Brenham editorially declared him innocent, and the editor of the *Brenham Banner-Press* predicted he would be re-elected in spite of the conviction. A more informed political observer, though, Roland Lindsey, head of United Press International's Austin bureau, figured that Mutscher was through. "It's not going to be a case of legislators jumping off the bandwagon," he said. "What you will see is the bandwagon throwing Mutscher off."

As you have seen, members of the press drew quite a bit of criticism from Mutscher, Haynes, Preston Smith, and many other persons involved either directly or peripherally in the trauma of the Year of Frank Sharp. "They created an atmosphere," "they focused their lenses," came the cries. Though the politicians probably felt the press corps sat back and collectively smiled a very smug smile after the Abilene decision, there was some disagreement and soul-searching going on in that profession, too.

Molly Ivins, writing beautifully about the trial in the March 31 issue of the biweekly *Texas Observer*, defended the actions of the press, but voiced her doubts about Mutscher's guilt:

> *While it is one thing to attack the press for a given instance of gross behavior, the events on the day the verdict was announced had nothing to do with the buckets of slop dumped on the Press by the defendants, their wives and their lawyers both before and after the verdict came in. Miss America of 1964 harassed the press throughout the trial in niggling little ways. Mutscher did a credible imitation of a martyr in his post-sentencing press conference. Haynes went on at great length about "suggestions and innuendoes" and those of us who "pillory people in public office who have no opportunity to defend themselves."*
>
> *A more specious argument I never heard . . . . The jury in Abilene didn't make Gus Mutscher guilty. The press in this state didn't make Gus Mutscher guilty. Gus Mutscher took the loans and passed the bills and made the profits. What he did makes him guilty, not what anyone else has done to him.*
>
> *But I am still not convinced that Mutscher is legally guilty. I have been convinced, ever since I made that first trip to Dallas to study the SEC documents more than a year ago, that he is factually guilty. But Mr. Bumble was right about the law. Had I been on that jury, I don't*

think I would have voted to convict. Take that, defense lawyers. (They freaked when they found an Observer reader on the jury panel.)

To me the recurrent theme in the trial was being seized by a ridiculous desire to leap to my feet and explain the House of Representatives to the jury. "Do you believe," a defense laywer inquired with insidious persuasiveness, "that 123 legislators would have voted for this bill if they didn't think it was a good idea?" And I wanted to jump up and say, "Yes, yes, of course they would, that's the way it works!" And the defense lawyers kept saying, "there was nothing unusual about the way the bill was passed." And I wanted to say, "Right. It wasn't unusual. No hearing. No debate. No one had read the thing. Just slipped through. That isn't unusual. That's the way Gus runs the House. That's what's wrong!"

Farenthold has been right all along. The significance of the Sharp affair vis-a-vis state government is not that it proves that Mutscher or Shannon or McGinty or anyone else was on the take: it proves that the way the Legislature runs is sick and that it has got to be changed. Unless Mutscher's conviction provides the impetus for reform, all of us might as well never have gone to Abilene.

Glen Castlebury, writing in the March 19 *Austin American-Statesman*, also defended the press and then bore down harder on the Legislature:

Yet, those involved, in and out of the courtroom, continue to berate the press. That dog just won't hunt. The facts are there, and the press didn't make those facts—it just reported them. No amount of crying can erase them. And with those facts, the public, much more than the jury, is equipped to make its judgement . . . .

[District Attorney Bob] Smith's "mess in Austin" speech was a beautiful, pointed summation of what the scandal lays bare about the state government and the men in it.

But Smith would be the first person to admit that the conspiracy law as written is nearly impossible to work with, not because there wasn't a good case, but because the law as written by the legislature was left with loopholes nearly as large as the stock scandal itself . . . .

It all leads one to wonder whether the alleged brilliant legal minds of the legislature—the Nugents, the Hales, the Halls, the Herrings— are really smart, or if in fact they are just dumb like foxes. If that is too strong an indictment, let it only be noted that it is no stronger than the stench of this scandal.

The legislative process was hit again by Sam Kinch, Jr. in the March 11 *Dallas Morning News*:

There is no doubt in this corner—as has been expressed here for 14 months—that Mutscher and his friends used positions of public trust for private gain. The question is whether they did something demonstrably, illegally wrong under the law . . . .

It is not simply the fact that Mutscher and his pals made a bunch of money off the deals. And it is not even the fact that Frank Sharp's bank bills were approved by the legislature when the profits were made.

It is rather, that something is seriously wrong with the legislative process if an affair like this is allowed to go on without scrutiny by the voting public.

Ernest Stromberger, the *Dallas Times-Herald's* Austin bureau chief, joined Kinch in criticizing the legislative process on March 12:

ABILENE—The defense in the Mutscher bribery conspiracy trial is scoring some points through a simple technique: Placing the quickie passage of the 1969 banking bills in the context of normal legislative routine . . . .

The defense's strategy is carried out by asking witnesses if there was anything unusual about the way the 1969 Sharp-backed state banking deposit insurance bills raced through the Legislature. With triumphant smiles, the defense attorneys await the certain negative responses from the State's own witnesses; they have no choice but to admit that the superficial look given to the Sharp bills is indeed typical in the Texas Capitol.

The defendants in the bribery conspiracy case, of course, cannot be convicted on the basis of the laxity of their colleagues in failing to scrutinize an obviously far-reaching piece of legislation. But it appears ironic that the defense is able to make such good use of the very weaknesses in the legislative system to which the current reform movement is directed.

One suggesting this before the trial would have been laughed out of Austin, but perhaps Mutscher would have fared better if the jurors had been members of the Capitol press corps. At least they know how the Legislature operates.

Payrolls and Postage Stamps:
To Keep the Voters Aware

There was little over two months between Gus Mutscher's "Ides of March" and other politicians' "May Day of Reckoning" but there was to be no let-up in publicity about the questionable activities of the Austin bunch.

Governor Smith called a very short special session of the Legislature to begin on March 28. The convicted Speaker resigned his position of power and the ensuing struggle found Rayford Price of Palestine sitting on top of the heap. Price, an East Texas conservative, had once been a loyal Mutscher-man (he even served as best man at Gus's wedding), but had fallen from grace when he began his own speakership campaign. After Price's victory, he replaced Tommy Shannon as chairman of the House Administration Committee with his supporter Ed Howard of Texarkana. The new regime allowed more public access to expense account records of the House members, and digging by newsmen led to more scandalous developments, one involving nepotism and one involving questionable expense account items.

Texas has long had nepotism laws prohibiting state officials from hiring their relatives, but somewhere years ago members of the House and Senate began hiring each other's relatives, thinking that since they were members of different bodies the law wouldn't apply. Years of existence sanctioned the idea, and when the scandal surfaced, many unsuspecting legislators were honestly unaware that they were violating the law. In retrospect, it appears that the vast majority of the hiring done this way, say, a representative's wife hired by a senator, was completely on the up-and-up, and a day's pay was taken in exchange for a full day's work. But, as the Secretary of the Senate Charles Schnabel said, "It could be we've been wrong all this time."

The rottenest apple of them all, though, caused even the most honest hiring arrangements to come under fire, and left the voters shaking their heads once again. The lead in uncovering this scandal was taken by the *Houston Chronicle*'s Austin staff of Bo Byers, George Kuempel, and Mary Rice Brogan.

While investigating a hiring relationship involving Senator David Ratliff of Stanford and Representative John Allen of Longview, who frequently hired each other's relatives, they discovered a number of Ratliff's relatives on his *own* payroll. The probe slowly moved as relationships between the Senator and his employees were examined, and it seemed in April of 1972 that the *Chronicle* had something new to report almost daily, either the finding of another of Ratliff's relatives on his payroll or some other juicy tidbit about the affair. Allen and Ratliff, for example, sometimes employed each other's children at a full salary while the children attended school full-time or held another job full-time. And Ratliff's practice of having his employee's checks delivered to him personally caused some problems for him, too. The *Chronicle* retained a handwriting analyst to examine some of the checks issued to Ratliff's children, and in the expert's opinion Ratliff himself had endorsed most of the checks.

The *Chronicle*'s withering blasts caused Ratliff to end his twenty-one-year legislative career late in April by resigning his office, and withdrawing from his current campaign. The *Chronicle* story reporting the resignation mentioned that they had found seven of Ratliff's relatives on state payrolls, including five on the Senator's own staff. The Travis County District Attorney Bob Smith, rapidly becoming the "Conscience of the Legislature," stated that a grand jury would make a full-scale investigation of the nepotism violations.

On April 19, Attorney-General Crawford Martin informed everyone that the law really meant what it said, thus declaring illegal what over seventy-five legislators had been doing for years. Legally the violation was only a misdemeanor, but for some of the politicians involved, the political penalty would be death.

Along with the nepotism disclosures, the newsmen burrowing through the mountains of documents unearthed some strange items that certain representatives had charged to the taxpayers. Representative Jim Earthman, a Houston Republican, had charged $74.85 for clock rental to the State in March of 1971. Representative Joe Hanna of Breckinridge had bought an $82, six-volume biography of Abraham Lincoln and charged it to the State. Many members used their expense accounts to purchase several-hundred-dollar sets of law books. Telephone and postage expenses soared for many legislators when they were in re-election campaigns, creating speculation that the State was financing their political races.

One former House member, Walter Knapp of Amarillo, had already been indicted by a Travis County grand jury on March 30 for allegedly using postage stamps obtained through his expense account to buy a pickup truck. At a trial in May, between the two primary elections, Knapp was found guilty by a jury after only twenty-nine minutes' deliberation. Prosecutor Bob Smith produced records showing Knapp had charged 145,000 six-cent stamps but only 6,000 envelopes to his expense account in 1970. After a car salesman testified that Knapp had paid him $1200 in stamps for a used pickup truck, Knapp's fate was evidently sealed. Later the jury sentenced him to four years in prison.

On the day after Knapp's sentencing, still another Travis County grand jury nailed four more political hides to the wall. Senator Ratliff and Representative Allen were both indicted on charges stemming from the nepotism investigations, and Representative Tom Holmes of Granbury and former Representative Hudson Moyer of Amarillo were indicted for alleged postage stamp misdealings. Holmes was charged with applying $1,995 in stamps toward the $3,195 price of a pickup truck, and Moyer with paying off a $6,000 bank loan with postage stamps. Both men allegedly got the stamps through their expense accounts.

District Attorney Smith, who by now might have been considering a "Legislative Wing" for the Travis County Courthouse, informed reporters that he would only prosecute future nepotism cases, because if he got tied up with past violations he would be in court for months.

This, then, is what the voters had been subjected to for over fifteen months as they walked into the polling places on May 6. Scandal after scandal, charge after charge, and denial after denial. By now the more imaginative voters probably had envisioned a fleet of moving vans backed up to the state Capitol with a stream of legislators carrying things out to haul off, stamps in their pockets, typewriters in their hands, chairs balanced on their heads, even the pictures from the walls of the hall.

It was as if the entire state had been called to serve on a huge jury panel, with over four million of them finally being selected to serve as jurors. Their sensibilities, their moral images, had been shattered by the months of outrage, and now the public servants had to walk barefoot through the jagged pieces laying on the floor.

Lynn Ashby told his readers:

> *Without question it was the Sharpstown Scandal that brought it all to light, that caused journalists to write and readers to read, for the rank-and-file to decide that things were rank enough . . . .*
>
> *Perhaps we all owe a great debt of gratitude to Frank Sharp and Gus Mutscher and Tommy Shannon and their cast of thousands because, however unintentionally, they nudged us into action . . . .*
>
> *Yet it cannot be said with all certainty that Frank Sharp & Co. toppled the Texas government. It may have been the last straw—the one that broke the voter's confidence, but all it really did was turn public attention to a situation that has been brewing for some time. . . . Oh, the situations had been there all along and had been pointed out again and again, only heretofore no one really gave a damn. But on May 6 they gave. It was that one time of the year when voters were allowed their say. It may not meet the equal-time rules of the FCC, but it works.*

PART TWO:
TRIAL BY BALLOT

Chapter 3

THE PRIMARIES

Texas is a one-party state. Ever since the old-time Texas Democrats regained control of the state from Reconstruction's Radical Republicans, they have dominated the governor's mansion and legislative halls. That overwhelming political fact has dashed many a good candidate's campaign against a brick wall. Oh, their dominance has been questioned and has even been shaky, but the Democrats have continued to rule.

Republican victories in Texas have been the product of either extraordinary circumstances or geographical accidents. The only two Republican presidential candidates to carry Texas before 1972, for example, were Herbert Hoover in 1928, and Dwight D. Eisenhower in 1952 and 1956, both being beneficiaries of abnormal circumstance. Hoover's opponent was a New York Catholic who favored repealing prohibition, and in 1928 that was a little too much for the average Texan. (That average Texan felt that his transgressions were woefully punished by a vengeful Democratic God, though, when the Depression came while Hoover was in office, and, as a result, more than one grandfatherly Texan has been known to say, "I promised the Lord that I'd never again vote for a Republican if He'd never send us any more Depressions.")

General Ike, a native-born Texan, ran against an "egg-head intellectual" who did not take Texas's side in the Tidelands controversy, and Ike was endorsed by the state Democratic Party.

Too, there are places where "un-Texan" cultures and ways of life happened to be ensconced in Texas. The German Hill Country in Central Texas was settled shortly before the Civil War by German immigrants many of whom remained loyal to the Union during the war, and whose offspring have remained loyal to the Republican Party ever since. And then there's that stretch of Kansas called theTexas Panhandle that really can't be persecuted too much for voting more like Kansas than the rest of Texas.

What all of this means, in political realities, is that the most important election in Texas is usually not the general election in November, but the Democratic Party primaries in May and June. Since the Democratic tradition is strong, almost all Democrats will defeat their Republican opponents (if they have any) without much bother. Though the November win is not as automatic as it once was, and though Republicans have elected one U.S. Senator and scared a few would-be governors, the election which really determines who will take office the following January is still the Democratic primary.

What it means, too, is that one-party politics usually means no-party politics. There are factions, of course, in the Texas Democratic Party, a Liberal and a Conservative faction. These factions have been doing battle for some time, and their bloodlettings are every bit as vicious as the Democratic-Republican feuds nationally. While the Conservative Democrats have usually managed to stay on top, the Liberals have kept on playing, winning a few, losing many, and having some sold out.

But these factions have never been either able or willing to bring a measurable degree of responsibility to the party elections. Political parties nationally have never been noted for their discipline, but they appear almost as military units when compared to wings, or factions of the Texas Democratic Party. There is, after all, no Conservative or Liberal majority leader, or minority whip, nor even a campaign committee. There is no research staff developing the issues, printing position papers, and pointing out inaccuracies in statements made by the other side. So, instead of responsible debates and reasoned choices, the party primary in Texas is more likely to be determined by personalities and irrelevancies. The one whose name is the most familiar, whose smile is the most photogenic, whose statements are the most appealingly bland, and whose stands on issues are the least forthright, is more than likely the one who will emerge on top. Since, in a popularity contest where issues are relegated to a minor role, money for television and billboards can make the difference, the Conservatives have always had the upper hand. Money, of course, won't win a contest all by itself, but a candidate without it, no matter how well qualified he might be, always has an uphill struggle. The 1972 elections provided more examples of proof for all these truisms of Texas politics.

The Big One:
The Race for the Democratic
Nomination for Governor

The race which really captured the attention of Texans (and even a few national observers) was the one for the Democratic gubernatorial nomination. There was an ample cast of characters, and enough drama, surprises, and excitement to keep the race high in public visibility. This 1972 election year would have undoubtably provided some surface changes, even without Sharpstown's impact, for the political currents had produced some new sandbars and rapids. The incumbent governor was a Conservative Democrat, but had never been a member of the establishment conservative Democratic team. The words "establishment" and "team" are hard to define successfully but almost any in-depth

observer of Texas politics knows beyond a doubt that they exist. The
players and performers change over the years, but the team keeps on
rolling. For the twenty or so years preceding 1972, the key players on the
team were Lyndon Johnson and John Connally. Connally was Johnson's
campaign manager back in that famous 1948 Senate race, and Johnson's
tainted 87-vote win propelled him on a career that took him all the way to
the White House. Young John then went off to make his fortune, and
didn't get back into active politics until the 1960s. He served for a while
as President Kennedy's Secretary of the Navy, then resigned to come
back home and win three terms as governor, and then began playing
footsy with the Republicans, serving President Nixon first as Secretary of
the Treasury and later as national chairman of the Democrats for Nixon
campaign organization in 1972.

The Texas Democratic Party in the 1960s was securely in the hands
of the Johnson-Connally team. Its well-oiled machinery controlled every
level of party structure from the precinct conventions to the state
Democratic Executive Committee. State party conventions were exercises
in un-democracy, with the man holding the gavel calling the shots any
way he chose to.

The heir apparent to the Johnson-Connally team was the young
lieutenant-governor, Ben Barnes. Everyone expected Barnes to try a move
up in 1972, as soon as he could decide whether to try for Smith's job or
the U.S. Senate seat held by Republican John Tower. Smith and Barnes
had never gotten along well, and most of the establishment people weren't
all that wild about Smith, so a good deal of pressure began coming to
Barnes, urging him to run for governor. The establishment didn't
particularly want to see Tower unseated anyhow, even though he was a
Republican, because his voting record was extremely pleasing to them
(that says something about establishment Democrats in Texas).

The political currents had not yet washed ol' Preston down the river,
either. He was proud of his record of sixes (six years in the House, six
years in the Senate, and six years as lieutenant-governor), and in normal
times he could have been expected to try to extend his service as governor
to six years. These were not normal times, though, and few political
observers expected him to try for a third term, especially after his
$62,500 profit on National Bankers Life stock came to light. But
Preston's maverick tendencies were well known, and if he decided to run
again, it might be surprising but it certainly wouldn't be shocking.

Another man of Preston's ilk was expected to run for the position.
Dolph Briscoe, like Preston a conservative Democrat, but not really a
team member, had spent a good bit of his money in a 1968 campaign, and
he had been planning ever since to run in 1972.

One other possible candidate was in the wings: Texas liberal
Democrats' old lion Ralph Yarborough. His bumpy political career had
led him to thirteen years in the U.S. Senate after three unsuccessful races

for governor back in the 1950s. Lloyd Bentsen had unseated him in the 1970 Democratic primary, and though he was 67 years old, he was planning to run for either Governor or U.S. Senator. His loyal band of supporters would make him a formidable foe for either position.

"Help Bring a New Day to Texas"

The first man to announce his decision was Barnes. Appearing before a press conference on June 14, 1971 (the same day Frank Sharp received his grant of immunity), the young lieutenant-governor said he would run for governor. "The greatest issue in Texas today is the loss of faith and confidence in our state government," he told the assembled reporters, and he said one of the reasons for this was the SEC lawsuit. He clearly felt that his election would help restore the people's faith in their government.

Barnes's Horatio Alger rise to fame was by then well known and well chronicled. He was the product of rural Texas, having been born in the small town of Gorman in Eastland County on April 17, 1938. His parents lived in the Comyn community a few miles down the road in Comanche County. His younger life was spent in this rural West Central Texas area where he graduated from De Leon High School. Ben's family was a farming family in this peanut-growing area.

Ben was a good student in school, and took an active role in school athletics, lettering in four different sports: football, basketball, baseball, and track. He also took an active interest in Martha Morgan, the class valedictorian, and they were married within a year after their graduation from De Leon High School in 1955.

His football prowess had drawn several college scholarship offers but a high school injury kept him from taking them. His injury was a good thing, though, Barnes later said; "otherwise I would probably be a football coach today."

After a semester each at Texas Christian University and Tarleton State College, he and his wife packed up and moved to Austin, where he entered The University of Texas in the fall of 1956. One of his campaign documents referred to their time in Austin as the "very lean years." Ben took business administration courses in the morning, worked for the State Health Department in the afternoon, and sold vacuum cleaners door-to-door on weekends and at nights. He and Martha also remodeled and painted a couple of old houses they bought with his father's help, and then sold them at a profit. After graduating with a Bachelor of Business Administration degree in 1960, he and Martha moved back home. Barnes later credited his job at the State Health Department with leading him into a political career. He came into contact with several legislators and this stirred his interest in political affairs.

After returning home with his degree in 1960, he began considering running for state representative. The incumbent in his district was not seeking re-election, but it would still be a tough fight because Ike Hickman, a Brownwood city councilman and businessman, was already in the race, and Brownwood, with 20,000 citizens, was the largest town in the district. Barnes talked to his De Leon friends about running, and one of them, C. H. (Ham) Locke, secretary of the De Leon Chamber of Commerce, recalled, "I was stunned, because the man already in that race was a well-known, personable man who had spoken to every ladies' group around here half a dozen times. I asked Ben if he had any money. He said, 'No, but I've got a friend who is willing to print me some cards and I know where I can borrow a little money. I think I can win it on shoe leather.'"

Ben and Martha campaigned hard together, passing out thousands of cards and running a true shoe-leather campaign. A Brownwood man, I.F. Bay, who was then a regional officer in the Texas Manufacturing Association, one of the establishment's more successful lobbying organizations, encouraged the pair, and, after an intensive door-to-door campaign, Barnes swamped the surprised Hickman by a five-to-one margin.

Ben did not make much of a splash in the storm-tossed 1961 session of the Legislature. He did, however, become completely lined up with the conservative, pro-business lobby team which dominated the House. The lobby was after a sales tax that year instead of Governor Price Daniel's more business-aimed tax package, and Barnes voted down the line for the sales tax and against Daniel's package. His friendship that session with Representative Byron Tunnell of Tyler later paid handsome dividends. Tunnell wanted to be speaker in the 1963 session, and Barnes began working, gathering up votes for him. Another contact made during this time proved valuable later on, too. John Connally, who had just resigned his Secretary of the Navy position to come back to Texas to run for governor, recalled that Ben Barnes was "the first man to greet me after I announced for governor." The two struck up a friendship, and Barnes began campaigning for Connally, too.

Tunnell, with Barnes's help, was elected speaker in 1963, and was assured of re-election in 1965. Ben enjoyed this trip into higher politics, and began plotting his own race for 1967. In the 1963 session, Tunnell rewarded his young friend by naming him chairman of the important Rules Committee and making him one of his most trusted legislative leaders. Barnes also helped the new governor, John Connally, in his dealings with the House, and voted down the line with the team in the House, thus keeping his conservative label almost spotless. The up-and-coming young politician was honored with a banquet in Brownwood on December 17, 1963, and he was praised by Connally, who spoke by phone since he was still recovering from the wounds he suffered during President Kennedy's assassination. The new president, Lyndon Johnson, wired his congratulations, and Speaker Tunnell,

Lieutenant-Governor Preston Smith, and dozens of House members found time in the busy Christman season to travel to Brownwood to pay their respects.

Those who traveled to Brownwood that December night were probably glad they did after a rapid-fire series of events left young Ben Barnes sitting on top of the legislative heap a little over a year later. It began as members of the Legislature gathered in Austin early in January, 1965, where the Fifty-ninth Legislature was about to begin its regular session. Barnes was looking forward to being a top legislative power again since he had helped Tunnell securely nail down his speaker's chair for the session. He was also hoping to lay the final plans for his own campaign for speaker of the 1967 legislative session. The series of events began on January 8, 196, when Tunnell abruptly resigned from the Legislature, and ended 36 hours later with Barnes sitting in the speaker's chair, after pulling off "the most amazing political coup in Texas history," according to Stuart Long, a highly-respected Capitol newsman. Governor Connally's guiding hand was firmly imprinted on the sequence of happenings. Tunnell's resignation came because Connally was appointing him to fill a vacancy on the powerful, prestigious Texas Railroad Commission, the regulatory body for the Texas petroleum industry. Tunnell called Barnes to tell him the news early Friday morning, two hours before a public announcement was made about the resignation.

Barnes seized the opportunity, and immediately announced his candidacy for the position in a Capitol news conference, and then hurried off to the Driskill Hotel. There he hurriedly had a bank of telephones installed and, along with some friends in the Legislature, began calling the other representatives asking for their vote for the office. Some of Connally's friends had been with Barnes at the news conference, including Frank Erwin, later to become a controversial chairman of the University of Texas Board of Regents, and two of Connally's staff members, Julian Read and Larry Temple. The establishment's support thus went solidly to Barnes, and, on Tuesday, January 12, 1965, 26-year-old Ben Barnes became Speaker of the House, one of the most powerful positions in Texas.

Barnes and Connally together ran the House without much trouble. The team's strength was such that a hundred votes, the parliamentary necessity for doing what you pleased, could be raised 'most anytime a little pressure was levied. Ben rode the establishment bandwagon to re-election in 1967, and thus had four years' experience in the powerful position at the age of 30.

He began trying to build good relationships with Texas liberals while he was speaker. A man who realized he had the votes on his side could afford to be magnanimous, and his door was usually open to them. He built a reputation as a good political fence-maker and mender at this time and it became apparent that he was destined to be the successor to

Connally on the establishment team. Press and personal aides who worked for the team were grooming the rough-hewn country boy, teaching him how to look, what to say, and how to say it. He took eagerly to the coaching, and this, combined with his awesome natural ability with people, soon made it clear that he was a force to be reckoned with, both individually and as a member of the team. The November 15, 1968 *Texas Observer* declared that Barnes "stands on the threshold of becoming Texas's most powerful politician," and that his support on both ends of the political spectrum allowed him to become "perhaps in ways Lyndon Johnson never did, in Texas, the consummate consensus politician."

During this time Barnes built up good relationships with the newsmen in the Capitol. Several of them were included in a small circle of his close friends, and he was very courteous, and quickly accessible to all the others. Sometimes he was too accessible, one veteran reporter recalled later. When something happened at the Capitol, Smith, Mutscher, and the others would go into hiding until they had the event analyzed and their reaction charted. Barnes didn't take the luxury of this thinking time. He would become immediately available, and sometimes his quick answers proved embarrassing later.

After serving two terms as speaker, Ben declared his candidacy for the lieutenant-governor's chair, and overwhelmingly defeated liberal Representative Don Gladden and one other candidate. Barnes got almost 80% of the vote; significantly, Texas's labor unions, afraid of his power, bugged out and didn't endorse Gladden so as not to antagonize Barnes. Many liberals had decided by now that he was unbeatable, and were saying "We'd better learn how to live with him, because he's going to be the main force in Texas politics for years."

That November, Barnes swamped his Republican opponent and became the first candidate in Texas history to get over 2 million votes, carrying all 254 of Texas's counties. Another notch was carved in his gunhandle, and he was heralded as one of the fastest-rising politicians in the nation.

The honors and accolades that fall upon the shoulders of those young men upon whom the establishment is smiling began coming in torrents. The Texas Jaycees had already honored him as one of five outstanding young men in Texas. The National Jaycees then laid their mantle on him, proclaiming him to be one of America's ten Outstanding Young Men. He was elected to the Board of Directors of the state's Urban Action Center, and to leadership positions in the National Legislative Conference and the Council of State Governments. President Johnson appointed him to the Advisory Committee on Intergovernmental Relations, and sent him abroad twice in 1968 to represent the U.S. State Department, once at a North Atlantic Treaty Organization conference in Brussels, and once at a United Nations meeting in Geneva.

His re-election in 1970 with only a Republican opponent to worry about clearly didn't hurt his luster, and by now the state's business and professional leaders had obviously pledged their pocketbooks and editorial support to the dynamic young man who, it was predicted, would wind up in the White House. More and more national attention was focused on him. Godfrey Sperling lauded him in the *Christian Science Monitor* as the "brightest rising star" in the Texas sky. The *Wall Street Journal* took notice of him, *Newsweek* called him the "heir-apparent" to the Johnson throne. United States Senator Fred Harris of Oklahoma, then chairman of the national Democratic Party, referred to him as the next President "to come from the South or Southwest," and Johnson added his personal blessing: "I just want you to know," said the President, "that I'm for you—money, marbles, and chalk." On another occasion Johnson stated, "I genuinely believe that Ben Barnes has what it takes to carry him as far as his ambition will carry him."

In those heady days before Sharpstown, Barnes could lean back and ponder not how, but when, he would go to, not run for, the U.S. Senate: "If I went up there next year, I think I might be able to exert some influence in the 1972 presidential convention. There might be a possibility that I could consolidate the South and the Southwest, so at least they wouldn't just ride us out of the party," he told Jimmy Banks, who recorded it in his excellent book, *Money, Marbles, and Chalk.* "I think there's a chance, as a result," he added, "for me to really do something for my state. Texas needs political influence. Then, too, every day you stay down here on the state scene you get a scar. You make someone mad . . . . Up there, it wouldn't be Smith and Barnes arguing over a one-year or a two-year budget." Even after Sharpstown had broken, Barnes still counted on a move to Washington, telling Harvey Katz in 1971, "Sometimes I think that Ted Kennedy will be ready to run for President in 1976. If that happens, it will open the door to another Massachusetts-Texas Democratic ticket. And you know what happened last time with that kind of ticket."

The glittering career of Ben Barnes was not entirely without tarnish, however. The most troubling, and persistent, questions were about his financial situation. He had come from a farming-working family, had been in what he called "dismal" financial straits in 1960, and had been on the state payroll at only $4,800 a year ever since. Yet he obviously had money, and had somehow financed some extremely expensive political races. So the obvious question was how did someone living on $400 a month do all that? Barnes had enrolled in law school at The University of Texas after completing his B.B.A. degree but he had completed only one year before getting too involved in his political career to continue, and so didn't have a law firm partnership or retainer income to point to.

His replies to financial questions usually mentioned Herman Bennett, a Brownwood contractor who had befriended him as a rich uncle might befriend a favorite nephew. Bennett, said Barnes, was his financial angel, allowing him to become a partner in his construction business and accepting non-interest bearing notes as part of the investment. Barnes had also acquired substantial holdings in motel franchises, real estate operations, and radio stations. Some of his partnerships in these areas were with lobbyists and posed interesting conflict-of-interest questions. In May of 1971 Barnes released a financial statement showing assets of $267,000, liabilities of $184,000 and corresponding net worth of $83,000. In January of 1972 he told the *Houston Chronicle* that his 1970 income had been $57,000, and an aide said that most of it came from his business association with Bennett.

Statements of this sort went beyond what Texas law required of office holders, but evidently not beyond what the voters wanted to know, for the sniping and questioning never stopped. The accounting practices used on the financial statements were unusual, and at least one large newspaper criticized him for this. No mention was made in either report of the Ben Barnes Club money. These clubs were made up of supporters in his home district who sent a $10-a-month contribution to help pay political expenses incumbent on a rising young politician. This fund raised an estimated $20,000 yearly and was administered, said Barnes, by people back in his home district. If he needed some money for a political reason, he would call them up and ask for money from the fund. The financial reports didn't mention another matter which tarnished Barnes's image, either—his divorce.

Somewhere along the line, his marriage to Martha had gone sour, and late in 1970 they agreed to an uncontested divorce. They had two children, and the financial terms of the divorce and child support were not divulged in the financial statements. Both Ben and Martha later remarried, Martha on April 15, 1971, to John Noble, an Austin insurance man, and Ben on July 26, 1971, to Mrs. Nancy Sayers, widow of former Representative and later Connally aide, Scott P. Sayers. She was 42 and Barnes was 33 at the time of their marriage.

Barnes did not seem to be worried about any of these tarnish spots when he announced for governor that June day in 1971. He still had that solid wall of establishment financial and editorial support going for him and many people began wondering how to deal with the man they thought would occupy the Governor's Mansion in January, 1973. He had kept the Senate liberals happy, and he now counted many of them on his own bandwagon. This, after all, was the next logical step in his ascendancy.

"A Man You Can Believe In"

The next man to announce for the Governor's Mansion was one who had never quit running since 1968, the millionaire rancher-banker from Uvalde, Dolph Briscoe, Jr. Reported at various times to be the largest single land-owner in the state, and to have over 1,000,000 acres of land in his domain, he proved to be an enigma to many people during the campaign. His name became known, all right, but not much was known about him or his political views.

Briscoe came from an old pioneer Texas family. There were Briscoes in Texas even before it declared its independence from Mexico. A Briscoe had been present at the Washington-on-the-Brazos convention in 1836, and had later fought at San Jacinto under Sam Houston in the rout of Mexican General Santa Anna. In 1891, the Daughters of the Republic of Texas was organized at a meeting held in the home of the San Jacinto Briscoe's widow. There was even a county, way up in the Texas Panhandle, named for a Briscoe. Dolph, Jr. was born in 1923 as the only child of Dolph Briscoe, Sr., a rancher who had seen both the ups and downs financially of the cattle business. He ended his first ranching business try by going broke in the early 1920s. Then in 1923 he formed a business association with Ross Sterling, who later was to become governor, but that partnership went broke during the Depression years. Dolph, Sr. picked up the pieces, though, began once more, and this time was successful enough to amass a tremendous fiefdom that extended all the way from Uvalde, a town some 80 miles west of San Antonio, to the Mexican border. A reporter in the 1960s noted that the Uvalde telephone directory listed no less than seven different Briscoe ranches.

Dolph, Jr. thus grew up in the ranching business. He was the valedictorian of the 1939 Uvalde High School Senior Class, and then went off to Austin to The University of Texas, graduating in 1943. He later married a girl he met at Austin, Betty Jane Slaughter, and "Janey," as she was known, proved to be one of the best campaigners in his organization. After a stint in the service during World War II, he came back home, and in 1948 won the first of four two-year terms in the Texas House of Representatives.

During his service in the Legislature, he was considered a liberal, but probably that is a comment more on what constituted a liberal in those days than on Briscoe's political philosophy. Briscoe himself told Jimmy Banks in 1969 that "I would consider myself to be conservative, now, very definitely," and, "I would take issue with having been a liberal while I was in the Legislature." "During the four terms I served in the Legislature, I represented a very conservative area—and during that time I never did have an opponent . . . . What I'm saying is that I represented a very conservative area and I did it in a way that satisfied my constituents."

Briscoe also told Banks that he was not "what you would call a part of the team," and had tried to retain some measure of independence. One of Briscoe's colleagues in those legislative years, a liberal who went on to serve in the United States House of Representatives, told his friends that Briscoe would probably be a "mildly progressive" governor. The Texas AFL-CIO gave Briscoe a good rating on his voting record, determining that he had cast 68 good votes and 14 bad votes, on the selected votes they thought to be important. But the liberal-conservative battle line in the 1950s was far removed from the battle line in the 1970s.

Briscoe's legislative record is also notable for the two rural-oriented programs he helped get underway—farm-to-market roads, and screwworm eradication. He and Senator Neveille Colson of Navasota jointly sponsored the Colson-Briscoe Act, an act setting up an annual allocation for the building of farm-to-market roads in rural areas. He also helped to get the state to commit itself to a fight against a pesky enemy of the cattleman—the screwworm. These worms, larvae of a type of blowfly, hatched from eggs laid in open sores or wounds of animals, can either kill or render useless the livestock which they infest. Although the program did not become fully operational until after Dolph's legislative career ended, he took an active part in sparking the program to life.

After retiring from the Legislature, Briscoe became president of the powerful ranch organization, the Texas and Southwestern Cattle Raiser's Association, and he built up a statewide friendship among people in the cattle business. His contacts in the financial world were also maintained, since he was chairman of the board of the First State Bank of Uvalde and of the Security State Bank at Pearsall, and a director of the Alamo National Bank in San Antonio. He also held offices in both state and regional chambers of commerce; he was rewarded for this by being proclaimed "Mr. South Texas" in Laredo in 1967.

Dolph never lost touch with the political world, either, often entertaining large crowds of the state's king-makers on his Catarina Ranch southwest of Uvalde. The name Catarina became known among the state's power-elite, and Dolph drew rave notices for his hospitality. Guests could hunt, fish in the many stock tanks on the ranch, or hang around the huge ranch house on the 165,000-acre spread and sample the South Texas ranch-style cooking while talking politics with other guests. John Connally planned his first governor's race here, picking Eugene Locke to be his statewide campaign manager, a fateful decision that may have cost Briscoe Connally's support in 1968. Ben Barnes had been here, too, being dubbed "the brightest young man" he'd ever known by Connally when Barnes was introduced to a room full of the movers and shakers in Texas politics.

As Dolph began laying the groundwork for his own campaign, he started inviting not only politicians, but labor leaders, reporters, and correspondents to enjoy Catarina's pleasures. More than one political article has been datelined "Catarina Ranch, Texas," and a state AFL-CIO president came back from a holiday season deer hunt with the glowing report that if Briscoe turned out to be "half as good a governor as he is a host, he'd be great."

His first return campaign was the 1968 free-for-all for the Democratic gubernatorial nomination. Dolph jumped into the race on January 25,

1968, and found himself in a very crowded field of candidates. Already running were then-Lieutenant-Governor Preston Smith, former Attorney-General Waggoner Carr, Secretary of State John Hill, and Connally's friend Eugene Locke, all rated in varying degrees of conservatism. One liberal, Don Yarborough, a Houston lawyer, later announced, and enough minor candidates entered to raise the total to ten would-be governors.

Dolph's campaign was a late blooming one, and he spent a large amount of his own money trying to get his message across. He compared his own political philosophy to that of John Nance Garner, the crusty Uvaldean who had served Franklin D. Roosevelt as vice-president during his first two terms of office. "Mr. Garner's philosophy was first to safeguard the lives and property of the people. Mr. Garner believed that each man should work out his destiny according to his talent," said Briscoe. The campaign had a rural tinge to it, and Dolph talked about the problems of the small towns even while working the metropolitan areas for votes. "Most city people came from the farm or small town," he said when asked why he was doing this, but his strategy backfired and he ran poorly in the big cities, picking up only 6,200 votes in Dallas and 8,800 votes in Houston.

He promised an "Open Door" policy if he was elected, a two-hour period every two weeks when anyone could see him about anything. He came out strong for law enforcement (as everyone did in 1968) and education. He told a Houston audience that stiffer laws were needed for pollution control, that the current laws weren't doing the job. During the campaign he was endorsed by the Uvalde chapter of the American Association of University Women.

A late-campaign media and telephone blitz enabled Dolph to end up with a respectable fourth-place finish, behind Yarborough, Smith, and Carr. Briscoe and the other defeated conservative candidates threw their support to Smith in the runoff making him victorious.

Briscoe amassed a total of 225,000 votes out of the 1.8 million cast that day, or a little over 12% of the total. His campaign slogan "Everyone Who Knows Dolph Briscoe Will Vote for Him" proved to be dangerously prophetic, since he carried only a handful of counties in his native South Texas area. It was a costly race for Dolph, who reported expenses of almost $700,000 to the Secretary of State, a figure of about $3 per vote.

Soon after the election, Briscoe let it be known that he would not try to buck Texas's strong two-term tradition, but would be a candidate for governor again in 1972. From this decision he never wavered. His 1972 campaign got off the ground much earlier, and he was figured by nearly every political observer to be a strong candidate in the race. Dolph officially announced in late September, 1971, by which time he had an enthusiastic crowd of campaign workers lined up in almost every section of Texas.

"Preston Smith Came To Serve"

The next major development in the governor's race came on Friday Nov. 19, 1971, when ol' Preston announced he would run for a third term. While Gus Mutscher sipped coffee and munched cookies at the Capitol, celebrating his 39th birthday, Smith told a crowd of reporters at the State Democratic Executive Committee headquarters that he thought he should be the hero of the Sharpstown mess instead of the villain because he had vetoed the bills. He mentioned the three-term tradition set by the last three governors, and said there is "no doubt in my mind that the people and Preston Smith will win." The announcement had been largely unexpected and it caught many people, including Preston's own staff and supporters, by surprise. His press secretary, Jerry Hall, had only recently resigned, leaving Smith to join a public relations firm that was handling Ben Barnes's campaign. Smith's core of voluntary workers had melted away considerably since the revelation of his $62,500 profit on the National Bankers Life stock, and most of them expected him to bow out without making a third-term bid.

There was almost universal agreement, too, that he wouldn't have a chance in the world to win another term. But Smith wanted vindication. The challenges of his honesty in the past months evidently hurt him deeply, and he wanted one more chance to prove the voters didn't think he was guilty.

If Smith won the race, it wouldn't be the first time he had fooled the experts. In the past, his support had come mainly from rural and small-town areas, and had always been difficult for pollsters to assess properly, so the newsprint was full of missed predictions about Preston. He was accustomed to fighting long odds, too. Indeed his entire life was a story of perseverance and hard work.

Preston was one of thirteen children born to the Charles Kirby Smith family, a poor farming family living in the Corn Hill Community of Williamson County. While he was still a boy, his father had given up on the Williamson County place, packed his family into an old Model-T pickup, and headed west. After traveling three days and nights, he stopped at Sunset, a wide place in the road between Lamesa and Seminole, and there he determined to raise his family. Preston's father was known for his farming ability, but this stretch of West Texas sand rarely provided more than just a marginal existence.

Four years later Smith packed his own bag, and, at the age of 17, gave up on the soil. He went in to Lamesa, walking the entire fourteen miles, and began working his way through the high school there. He was evidently a good student, and his ability plus his ambition carried him through Lamesa High School and then through Texas Technological College in Lubbock. Preston says he had already determined his goal in life and that was to reside in the governor's mansion in Austin. This monumental decision had been made back on the old Williamson County farm. "I was walking down a cotton row behind a span of mules and reading an old newspaper about Governor Jim Ferguson. That was the first time I'd read about a governor and I decided right then and there I wanted to be governor." At the time, Smith was nine years old.

In college, Preston Smith was quite an entrepreneur. He pumped gasoline, fixed flats, hired out on odd jobs, and sometimes got into the real estate business by renting old houses and then renting rooms in it to other students. He also met a pretty young girl from Ralls, Ima Smith, when they were put next to each other in a class by a teacher who seated students alphabetically, and, after persuading her to break an engagement with someone else, convinced her she should be Mrs. Preston Smith. They were married in June, 1935, about a year after their graduation.

The same year he was married, he went into the movie business, opening up a "movin'-picture" theater across the street from the Tech campus. The start of this new enterprise was very shaky, but it soon began to prosper, and the young entrepreneur could afford to become active in the affairs of the new and growing town of Lubbock.

A few years later he began thinking about that nine-year-old boy in Williamson County, and jumped into politics. He won a race for the House in 1944 and served three full terms there. In 1950 he tried to flex his political muscles a bit early, and wound up losing a state-wide race for lieutenant-governor. He wasn't embarrassed by his showing, though, since he finished third in a thirteen-man race. Back to Lubbock he went, and two years later suffered his second political setback when he lost a race for the state Senate by a slim margin to the incumbent, Senator Kilmer Corbin.

Instead of licking his wounds and retiring with a bitter taste in his mouth, Smith immediately began planning to challenge Corbin again in 1956. He was not far enough removed from the West Texas soil that he didn't know how to relate to people, and he began traveling around the district, meeting people, making friends, shaking hands, visiting with the voters. He liked this style of campaigning more than any other, and years later, when the mass media had completely taken over politics, he still loved the personal type of campaign. ("Briscoe may win," he told a reporter late in the 1972 race, "but he doesn't know the people like I do.") Since the small West Texas towns were often bitter rivals, he organized his campaign leaders by towns, not by counties. He concentrated on West Texas issues, and waited for 1956 to roll around.

When it did, he sprang a few tricks on Corbin, such as a 30-minute television political show. This was a first in West Texas politics, and to make sure people watched it, he bought the same slot of time on both the local stations, a practice that would cause media men in the 1970s to shudder. The program itself was a personal visit with Smith and his family.

These tactics proved to be successful, for Corbin was eliminated in the first primary, and Smith defeated Lubbock attorney Carroll Cobb in the runoff. After this race, Preston began more seriously planning his moves to fulfill the wishes of the farm boy in Williamson County. Realizing that he would be spending most of his time in politics, he merged his theaters with those of some of his competitors, giving them the management responsibilities and a 69% interest, and retaining a 31% interest for himself.

After serving six years in the Senate, Preston got the urge to move up and entered what he later called "the toughest political race that I have ever run and been successful with winning." Ben Ramsey, a man who had served for six terms as lieutenant-governor, decided to move on to the Railroad Commission, and a dog-fight ensued for the vacant chair. Jumping into it along with Smith were three other state senators, Crawford Martin, Jarrard Secrest, and Robert Baker, plus House Speaker James Turman. The political spotlight that year was on the governor's race, where John Connally was trying to unseat Price Daniel, and Smith's campaign, as he admits, had a hard time getting off the ground. He managed to slip into a runoff with Turman, though the Speaker had a sizable 70,000 vote lead. With the help of a reporter who uncovered a questionable travel item that Turman had charged to the State, Smith overtook Turman and defeated him by about 50,000 votes.

The six years that Smith enjoyed as lieutenant-governor were spent in the shadow of Connally. Especially after his near-martyrdom in Dallas on November 22, 1963, Connally's name was a household word and his popularity was a Texas legend. John was smooth, polished, urbane, and sophisticated; he was a mover in the establishment's inner circles. Preston was plain, colorless, country, and bald; he was not a fixture in anyone's inner circles. Or at least this was the conventional wisdom. Those who knew Preston would not rate him that badly, but not that many people knew him.

He was never a conservative of the Connally-Barnes stripe. Both Connally and Barnes, darlings of the business establishment, knew the rhetoric of progressives, and could spew it flawlessly. They could spin smooth promises about excellence in education and improving the environment, yet when it came time for action, their proposals would fall far short of their promises. Preston never learned to use the rhetoric the way they did. If his speeches were not as uplifting, at least they were honest. He was the kind of conservative who felt, as one man stated, "that the government really shouldn't do very much about anything at all." Preston remarked to an interviewer once, "Contrary to what many feel, it is my belief that the governor's office does have sufficient authority . . . I don't know of any way you could improve upon the executive branch of our government." When the interviewer asked his position on constitutional revision, Smith replied, "It is my feeling that we have a good constitution in Texas." Barnes, on the other hand, said the constitution put the state in a "strait-jacket," and we "very desperately" needed to revise it. He could also tick off many ways in which the governor's power should be strengthened.

In spite of the difference in rhetoric and style, Preston certainly came closer to understanding the average Texan than Connally did, and probably came closer than Barnes. Smith loved to refer to himself as "just common folks," but he was certainly an uncommon politician.

His next political move came in August, 1967, a daring, gutsy announcement that he would run for governor in 1968. It was a daring move because Connally had not yet made up his mind about trying for an unprecedented fourth term. Most political people figured the popular Connally was a shoo-in if he tried, and most of them also figured he'd try. Several months went by before John announced he was retiring, and that announcement brought forth a host of candidates, but Preston always thought he had gained in the public image because he announced his decision without waiting for John to decide.

The 1968 race essentially boiled down to a liberal-conservative battle with one liberal and many conservatives. The liberal, Houston lawyer Don Yarborough, was generally conceded to have a runoff berth won, and those concessions proved accurate when he led the ticket on May 4 with 24% of the vote. The real battle in the first primary was among the conservatives, with the winner being assured of a runoff place and a good chance at victory. Among the conservatives thought to have a shot at winning were three political veterans (Smith, former Attorney-General Waggoner Carr, and Secretary of State John Hill) and two political newcomers (Dolph Briscoe, and Eugene Locke, a deputy ambassador to Vietnam and a friend of Connally and Lyndon Johnson).

Locke's campaign was well financed and grabbed attention through the use of a catchy jingle proclaiming "Eugene Locke should be governor of Texas, the governor of Texas should be Eugene Locke." Locke was generally considered to have the tacit support of John Connally, though at least two of Connally's more visible supporters, Will Davis, the State Democratic Party Chairman, and Frank Erwin, but now a member of the University of Texas Board of Regents, were lined up in Smith's corner. In a typically Texan, non-issue, personality-oriented campaign, Smith's experience and years of campaigning paid off for him: he finished with 21% of the vote, well ahead of Carr, his nearest competitor.

Smith went into the runoff planning to wage a bland, let's-come-together campaign designed to weld a victory from disappointed supporters of Carr, Briscoe, Locke, and Hill, all of whom had endorsed him. But, after a joint appearance with Yarborough on May 11 turned into a bitter personal confrontation, Smith took the offensive and mounted a campaign designed to paint his opponent as a wild-eyed radical. He pictured him as a radical-liberal who was controlled by the "big Eastern labor bosses," and Yarborough's fate was sealed. The establishment newspapers rallied editorially to Smith's defense, and the whole runoff became more a comment on the asininity of political labels in Texas than a serious contest between two men. When the nonsense died down, Smith was standing victorious with a 55% margin, a win based largely on the rural areas of the state.

The general election that fall brought the first of two serious challenges to Preston by a Republican, a Wichita Falls oil and gas attorney named Paul Eggers. Eggers mapped out an expensive campaign, hoping to ride in on Richard Nixon's coat-tail. It was a presidential election year, and the Republicans thought they had a good chance in Texas because of the disarray the Democrats were in after the Chicago convention.

But Eggers was a lot like Smith in that he could never develop any distinctive issues, and on election day the Texas voters showed once again that, given the choice between two conservative candidates, they'll pick the Democrat every time. It was a frustrating and expensive lesson for the Republicans which was repeated in 1970 when Eggers challenged Smith again. Although Smith's winning margin in either race was not great (56% in 1968 and 52% in 1970), together they were enough to fulfill the wishes of that Williamson County farm boy from long ago. And that farm boy was sitting in an office which he felt was powerful enough, waiting for the Sharpstown curtain to signal the end of his political career.

"That Lady for Governor"

Mrs. Frances Farenthold, a leader of the legislature's "Dirty Thirty" ethics coalition, was also thinking about running for higher office. Newspapers began carrying stories about the possibility in October, and she too began traveling the state to discuss the matter with her supporters. She was aware of the tremendous problem she would face in simply becoming known around the state. The political observers knew who she was by now, but the average voter did not. In the months between October and the February filing deadline, she considered running for governor, senator, attorney-general, and railroad commissioner. She announced that she would not run for any office that either Yarborough or Bill Hobby sought. In January, Yarborough, who had always wanted to run for governor, gave in to his advisors and announced for the Senate. Hobby, whose family owned the *Houston Post* and whose father had once been governor, had announced for lieutenant-governor, and the options available to Sissy narrowed to governor, attorney-general, or railroad commissioner.

In December Sissy remarked to a reporter that "not within my time have we had the opportunity to overhaul state government as we do in 1972. These aren't new problems [the Sharpstown Scandal], but there is a new awareness of them." A look at the last decade's government, she said, would lead one to think that "only about twelve white Anglo males were equipped to run the state."

Go for attorney-general, some of her advisors said; Crawford Martin is vulnerable and you'll have a good chance to beat him. No, said others, go for governor, that's where the action and publicity are, and no one's going to pay any attention to that attorney-general's race.

She listened, and thought, and talked to her husband, and finally, on the last day to register, February 7, she announced her candidacy for governor. And Texas politics would never be quite the same again.

Seven months later, speaking at a dinner honoring Sissy in Corpus Christi, State Land Commissioner Bob Armstrong was introduced as a "young man with a great future." He got up, looked pensively over the crowd, and said, "I don't know if I want to be called a man with a great future, because I remember what Sissy did to the last guy they said had a great future."

Armstrong knew whereof he spoke, too, for he had attained his high office as a result of a Farenthold crusade against the incumbent land commissioner. In fact, any number of men had already cowered under the withering onslaughts of this determined woman in her short but remarkable political career.

Sissy was a South Texan, a native of Corpus Christi. She had family ties to three of the oldest and most prominent families in the area. Her father was Dudley Tarlton, a Corpus Christi lawyer. The Tarlton name was well known in Texas history, one having served as a legislator in the 1880s, then on the Court of Civil Appeals in Fort Worth. The same man, who was Sissy's grandfather, also served as a professor at the University of Texas Law School after losing a campaign for the Texas Supreme Court, and the library there is named after him, Benjamin Dudley Tarlton.

Sissy's mother is Catherine Bluntzer Tarlton, the Bluntzer name being every bit as prominent regionally as the Tarlton. A Bluntzer first came to the area while Texas was still a Republic, and they have been involved in the region's civic, political, educational, and medical affairs ever since. One Bluntzer is listed in Pleasanton's South Texas Cowboy Hall of Fame, and one served as a Texas Ranger many years ago.

She can also claim allegiance to the Dougherty family name. Her grandfather, Robert Dougherty, came to South Texas from Ireland in 1854, and the Doughertys, too, have been prominent in the region's educational, political, and philanthropic affairs since then. One of Sissy's aunts, Miss Lida Dougherty, was the first woman school superintendent in Texas.

One would not be surprised to find a daughter born into such an environment turning into either an outspoken maverick or a society-conscious Junior Leaguer matron. Sissy's early days gave no real clue about which direction she would take. She attended both the public and parochial schools in Corpus Christi, then, as befitting a daughter of the establishment, went off to the select Hockaday School in Dallas, graduating in 1943. From there she went to the ivy-league Vassar College, where she received a Bachelor of Arts degree in 1945 at the age of 19.

She came home to Corpus Christi, refused to make her debut, and went off in the family tradition to the University of Texas Law School. She got her law degree in 1949 and came home again, this time joining her father's law firm. Her marriage in 1950 to George Farenthold quickly took her away from any active practice of law into the child-raising duties of a mother of five.

Belgian-born George Farenthold came to Texas in 1936 and became a U.S. citizen in 1940. He was a man of the world, having attended schools in Switzerland and France, and spent time in North Africa where his family owned some land and a large house, Villa Jolly. The house is now the official residence for Algeria's president. "We were not exactly paupers," says George.

He was not exactly a sunshine soldier, either, and his exploits in World War II for his newly-acquired homeland won him a Bronze Star. He served in the U.S. Air Force as an intelligence officer, spending most of his time in North Africa and Europe, and finishing his service as a captain.

The fortunes of love brought George to Corpus Christi and Sissy, though it was not their own love at first. His first wife, whom he had met in France, was Annie Blake Morgan, daughter of pioneer Corpus Christi farmer and oilman Rand Morgan. After the war the marriage went bad and they were divorced in 1948. (She is now married to Corpus Christi lawyer Hayden Head, a prominent conservative political king-maker.)

After George and Sissy's marriage, they quickly fell into the baby-a-year routine. George recalls that "the company I was with kept sending me overseas—I still travel a lot—and our first child was born on an August 23. The next year our second child was born on August 22, and a year later we had one on August 21. Finally my company told me I couldn't come back to the states in any November." The next August went by without another child, but the following February Sissy gave birth to twins. With five small children, the 1950s became a decade devoted to motherly duties for Sissy.

The 1960s saw both George and Sissy dabble in politics, with only Sissy being successful. George made one try at Nueces County Democratic Chairman and was convincingly defeated. "With a name like Farenthold," he says, "and an accent on top of it, I didn't have a chance."

Sissy's first venture into political and civic affairs had a tragic background. All of their children suffer from a form of hemophilia, which proved fatal for one of the twins, Vincent. After an injury in an accident in the home, he died shortly before his fourth birthday. "She was terribly torn up, it crushed her, so I suggested that she get into politics, just to get her mind on something else," remembered George.

Her public life, like that of many establishment wives, began with organizations such as the Goodwill Industries, the Corpus Christi Art Foundation, and the Corpus Christi Human Relations Commission. Five years' experience on the Human Relations Commission helped her gain an understanding of the problems of ethnic minorities and the poor, but it remained for her next public experience to color her life permanently. In 1965 she signed on as director of Legal Aid for Nueces County, partly because it was a job no other lawyer would take.

"It was a soul-searing experience," she recalled later. "I don't think I would ever have gone into politics except for that. I've lived in Corpus Christi all my life, but I saw and became aware of things I just hadn't known about until I got that position. From the outside one tends to think, 'Well, we've got institutions to take care of these problems—there's a hospital and a welfare program and all these programs to solve people's problems.' It's not until you get on the inside that you realize—it's just not enough. The programs aren't working.

"I never will forget a Chicano woman who walked from Robstown to my office (about 15 miles) for help. The plight of the unskilled woman with her children—Black, Anglo, Chicano—that's the problem. I'd say 90% of my clients [at Legal Aid] had welfare-related problems. I realized that it wasn't the case workers causing the problem." It was the policies up in Austin, she concluded.

The elective part of her public career began in 1968. On the day before the filing deadline a friend called and asked her to run for the Legislature. She thought it over, called back in a couple of hours, and then mounted what she later confessed was an amateurish campaign. A friend of hers from the Human Relations Commission took over as campaign manager, and the major concern of her effort became the "Four E's—Education, Ecology, Ethics, and Efficiency." "Live in '68, Plan for '78" was the slogan at the top of her campaign handouts, and some of her policy stands included lowering the voting age to 18, annual sessions and more staff help for legislators, and a strict code of ethics for elected officials. "If elected," she said, "I plan to file with the Secretary of State a copy of my income tax return." She also favored stricter pollution controls and an "equitable" tax bill.

She recalled later that she had a good many professional advisers (though she didn't usually follow their advice) and that she had a hard time learning to ask people for their vote. Her advisers, for example, wanted her to put up billboards, and were perplexed when she refused. "I thought, 'Well, if I'm going to come down on business for using them, I

can't do it myself.'" George finally came up with a plan to get her out with
the people by driving her to a shopping-center parking lot, putting her out
of the car and giving her 1,500 campaign cards and a dime. "When
you've given all these out," he told her, "call me and I'll come get you."

There were two opponents in the first Democratic primary, and
although Sissy came within ninety votes of capturing a majority, she was
forced into a runoff. Her opponent in the second primary was a Chicano
businessman, and she handily defeated him, winning almost 60% of the
vote.

The November general election pitted her against the Republican
incumbent Charles "Chuck" Scoggins. He was a two-term veteran, the
minority leader in the House, and he stressed his seniority and experience
in the battle. Nueces County is normally a Democratic stronghold, and a
big push was made that year on behalf of the entire Democratic ticket.
Sissy defeated Scoggins, easily, winning 61% of the vote, though she
admitted later that "I went over with the ticket. It was November, 1968,
and I don't fool myself."

Thus the "roadrunner days" began for the only female in the Texas
House of Representatives. She and George maintained their home in
Corpus Christi, and rented an apartment in Houston, where his work had
taken him. He is employed by the Crispin Co. in Houston's World Trade
Center, a steel import-export company.

She attracted a little attention in Austin as the House's lone woman,
but for the most part, the first days of her legislative career produced no
parliamentary bombshells. As might have been expected, the male
members had a poem dedicated to her on Valentine's Day, but she
introduced her bills and went about her business.

Of the less than a dozen bills she introduced in that first session, over
half were concerned with "guaranteeing human rights." Her legislation
would have allowed higher pay for jurors with economic hardships, given
aid to indigents in both civil and criminal cases, knocked out legal
discriminations against women, and created a Texas Human Relations
Commission. Her experiences on her own city's Human Relations
Commission gave her "an awareness of the need for such a commission on
the state level." She also joined with the other Corpus Christi legislators in
sponsoring a bill to create a senior college for Corpus Christi.

Sissy attracted more attention in her first term, though, for her votes
on other bills and resolutions than she did on the ones she sponsored. One
of her best-known votes came on a resolution inviting former President
Lyndon B. Johnson to address the Texas House. The invitation was fine
with her, but a commendation (in the resolution) of Johnson's
administration was not.

She was not an early critic of the Vietnam War, but, by this time, she
was questioning it. "I paced the floor for an hour on that and finally voted
against it." Her courageous vote, tweaking LBJ's nose in his home

country, was the only one cast against the measure, and it provided fodder for many a letter-to-the-editor in her later campaigns.

Another controversial vote in that first session proved to be a favorite of the letter writers, too. It was her vote against (this time there were eleven other hardy souls) the campus disruption bill. Lest anyone forget, 1968 was a law'n'order election year. The explosions of Newark, Detroit, and Watts were still vividly etched in the minds of the voters, and the battles between Mayor Daley's policemen and the long-hairs in Chicago had only recently faded from the nation's television screens.

Texas had never been the scene of any major campus riots, and anyone familiar with Texas campuses could have safely predicted that it never would be. But, the state was sore afraid at this time. Political observers all over the country were noticing that Americans were scared, and the farther removed they were from the possibilities of violence, the more they seemed to be afraid.

The Texas psychological climate was such that in February of 1969, Major General Thomas Bishop of the Texas National Guard announced (and was given generous coverage by the Texas press) that he could have 11,000 men anywhere in the state in sixteen hours except El Paso, Amarillo, or Texarkana, and it would take possibly another six hours to reach those cities. But, he said, "We discount the possibility of three simultaneous riots, so we feel we can handle anything but a revolution." Presumably he said this all with a straight face.

It was in this kind of an atmosphere that Representative Joe Shannon, Jr. of Fort Worth introduced his campus disruption bill. Shortly before it was acted on there was a flurry of violence at a few scattered campuses around the nation, and then one of the few episodes to hit Texas, a tragi-comic affair at Wiley College in Marshall in Deep East Texas. It was a poor, small, black college run by an autocratic administration, and protest began over such serious academic matters as the elimination of athletics. The good citizens of Marshall, envisioning Black Panthers marching in perfect ranks into their downtown area, called for help. In a textbook example of over-reaction, fifty shotgun-and-rifle-carrying state policemen marched onto the campus and into the ten o'clock news around the state, but after a few tense moments the problems of Wiley College were forgotten.

Shannon's bill was not forgotten, though, and it was hastily brought up into action the next day. It had not been scheduled for debate, nor had it been printed, so the House members did not even have copies to examine, but after suspending all the rules of the House, the bill passed 135-12.

Sissy's explanation of her vote accused the bill of being an ill-conceived, poorly drafted, and emotionally amended piece of legislation. "It wasn't needed. Our college can call in state police at any time to keep order," she said, pointing out that the bill's support to law enforcement was "more psychological than governmental." Present laws were sufficient to deal with problems, she said, and this new law's attempts to define "disruptive activity" created some constitutional questions that the House did not get answered in its haste to pass the bill. The fact that the Senate recalled this first bill after passing it and substituted another version because of those nagging constitutional questions gave credence to Sissy's explanation, but that was difficult to explain to those letter-writers.

On Palm Sunday, she and two of her sons traveled to Del Rio where she became the only Anglo legislator at a Mexican-American rally protesting the removal of VISTA workers from Val Verde County at the request of the county commissioners. This action too might have troubled some of her more conservative constituents, "but I'm glad I went and saw what I did," she told AP's Angela Penna later. "There was a lot said about the 'gringo' or white man that offended me," but ". . . problems were expressed and they were problems we need to heed."

Sissy also told the reporter that being a woman wasn't too much of a handicap in the legislature "unless I'm hit between the eyes with it." She had been barred once from one of her committee meetings because the chairman had called it for noon in Austin's Citadel Club, a private club that refused to let women in until 1 : 30 p.m.

The next week she testified in favor of a constitutional amendment concerning equal rights for women. The State Bar President, Ralph Brite of San Antonio, spoke against the measure, asking rhetorically if we let them in men's clubs, what about men's gyms? Sissy reminded him in an exchange of words that she "was not trying to get in the men's gyms," she was just trying to attend her committee meeting. And, she went on, "I recall I was able to get a license to practice law before I was able to serve on a jury." Did the State Bar, she queried the startled attorney, also oppose women as jurors?

In many ways her first session was disappointing to Sissy. There were few victories after it was all over. "It's like going through plate-glass that isn't shatter-proof," she said, and added that she learned the hard way that an "obviously pressing need is not sufficient to pass legislation." "I really thought when I came up here" [to Austin] she told the *Texas Observer*'s Molly Ivins, "I would be able to involve myself in welfare reform." Her attempts at it were fruitless, though. Her resolution that would have created a committee on welfare, for example, was one of the session's casualties. "We have a standing committee on cattle, but not one for the children and the incapacitated of the state," she told her constituents when she announced for re-election in December of 1969, saying that she planned to reintroduce the resolution.

Her first bit of statewide attention as well as her first great show of legislative determination came in the summer of 1969, and revolved around the incredible, true-to-life adventures of "Jerry and the Pirates."

It all began over 400 years earlier, in 1553, when four treasure-laden galleons bound from Mexico to Spain ran afoul of a hurricane off the lower coast of Texas near what today is Padre Island. The ships went under well inside the ten and one-half mile line out from shore that is under Texas jurisdiction, and lay there quietly, stirring intrigue for four centuries.

The Jerry mentioned here is Jerry Sadler, a snuff-dipping, catfish-farming politician from the East Texas Pineywoods town of Palestine. He had been in and out of elective office for years, running variously for governor, railroad commissioner, state representative, and, finally, land commissioner, to which he was elected in 1960. He built up a fiefdom in the office, a little-known and less-understood position. Unlike other states, Texas kept title to its public lands when it entered the union, and income from the land was dedicated to the public school system of the state. Discoveries of vast quantities of oil, gas, sulphur, and other minerals later gave the land commissioner probably more economic power than any other office in the state. The mysterious sub-surface world of drilling rights, claims, and petroleum law made the office even more invisible, and thus more susceptible to questionable deals. The office has provided the scene for more than one scandal.

In late 1967, Sadler became aware that someone was trying to get at the treasure in those sunken galleons, and he jumped into the fray "in the name of the school-children of Texas," as he was wont to do. Claiming jurisdiction under his power to regulate offshore oil and gas production, he investigated and found an Indiana salvage firm, Platoro, Ltd., busily extracting treasure. The firm evidently got a large amount of the booty out before an injunction against it was issued in January of 1968.

From that point on, confusion becomes the only certainty in the entire affair. In October of 1968, Sadler said he made a contract with Platoro for the state, and a 50-50 split of the treasure was agreed on. He later refused to show the contract to a House committee looking into the matter, and finally flatly denied ever having made such a contract. Platoro, which had taken the treasure to Indiana, reluctantly sent it all back to Sadler when the contract fell through. Then they decided that since Texas had no antiquities code making such relics state property they should get it all, so they filed suit in federal court asking for title to all the property.

The treasure was supposedly locked in a vault in Sadler's office, but questions about how much loot was recovered, whether the recovery methods were scientific, where the artifacts should be displayed, and who should make a contract for the state remained unanswered. The state archaeologist, concerned that the treasure might physically deteriorate if not stored properly, asked to see the items but never got permission from Sadler.

Sadler appeared before the committee looking into all of this, but when the questions got rough, his answers became "a little bit evasive," as he admitted later on. Sissy was on the committee, along with several more or less establishment legislators, and they all became incensed at the way Sadler treated them.

Once when the committee, along with the governor and lieutenant-governor, went to inspect the items, the two top officials departed while the committee was still asking questions. As soon as they left, Sadler became very rude to the legislators, refusing to answer any more questions.

Another time, Sissy and Representative Jake Johnson went along with a three-man commission appointed by a Corpus Christi district judge to inspect the treasure, and Sadler stepped in the doorway blocking their entrance. He told the two they could not come in, and when Johnson asked why, Sadler reached for his throat and began choking him. An astonished newsman with a tape recorder said, "Mr. Sadler, were you going to choke the representative?" When Sadler made a menacing move toward the newsman, he asked, "Are you gonna choke me now?"

The angry representatives went back to the House where Johnson denounced Sadler in a personal privilege speech, stating he'd "offended the dignity of this House." By now the affair had taken on comic overtones, with Sadler announcing that mini-submarines were raiding the other galleons, and that the Mafia had warned him to back off. Both Johnson and Sadler had come up with further charges against each other, and Johnson wanted a grand-jury investigation of his charge that a Land Office employee on the state payroll was running Sadler's motel in Palestine.

The fun and games became a little more serious, though, when Sissy introduced a resolution censuring Sadler in a special session on August 20, 1969. The resolution charged Sadler with violating state law and misrepresenting facts before a legislative committee. As far as anyone knew, the Legislature had never before even thought about censuring a state official, and, in spite of Sadler's actions, the team in the House was only lukewarm about the resolution. If the boat gets rocked, we all might get wet, they reasoned.

Speaker Gus Mutscher sent the resolution to the Rules Committee, and after a public hearing, it went on to a subcommittee. In the hearing, Sadler admitted telling the Platoro officials not to respond to the legislative committee's inquiries. He also said the State of Texas had a contract with Platoro, but "I did not say Platoro had a contract with the State of Texas," and he offered to resign if anyone could produce a contract signed by him.

A vote was never taken on the resolution in the special session, but when a second special session was immediately called, Sissy, against the advice of almost everyone, re-introduced the resolution. After another hearing, and after the toning down of the resolution from a "censure" to a "reprimand," it finally came up for a vote on Sept. 9, 1969, just before the session ended. The fact that it ever came up at all is a tribute to Sissy's determination and the rightness of her position. And when she finally got it up for a vote, at least seven representatives turned tail and ran. After voting down an amendment which would have gutted her resolution, the House proceeded to vote on the reprimand. Between the two votes, seven members were excused "on account of important business." With only 113 of the 150 members voting, her resolution passed 64-49, and Sadler became the first state official in history to be reprimanded by the House.

This "will cost him his office," said Jake Johnson. "You're going to destroy him," Representative Temple Dickson told the House. "I never felt better in my life," said Jerry Sadler. "She shamed them," said one of Sissy's close friends. "She shamed them into doing something that they knew they should do."

Johnson's remark proved prophetic, as a young Austin representative, Bob Armstrong, who had voted with Sissy, challenged and defeated Sadler in the next Democratic primary. Sadler thus became the first state official to suffer the consequences of incurring Sissy's wrath.

The day after the reprimand vote an Antiquities Act was finally passed by the Legislature, and Sissy found herself being praised editorially by her hometown newspaper, the *Corpus Christi Caller*. Both the reprimand and the Antiquities Act were "almost entirely due to Mrs. Farenthold's courage and perseverance," said the *Caller*.

While the Legislature was not in session, Sissy focused on activities of state agencies, often attending public hearings. She was especially concerned with oil spills and oil well discharges into coastal waters. She was also a legislator who couldn't say no to a person with a problem and thus spent an inordinate amount of her time (and her contingent expense allowance) working to solve all sorts of governmental and consumer problems for her constituents. In March of 1970, the Texas Intercollegiate Students Association voted her the "outstanding state legislator."

Going into the 1970 election, Sissy was the only one of Corpus Christi's four representatives to have an opponent, and she drew two, one in the primary and one in the general election. Neither of the challengers, Democrat James Rehfield and Republican Clyde New, mounted effective campaigns, and she waltzed to a win over both by similar 2½ to 1 margins.

Then January, 1971, rolled around, and after her second term began, Frank Sharp, Mutscher, Smith, Sharpstown, and all those other things mentioned in Chapter 2 became a blur. She had introduced a number of bills, with most of them again about human rights, but the "Farenthold Resolution" proved to be about the most significant item considered by the House that session. And, as most other Dirty Thirty members did, she found out that the penalty for questioning the Mutscher team (while he was still in control) was having your bills die ignominiously in some committee somewhere.

As the session rolled, and she became known as the "Den Mother of the Dirty Thirty," a few liberal politicians began hoping she would bring some measure of organization to liberals in the House. Sissy was among the small handful of the Thirty that was responsible for planning and strategy, but she drew mixed grades on her leadership abilities. (One is reminded here of a remark by Bob Eckhardt, the last effective liberal leader in the Texas House, that "trying to organize liberals is like trying to organize quail to fight the bird dogs.") Her courage and doggedness, though, made her one of the few who would keep on trying.

After the session came her Autumn of Discontent. She watched the governor's race fill up with candidates, tried to decide what to do, then one day while driving in Houston she saw a sign that helped her decide. "Help bring a new day to Texas," said a Ben Barnes silently staring at her from the billboard. That was the last straw, she said as she jumped in to give Texas a choice between "two contaminated candidates and a legislator from the fifties."

The First Primary

After the filing deadline had passed, the rest of February was devoted to all sorts of political jockeying behind the scenes. Campaign plans and issues had to be firmed up, financial supporters had to be rounded up, and press and public relations help had to be signed up.

Although three other minor candidates entered the race, (Robert E.L. Looney of Austin, Gordon F. Wills of Crockett, and William H. Posey of Houston) the four names previously mentioned were the only ones to be taken seriously by the press and the public.

The person considered to be the front-runner at this point by almost everyone was Ben Barnes. The youthful, energetic lieutenant-governor's campaign organization was already humming smoothly, and there was a seemingly inexhaustible supply of wealth and talent to keep it running. Barnes publicly estimated that it would take at least $750,000 to run a "good media campaign" and he indicated his plans to do that. Some of the best known political public relations advisers were in his talent pool already. Julian Read, one of former Governor John Connally's closest advisers, was there, along with George Christian, a former aide to Connally, former Governor Price Daniel, and former President Lyndon B. Johnson. Christian had also been a key adviser in Lloyd Bentsen's successful campaign in 1970 for Ralph Yarborough's seat in the U.S. Senate. Also helping in the Barnes campaign were Jerry Hall, a former press aide to Governor Preston Smith, and Sam Kinch, Sr., a recent retiree from the *Fort Worth Star-Telegram*'s Capitol staff.

The Barnes race never lacked for money. His card file of campaign contributors yielded a large number of major donations. He had been building his organization for years, and he already had lined up many of the state's top political and athletic personalities for his campaign rallies. Many of the senators who served under his gavel were lined up with him, including some liberal senators who had begun to feel uneasy about their commitment after Farenthold announced.

Some of the state's labor leaders and minority group spokesmen were also committed to Barnes and likewise felt uneasy after Farenthold jumped in. But with only minor exceptions, they quenched their uneasiness and stayed with Barnes.

The man considered most likely to wind up in a runoff with Ben was Dolph Briscoe. His campaign organization was not moving at full speed, but it had never completely shut down after the 1968 race, and a great infusion of money would bring it to a gallop at almost any moment Dolph chose. He had not been in office during the Year of Frank Sharp, and would undoubtedly pick up many votes from conservative Texas Democrats who couldn't bring themselves to vote for any of the incumbents. The Briscoe organization of personal friends and acquaintances had by now been built into a formidable campaign structure. The professional talent that Briscoe retained was not as well known in Texas politics as the Barnes men but by the end of the campaign they had proved themselves just as capable. An engaging, curly-haired young man named Jack Canson was hired to handle press releases and speeches. Canson was an East Texas product who had been in the Austin environment for some time. He had worked for Preston Smith two years earlier, and had also helped some Austin area candidates considered to be liberals. Jack had signed on with Dolph in late 1971 and his fast-paced campaign style (runnin' and workin', he called it) provided a much needed spark to the Briscoe entourage.

Dolph's television blitz was handled by Deloss Walker, a forty-year-old Memphis image-maker with a national reputation. Best known for handling Dale Bumper's upset defeat of former Gov. Orval Faubus in the 1970 Arkansas governor's contest, Walker's mellifluous voice would become very familiar to television-watching Texans during the race. He occasionally drew barbs from the public (and from Briscoe's other aides) because he was too oriented toward "bought" media, and was not concerned with other campaign tactics. Some of these barbs were hard to ignore, and, at one point in the campaign, Briscoe's voice was substituted into the television spots in place of Walker's more professional-sounding voice as a response to charges that Dolph was hiding behind his image makers.

Briscoe also hired former *Houston Post* political reporter Bill Gardner, and, in the runoff, Bill Harding, another Texas newspaper and public relations worker. George Lowrance, a veteran of Lloyd Bentsen's 1970 victory, was also working out of Briscoe's state headquarters.

Like the Barnes effort, the Briscoe campaign never lacked for money. Unlike the Barnes effort, though, most of the money spent on Briscoe came from the candidate, especially during the first primary. After Barnes was eliminated, many of his supporters sent checks to Briscoe hoping to keep a friendly contact in the governor's mansion.

Despite small changes brought on by criticism, the Briscoe campaign was truly a "bought" media effort from start to finish. Most of his appearances in person came at carefully planned dinners and barbecues where his remarks would be straight from a script. He shied away from press conferences and from interviews with reporters, preferring to run instead on television screens and newspaper advertisements where a statement of bland generalities would not bring a sharp question.

The third candidate, Governor Preston Smith, was beginning a campaign that almost everyone in the state thought futile and senseless. He brought his son Mickey back from Colorado to manage the campaign, and put two of his veteran advisers in charge of the campaign press relations. Otice Green of Lubbock had worked in Smith's races ever since the 1956 Senate win, and Jerry Conn of Austin had been working in the Smith camp since 1967. Conn had even written a master's thesis on Smith at The University of Texas, which was published during the campaign under the title *Preston Smith: The Making of a Texas Governor*.

Preston had a much harder time getting money than did Dolph or Ben, and consequently did not run as much television time as they did. One of his spots, though, was hailed as one of the best political spots in Texas television history: A voice over a picture of Preston in the Capitol gravely intones that some men came here to rule, some to govern, but "Preston Smith came to serve."

The fourth candidate, Sissy Farenthold, was the only one who had never been in a statewide race before, and thus the only one without at least the bare outline of a statewide organization. She was able to recruit a few volunteers from Ralph Yarborough's old campaign structure, however, and, very late in the game began trying to put together her own machine. Creekmore Fath, an Austin attorney who had managed several Yarborough races, was persuaded to take the job as campaign manager. Her race was obviously going to be a low-budget one, but she was able to come up with enough pledges to get Fath to take on the job. There was not enough money for any high-powered public relations firms, though, and a handful of full-time workers supplemented by throngs of usually youthful volunteers had to perform all of the tasks handled by experienced professionals in the other three camps.

She had no television spots at all until just before the first election date, and then they were amateurish, and "godawful", in Sissy's words. Her campaign never lacked for enthusiasm, however, and many words were written about her grass-roots appeal. She "has stirred more excitement among insurgent voters than any recent challenger of the status quo," proclaimed one San Antonio newspaper.

Early in March, Joe Belden's Texas Poll released a survey it had taken during the month of February. According to a study of 510 "likely" Democratic voters, said Belden, the most popular figure in the race was Barnes.

A question designed to measure the number of voters "aware" of the candidates produced these results:

Candidate:	Percentage Aware:
Preston Smith	97
Ben Barnes	92
Dolph Briscoe	65
Frances Farenthold	28

The governor and lieutenant-governor were recognized by almost all the voters while the man from Uvalde had more of a name identification problem. The lady from Corpus Christi was known by only about one out of every four voters, and clearly had the biggest name identification task.

Then a question on the opinion of each voter about the candidates was asked. It produced these figures:

Candidate:	Percentage liking:	Percentage disliking:
Preston Smith	45	45
Ben Barnes	60	24
Dolph Briscoe	43	9
Frances Farenthold	16	7

Hindsight tells us that the most important statistic in this chart is the 9% who disliked Briscoe. Both Barnes and Smith had built up a considerable pool of enemies. Smith's 45% was staggering, in fact, and was a clear signal of things to come. Briscoe was liked by almost one-half of this sample, and was disliked by a very small number. And in a throw-the-rascals-out year, this easily made him a prime contender. Back when the pool was taken, however, most people were still blinded by the brilliance of Barnes's ascending star, and they thought the key to the chart to be the 60% who liked Barnes.

Barnes had already provided a sample of the type campaign he had planned, an elaborately-planned, lavishly-furnished train trip—the Ben Barnes Victory Special. In the last week of February, the Barnes entourage had clambered aboard a four-car chartered train in Amarillo for a three-day whistle-stop tour of Texas. Aboard for the junket were Barnes's wife Nancy, two doctors, several professional football players, a number of Texas's political reporters, and over two dozen of Barnes's own "staff and support personnel." The train cost over $25,000, but created quite a bit of publicity for the young peanut farmer. The athletes on board created a lot of excitement by themselves, and one of them was usually in charge of presenting Barnes to the audience. Barnes let the scene determine the scope of his brief remarks, talking about feedlots in West Texas, new industries in the small towns, storm insurance problems in the coastal areas, urban problems in the cities, and welfare everywhere. The impressive crowds and professional atmosphere surrounding the junket got Barnes a pretty good press, and the only hitch during the ride, a burning trestle that halted the train four miles short of the end of the 758-mile journey, was countered so effectively that it was to Barnes's credit. He merely stopped the train, got in a helicopter that had followed the entire trip, flew the last four miles to the windup rally in Houston, and told the crowd it would take more than a "burning bridge to keep Ben Barnes from being governor."

Ben did suffer some sniping from Sissy Farenthold during his trip. Beginning a tactic of getting as much publicity as possible from other candidates' actions, she said that while Barnes was traveling around the country he could tell people "why he rammed through the 'Barnes Bread Bill' that put a sales tax on groceries," and why he tried to get a "two-cent per gallon increase in the gasoline tax that was uncalled for and unnecessary." He could also explain to the taxpayers where the money to rent the train came from, she said.

Ben ignored most of her jibes (he was to hear them time after time during the campaign) and rarely mentioned his opponents. The last speech of the journey, made at Houston, found Barnes singling out Preston Smith and Frank Sharp for the first time. Accusing his opponents of trying to smear him, Barnes charged, "They cannot tie me to Frank Sharp because the truth is that I don't know Frank Sharp and never bought any of his stock. That was Preston Smith, not Ben Barnes, and nothing he does can change it."

The savvy governor answered Barnes a few days later on a thirty-minute statewide television show. His March 1 telecast presented what Smith called a "full factual disclosure" of the Sharpstown affair, and charged Barnes with being responsible for the two Sharpstown bills having passed the Legislature. The charges were pretty well torn apart by the state's political reporters. The *Houston Chronicle's* Bo Byers called Smith's explanation a "Pollyanna story" in which he failed to tell the whole truth. The Governor held copies of the two bills up for viewers to see, pointed to the signature of Barnes on the documents. "I did not introduce the bills," he said, "and the only place my signature is on this bill is under the veto message." He also attacked Barnes for giving the bills (which by any possible measure must be the two best-known bills in Texas legislative history) special treatment in the Senate.

Political observers were quick to point out that Barnes, as presiding officer in the Senate, really had no choice but to sign the bill. They also called attention to the fact that Smith's veto came twenty days after the bills had passed, and seventeen days after his National Bankers Life stock had been sold at a good profit. Ben Barnes was also quick to reply to the charges, accusing Preston of using a "cheap political trick" . . . "to mislead the people in his desire to drag me into the Sharpstown mess he helped to create."

By now the trial in Abilene had started and for a few days the public's mind seemed to be sitting outside the bar in that courtroom. The governor's race was thus out of the spotlight, but a pattern had emerged that showed what much of the race would be like at least through the first primary. Ben Barnes was clearly thought to be the front-runner and the one to beat, and he would be the main target of the other candidates' pointed remarks. And though he was the focal point of the campaign, he didn't have nearly as much freedom in determining the battle ground as he would have like. For in addition to delineating his own positions, he had to spend much time worrying about whether or how to respond to his opponents' barbs. Most of these barbs were coming from Preston and Sissy. Briscoe stayed above the fight for a long time, choosing to utter platitudes about leadership, ethics, and responsibility when he finally did break loose. His was an extremely issueless campaign, one of glittering phrases and banal generalities, and one completely without substance.

The Race Gets Warmer

The first weekend in March saw all of the candidates have an opportunity for joint appearances at important conventions, the first being the Texas Association of Broadcasters fest in Houston, and the second the Texas AFL-CIO's political convention in Galveston. While Ben, Preston, and Sissy showed up for a few remarks in Houston, the Galveston convention clearly stole the show, and Sissy clearly stole the hearts of the delegates to the convention.

At stake was Texas labor movement's endorsement, the key to labor's campaign chest and supply of volunteer workers. The Texas labor leaders were facing a problem about the governor's race. Farenthold's late filing announcement had caught them unawares, and though she had a perfect labor voting record, they had already decided to concentrate on Ralph Yarborough's race for the U.S. Senate, and state Senator Joe Christie's race for lieutenant-governor.

Both men were naturals for the labor endorsement, especially "smilin' Raff." He had been their hero, and it was evident when he walked into the convention that he was still their hero. The state AFL-CIO president, Roy Evans, had planned to recommend a full endorsement (and thus money) for those two, and, according to the *Texas Observer*'s Molly Ivins, labor had decided not to put any money into the governor's race before Sissy announced.

As delegates began arriving for the convention it was clear that many of them strongly supported Sissy and might be inclined to buck Evans's recommendation about staying out of the governor's race. Her fledgling campaign had obviously caught fire by now, and she picked up an endorsement from the United Steelworkers of America and the Communications Workers of America on Thursday night at their caucuses. Friday morning she got the nod from the Oil, Chemical, and Atomic Workers (OCAW), and those three endorsements gave her almost one-fourth of the delegates to the convention.

Ben Barnes also had some supporters present, though obviously not nearly as many as Sissy. His people began a move to keep Sissy from getting the endorsement, and were able to bring about a change in the OCAW vote. Dallas state Senator Oscar Mauzy, a liberal who served under Barnes's gavel, helped get his countermovement started, aided by Gerald Brown of the Texas Building and Constructions Trade union. They were able to get the OCAW to caucus again a few hours later and reconsider the endorsement. The elapsed hours enabled them to persuade some of the rank and file, and the second caucus failed to endorse her by two votes.

The Farenthold supporters there began to realize by Friday night, according to Ivins, that they couldn't win a floor fight for endorsement. It would take a two-thirds vote to do so, and she just didn't have that much support. Her friends felt she could get around 60% in such a fight, but they were also aware that if a candidate lost an endorsement fight, the AFL-CIO rules would then prevent any local from endorsing the candidate.

All four of the candidates had already addressed the convention. Barnes, Briscoe, and Smith had received a polite round of applause as they spoke. Barnes had led off the list of candidates and had talked about becoming a leader in the Texas Democratic Party. He finished by saying "it's time to get Dick Nixon." Briscoe told the assemblage that he was proud of being a "legislator from the fifites," the tag Sissy had put on him, and that he was "sick at heart" that today's Democratic Party had become "soiled and divided" by the actions of the incumbents. Smith listed the achievements of his administration, slammed Barnes for his support of the sales tax on groceries, and concluded "an acre of performance is worth a world of promises."

Then the lady from Corpus Christi brought the crowd to its feet cheering when she walked in. Her remarks were punctuated by thunderous applause a half-dozen times, and were followed by a standing ovation. "There are those," she began, "who say we must discuss issues and stop dealing with personalities, but unfortunately the personalities have become issues themselves."

"We need a governor who will maintain his perspective" between the interests of the people and his partners. "We need a legislature that is as responsive to the people as it is to the corporate lobbyists . . . We need a revitalized Democratic Party that will work actively on behalf of the national as well as the state ticket. I know we have Democratic voters in this state, but I sometimes wonder if we have a Democratic Party," she concluded.

After making the decision that an endorsement was out of the question, Sissy's workers planned to seek a resolution commending her. And, after some more haggling and after the lines of communication were straightened out, the convention did just that, commending Sissy "for her exceptional record of public service, her indomitable courage, and her exemplary campaign for continued public service."

Whether it was a victory for Sissy or Barnes was debatable. After the convention, Sissy was asked if she thought the resolution was a victory. "Indeed I do, considering the skepticism among my friends and cynicism among others when I entered this race." Other viewers thought it to be a victory for Barnes, since it allowed him to keep the support he had among leaders. One disappointed Sissy supporter told the convention, "We're telling the one candidate with a perfect labor record that we're standing aside and letting her go it alone."

Roy Evans told reporters, "I had no idea there was this type of feeling for Sissy. There's no question that her campaign is on fire."

The AFL-CIO COPE convention in Galveston came about two months before the first primary. By this time, at least a little bit of each candidate's organizational structure (and problems) was beginning to emerge.

A casual visit to each of the four gubernatorial candidates' Houston headquarters on the Saturday that the Barnes and Farenthold labor forces were battling it out for the COPE endorsement in Galveston proved to be a telling commentary on the campaign so far.

The only place with much activity was the Farenthold headquarters. Located in an old building in the 2300 block of Travis, it had the look of an organization run largely by volunteer workers. Maps, newspaper articles, and posters were tacked all over the walls, the phones were constantly ringing, and there was a wide assortment of people coming in and out. An older woman wearing a sequined black turban on her head was answering telephones and talking about raising money. Fath had given them a quota far above what would be needed in Houston, she said, and the extra would go to the state headquarters in Austin. Behind her on the wall was a large, freshly done oil painting of Sissy abstractly superimposed on the Lone Star of Texas. A teen-aged girl with long blond hair and blue jeans wandered in and out, clutching a tiny kitten. An older, bearded, hippie-shirted man helped move in a desk to one of the already crowded rooms. A man in a business suit passed through (He's the landlord," said the lady of the turban, "and he's for Sissy, but he also rents to Preston Smith's people, so he can't come out for her publicly"). A blackboard on the wall in another room was crammed full of notes ("daily staff meeting at 2:45, list of precinct captains, $1,000 club"), and several people came by to pick up bumper stickers and buttons from a dwindling supply ("Bumper Stickers $1, Buttons 25 cents" said the sign). Sissy's statewide headquarters had only recently been cranked up and was having a hard time getting campaign material out to the city and county volunteers.

A trip around the block to visit Preston Smith's headquarters in the 2300 block of Main found it locked tight with the blinds drawn shut. Considering his poor finish in Harris County later, it is doubtful what his organization could have accomplished anyway. (At least they had a building, though; in most other Texas cities, Preston didn't even have a campaign headquarters.)

On out Fannin, in the 4900 block, the Dolph Briscoe headquarters was located in a large building. The front door opened onto a business counter with huge piles of buttons, bumper stickers, and full-color brochures (it had a picture of Dolph, a biography, a few general remarks, and it was about the only piece of literature put out by Briscoe in the entire campaign). It was an obviously more affluent place than the Farenthold operation. Only one man was in the building, and he sat in a back office, concentrating on a telephone conversation, oblivious to visitors. There were rows of desks, each with its own typewriter. All of the desks were loaded down with computerized lists of registered voters, and a few had boxes of expensively printed invitations to "Key Members" of the Greater Houston Builders Association, the Houston Apartment Association, and the Houston Board of Realtors, urging them to "Please Attend for Texas" a reception for Dolph on the next Monday. On this Saturday, though, there were no visitors to pick up the campaign buttons and literature, and the Briscoe headquarters was a quiet place.

Ben Barnes's headquarters on this day was out on West Gray, but a sign told of a planned move the next week to a permanent home in the 3000 block of Louisiana. His was an obviously affluent campaign, too, with boxes and boxes of buttons, bumper stickers, yard signs, newspaper supplements, and Nancy's cookbooks. One smartly dressed woman was present, and she cheerfully offered a visitor handfuls of any of the literature available. The affluence of the Barnes camp was evidenced not only by the boxes of expensive, full-color brochures, but by a number of billboards and bus signs. Barnes was the only candidate to have this type of advertising in the Houston area this early in the campaign, and his "Help Bring a New Day to Texas" slogan was facing motorists all over the city. (Briscoe soon caught up in the billboard race, though; later in the campaign it was difficult to drive many miles in Texas without coming under Dolph's gaze from a billboard. Farenthold, as she did in her legislative campaign, refused to use billboards anywhere, on environmental grounds.)

A visit to each candidate's state headquarters in Austin a few Saturdays later gave an almost identical glimpse into their organizational weaknesses and strengths.

Preston Smith's statewide headquarters in the Stephen F. Austin Hotel, on a Saturday less than a month before the election, was locked up tight. Dolph Briscoe's headquarters on West Sixth was open, and rows of desks with typewriters gave the building a busy look. There was only one person present (the rest of the staff was having a private meeting with the candidate) and she could gladly hand out any number of buttons, bumper stickers, and full-color brochures.

Ben Barnes's headquarters on West Fifteenth was a beehive of activity. There were stacks and stacks of paper everywhere—biographical sketches, campaign rhetoric, statements, positions, reprints of editorials, copies of flattering articles. By the hundred they were stuck in their pigeonholes, all printed upon the red and blue Ben Barnes letterheads. A couple of dozen workers were hustling around, most of them young people, but most of them in the dresses and suits and ties of paid office workers. Visitors were met graciously, and were offered samples of the unending supply of campaign paper and materials.

Frances Farenthold had set up her statewide headquarters in an old, spacious, high-ceilinged, two-story house on West Thirteenth. It was every bit as busy as the Barnes building, but the tone of the operation was quite different. Most of the workers were young, but instead of the formal office garb, most of them wore blue jeans and casual clothes. Paper was everywhere, too, since the Farenthold staff had been cranking out position papers right and left. A collection of obviously donated furniture was serving passably for office equipment, but some of the people were trying to work from couches and chairs not really designed for office work. A playful black kitten was running through the office of Susan Longley, the Farenthold staffer in charge of itinerary, trying to catch the hem of a long granny dress on one of the young workers. Here, visitors (of which there were many) were met graciously, too, and were given campaign literature from a large supply. This obviously was a low-budget, volunteer operation, and the enthusiasm of the volunteers would have to go a long way to match the professional, well-oiled machines on West Fifteenth and West Sixth.

By the second or third week in April, the campaign had begun to have at least a blurry outline. The edges were not very clear, and wouldn't be until after the votes were counted on May 6, but a few generalizations could be drawn about the battle so far.

For example, it was clear by now that the entire race was revolving around only two candidates, Ben Barnes and Sissy Farenthold. They were the lead players in the campaign drama. The major events, charges, statements, countercharges, excitement, thrills, spills, and enthusiasms were coming from the camps of these two. And it was just as clear that the other two candidates, Preston Smith and Dolph Briscoe, were drifting along on the campaign tides as bit players, either responding to or running

from the latest charge or statement from the lead players, Barnes and
Farenthold.

The Barnes Campaign

Barnes's role as a major player in the campaign drama was not
surprising. He was still considered by most observers to be a front-runner
in the race, the only one almost assured of a runoff spot. It was not only
his political efforts keeping him in the spotlight, either: it was the darts
being thrown his way by the other candidates. For as the front-runner, he
became an automatic target for the other candidates, and they struck at
him with all the force they could muster.

His twelve years' experience in Austin had given him a good working
knowledge of Texas government. His mind worked quickly, and his easy,
effortless answering of questions during interviews showed that, if nothing
else, he had at least done his homework on the issues of the day. The
Barnesian rhetoric in his campaign literature demonstrated his knowledge
of governmental problems:

*About Constitutional Revision: To Ben Barnes, constitutional
reform remains one of the unsolved needs of Texas. Barnes supports
annual sessions of the Legislature, a strengthened Executive Branch
and basic revision of our 19th Century Constitution...*

*About Ecology: Ben Barnes believes that environmental protection
is one of the most important issues of the 1970s ... He calls for strict
enforcement of existing anti-pollution laws and advocates new
legislation to save the environment.*

*About Reform: Ben Barnes has initiated legislative reforms ... He
has fought for joint rules for the Senate and the House which would
govern conference committees so that ten men would not have the
power to write, behind closed doors, most of the major legislation,
notably state appropriations.*

*About Integration and Busing: Ben Barnes's record on human
rights is clear and consistent. He has long been outspoken against
discrimination and bigotry in all of its forms. He has opposed busing
children.*

*About Elections and Voting: Ben Barnes was instrumental in
obtaining passage ... permanent voter registration ... and swift
Senate ratification of the 26th Amendment ... [lowering the voting
age to 18]*

*About Welfare: Calling the State's welfare program "the biggest
mess in the world," Barnes advocates creation of a single
administrator... who is directly appointed by and accountable to the
Governor.*

About Tax Reform: Ben Barnes advocates revision of the Texas taxation system, although he does not favor a state income tax.

About Education: Ben Barnes believes . . . vocational and technical training should be among the top priorities . . . in the field of education. Ben Barnes has long supported salary increases for Texas school teachers and for University faculties. Ben Barnes believes that Texas colleges and universities should employ due process procedures in administrative disciplinary proceedings . . . he believes that the campus newspapers should be run by and for the students and should be unfettered and uncensored.

About Drugs and Abortion: I do not believe that the solution to the drug problem is to throw all of those who have experimented with marijuana into jail. I feel that felony punishment for drug experimentation is too severe . . . I don't believe Texas should become an "abortion Mecca," but I do believe our laws should be in keeping with changing medical and social viewpoints . . .

About the Stock Scandal [a three-page letter on this was published]: Barnes never owned a share of National Bankers Life stock. He did not make any "quick profits" as some other public officials did. In fact, Ben Barnes has never met Frank Sharp in his life.

Barnes mentioned all of these things in his travels around the state, sometimes adding or subtracting a few comments to fit the audience. He came out in favor of a state water plan and rejuvenation of small towns, for example, during a swing through dusty West Texas. He came out for limitations on conference committees in the Legislature during an appearance in Houston, also telling a group of students that he favored a state-wide system of daycare centers for children, an enrollment limitation on The University of Texas at Austin, not reappointing crusty Frank Erwin to The University of Texas Board of Regents, and an immediate withdrawal of the troops in Vietnam.

Everywhere he went, Ben also brought up the Sharpstown mess, trying to convince the people that he really was not one of the guilty parties. This was perhaps the most difficult and elusive issue with which he had to contend. He repeated those words "I never met Frank Sharp" many hundred of times over the state, bringing the issue up himself if no one asked a question about it. Over and over, Ben Barnes has nothing to hide, Ben Barnes was investigated by every agency involved and got a clean bill of health from all of them, Ben Barnes never made any profits as the others did.

Under the circumstances he really could have done little else, but also under the circumstances, his explanations had little effect on the voters. They were mad and looking for someone to place the blame on. "You know how he gets all the money to ride around in that helicopter?" an old man in a small Panhandle town asked *The Dallas Morning News*'s John

Geddie one day as the Barnes entourage town-hopped. "He made it on all them stock deals." This attitude, sometimes spoken, sometimes unspoken, existed all over the state, and in the end proved to be too elusive for Ben to handle. In fact, every time he repeated his lines, he may have just reinforced the attitudes in the minds of the unbelieving public.

He was undoubtedly not helped in his fight to get a clean image by the other three candidates. "As far as I'm concerned, Abilene was only the tip of the iceberg," Sissy Farenthold told one crowd. "There is a saying in Austin when speaking of legislative passage, which concerns the speaker of the House, the lieutenant-governor and the governor," she said, telling the enthusiastic crowd that the saying is "It takes three to tango."

Dolph Briscoe, who by late April was running as if Barnes were his only opponent, made honesty and integrity key points in most of his speeches. He, too, mentioned Frank Sharp many times, trying to tie him around the lieutenant-governor's neck: "Our state has been disgraced by the Frank Sharp banking legislation. As governor I will veto any legislation passed without public hearing. No more Frank Sharp legislation can become law, and people can know what's going on." In his speeches he rarely mentioned Barnes (or any of the other candidates) by name, choosing instead to talk in general terms about the "mess in Austin" or the "lack of leadership at the top level of state government."

Sharpstown did not pose the entire problem for the young politician, however. Another issue that hurt him badly was his support of a couple of almost-enacted tax bills in past legislative sessions. The most damaging bill was one that Sissy Farenthold called the "Barnes Bread Tax." It became a stock phrase in her speeches, and it invariable brought whistles, cheers, and waves of applause when she used it. The bill itself had been designed to remove the exemption for groceries from the sales tax in Texas, and, with some uncommonly heavy arm-twisting from the lieutenant-governor, had passed by a 15-14 margin in the Senate in the wee hours of Sunday, August 24, 1969. News of the Bread Tax, as the *Houston Post* immediately labeled it, jumped from the Sunday morning newspapers onto breakfast tables all over the state, and the ensuing barrage of phone calls, telegrams and special delivery letters struck fear into the hearts of many normally pliable representatives. And thus the House leaders, realizing on Monday that they didn't have the votes to pass it, never brought it up for a meaningful vote, so it died.

The bill had passed the Senate, though, and Barnes couldn't hide from this fact. Sissy and Preston hit on this over and over, Sissy even choosing to make it the subject of those "godawful" television spots of hers. In all fairness, it should be stated here that Smith's use of this issue was a bit of pure demagoguery since he had publicly announced before it was considered that he would sign the bill into law if it passed.

The other tax bill that caused some problems for Barnes was one levying an additional two-cent per gallon tax on gasoline sold in the state.

It had mysteriously come out of the Sixty-second Session of the Legislature, even though neither the Highway Department nor their lobbying arm had asked for it. After it had passed both houses, Preston Smith bluffed the solons down, threatening to veto the entire tax bill unless that one portion was removed, and the Legislature meekly withdrew it. But Barnes's role in its passage was drilled home to thousands of voters by Sissy and Preston before the campaign was over.

Barnes was no pushover in the race, however, and though he suffered from some of the above blasts, he also managed to get off a few shots of his own. Most of his bullets were aimed at Dolph Briscoe, the silent candidate whom Barnes saw as his major opponent. Oh, he didn't entirely ignore the other candidates, and he would occasionally take a swipe at one of them. After Preston Smith's major shot of the whole campaign, the speech promising "no new taxes," Ben charged it was "pure demagoguery." And he sometimes tried to mention Preston's role in the Sharpstown Scandal, telling one crowd in the Valley, for example, that Preston's veto of the bills "probably kept him from following the same route the Speaker did." After all, he said, didn't the prosecuting attorney in Abilene say Preston was a co-conspirator? "What did Smith do different from Mutscher, other than veto the bills?"

Barnes also took a poke or two at Sissy, saying once early in the race that she didn't really want to be governor, she just wanted to keep Barnes from winning. He also chided her for her different political philosophy, but, he grudgingly acknowledged, at least "she's not hiding, she's got some programs."

Briscoe was in hiding, however, and nothing Ben could say or do ever managed to smoke him out. His grasping for Briscoe was not unlike, say, a peach-fuzzed young FFA'er from De Leon trying to catch a calf in the scramble at the State Fair. He had the zeal, and he lunged every time he got close enough, but he never came up with anything but a handful of air.

Dolph's low-key, issue-less campaign was a tough one to fight. Barnes began by calling him a "phantom candidate." It's high time Dolph "stopped being a phantom candidate and began telling the voters how he stands on the issues," he said in Houston over a month before the election. A man of integrity, he continued, "ought to come from behind the log and face the issues." In Dallas a week later, he scolded Briscoe for buying television spots "to sell a candidate like you try to sell a bar of soap." "The prerequisites that go into making a good governor aren't necessarily having the money to buy television spots to sell a celluloid image," he repeated. Some variation of these remarks became a fixture of his campaign speeches, much like the I-don't-know-Frank Sharp remarks, and he uttered them over and over throughout the entire race.

It was a frustrating way to fight, and the punches never really registered on either Briscoe or the voters. "Who is Dolph Briscoe? Where is Dolph Briscoe? What is Dolph Briscoe?" he would ask. "Who's heard

Briscoe on TV? All you hear is a paid professional voice." That last glancing blow did hurt enough for Briscoe to change his television commercials in midstream, substituting his own voice in some places for the beautiful baritone of Deloss Walker. But that one blow was not much punishment, and Barnes had to get much stronger before he got much more of a reply than that.

In the last week or two of the race, Ben began attacking Briscoe's credibility on financial matters. Dolph himself furnished the ammunition by declaring his net worth to be around $2.5 million, and his 1971 income to be around $79,000. Barnes then revealed U.S. Department of Agriculture figures showing Briscoe had received $52,000 in crop subsidies in 1971, saying, "I find it highly unlikely that one of the largest land-owners in Texas made only about $27,000 last year." He also challenged the $2.5 million net worth figure, claiming to have seen a 1964 Briscoe statement showing a net worth far more that that, and criticized Dolph for turning in a statement for campaign purposes that listed assets without their dollar value.

At one point Ben made Dolph a public offer of $3.5 million for all of his holdings, thus allowing him a $1 million profit. Briscoe's refusal and remarks that a man with Barnes's financial connections wouldn't have trouble raising that amount of money helped to minimize the damage from these credibility charges.

Barnes also fired two other salvos at Briscoe, but neither proved to be any more effective than anything else he tried. One involved a "road to nowhere" and the other a tax fight with a small South Texas school district.

The "road to nowhere," said two of Barnes's loyal state senators, Oscar Mauzy of Dallas and Bill Moore of Bryan, was state-built FM 2688, a 13-mile stretch of Dimmit County pavement that served only the "hunting lodge" of Briscoe.

A Briscoe ally, H.C. Petry, Jr., of Carrizo Springs, was chairman of the Highway Commission when the road was authorized, said the two senators, and that authorization appeared to involve cronyism and favoritism. Briscoe's retorts that the road served about ten ranches, was a school bus route, and had also been requested by the National Aeronautics and Space Administration because of a nearby satellite tracking station took the sting out of the charges, and Barnes was not able to make much political hay out of the incident.

The other story, usually attributed to the Barnes camp, was that Dolph had brought the Eagle Pass School District to its knees financially in a suit over their taxation procedures, but a statement from the school district's lawyer that "Briscoe was the hero of the situation" and had helped the school district maintain its solvency neutralized this issue.

Ben still took Dolph very seriously, and on the Sunday before the first primary predicted the two of them would be in a runoff. In the runoff, he said, "Dolph is going to have to come out and face me and talk about the issues," although neither phantoms, nor money, nor roads, nor school tax suits had forced Briscoe to do much so far.

In addition to exchanging pot shots with the other candidates, Barnes also did a commendable job of just plain appealing to the voters. In football-crazy Texas he doubtless made a few points with his lineup of athletes: Bob Lilly and Walt Garrison, two of the most popular members of the Dallas Cowboys, Darrell Royal, coach of the University of Texas Longhorns, and Brownwood's Morris Southall, one of the state's better-known high school coaches.

His ties with the state's minority groups were excellent, and he was expected to run well in Black and Mexican-American areas. Judson Robinson, a Black city councilman in Houston, and Dr. Emmet Conrad, a Black school board member in Dallas, were on his team, and he had campaigned hard in those areas. There had been one serious defection from his camp in the person of State Senator Barbara Jordan. He had helped carve a Congressional district for her in Houston's Black area, and was hoping to have her support, but she announced before the first primary that she was supporting Farenthold.

Barnes also thought he could do all right with the state's Mexican-American voters, in spite of Briscoe's and Farenthold's obviously strong followings. A couple of young county judges in the Valley, Ray Ramon of Cameron County and Ed Gomez of Hidalgo County, endorsed him heartily, but most Mexican-American leaders were in either the Farenthold or Briscoe camp.

In a hands-offish sort of way, Barnes was endorsed by former Governor John B. Connally, then Richard Nixon's Secretary of the Treasury. On April 14, Connally traveled to Fort Worth to attend a dinner honoring Robert Calvert, the retiring Chief Justice of the Texas Supreme Court. He told a press conference that he had a "very high regard" for Barnes. "I have no question about his integrity and ability," he said, voicing concern over attempts to paint Barnes with "the brush of guilt by association." To reporters who asked his opinion of Smith and Briscoe, he replied, "You might not get the same answer." Connally's statements appeared later in ads for Barnes under a bold heading "We Agree with John Connally About Ben Barnes." Ben was careful to proclaim himself a loyal Democrat, however, saying he would campaign for all the party's nominees in November. And he always said, "I never asked John Connally to campaign for me."

From beginning to end, the Barnes campaign was quite professional, and as election day approached there was no reason for anyone to think he wouldn't be involved in a runoff with someone, probably Briscoe.

The Farenthold Campaign

The other lead player in the election drama, Sissy Farenthold, was given little chance by anyone to make the runoff when she began her campaign. But the longer she ran, the more enthusiasm she stirred up, and the more she began to worry the other candidates. Hers was a decidedly amateurish effort, but her supporters' enthusiasm, warmth, and zeal made the other three campaigners appear computerized and mechanized.

Sissy had a good press throughout the entire campaign. There were at least two reasons for this: the "novelty" of a woman candidate, and her remarkable candor. Being a woman candidate was enough to attract not only statewide but national attention. The more it became clear that she was indeed a serious candidate, the more attention she attracted. Early in the race, the Texas newspapers seemed to have a hard time deciding whether to send political reporters or women's news reporters to interview her, and on more than one occasion, Sissy wound up on the women's page instead of in the political news. Later in the campaign she did indeed make the political page, but still had to face reporters' occasional mention of her dress color or hair style. "Just once I'd like to see a news story mention the color of Ben Barnes's suit," said one of her supporters one day after reading a political story where Sissy's dress received attention.

Sissy bore the burden of her womanhood gallantly, sometimes wondering what things would be like if her name were Frank Farenthold, but always answering the inevitable questions about women in politics forthrightly. Texas, of course, had already had one woman governor, but she had ridden her husband's coat-tails into the office. Could a woman running on her own win an election in a state where the "*machismo*" idea and the "barefoot and pregnant" theory still held sway? This question was in the minds of voters and the queries of reporters.

The aforementioned forthrightness was another reason that she got a lot of publicity. Sissy was a favorite of reporters. She fielded any of their questions without reluctance, always speaking honestly and plainly. She stood in refreshing contrast to Briscoe's refusal to discuss the issues and Barnes's professionally programmed answers. "If you travel with the Farenthold campaign for a couple of days," said one reporter, "you get to talk with her at length. You will know how she feels on many, many issues, and you can usually determine how she stands on the others." Sissy's candor got her in hot water several times, and her staff members would often wince when a difficult question was asked, afraid her answer might get her in more trouble. One columnist, after noting the dictionary definition of *candid* as being "free from bias, prejudice, or malice, marked by concern for the truth and justice," stated "by those terms, Sissy is indeed a candidate."

Her supporters, thus, could say truthfully that their candidate's positions on the issues were clear. Sissy's tiny Austin staff got busy and cranked out lengthy position papers on higher education, taxation, the environment, the arts and humanities in Texas, public school financing, welfare reform, and mental health. These papers, three to seven legal pages in length, made the other candidates' position statements appear almost as "capsule commentaries" on their topics.

Higher Education: This long, complicated paper delved deeply into the problems of the schools in The University of Texas system, having entire sections dealing with standardization of schools, financial irregularities, stifling of the intellectual environment, neglect of students, neglect of individual schools, and problems of discrimination on campus. It all reflected her dismay at the deterioration of the academic environment in Texas. Her proposals included a separate Board of Regents for each institution, full disclosure of financial interests by those regents to avoid conflicts of interest, allowing these local boards to control business affairs of their schools, recognizing the right of the local faculties to administer the schools and determine educational criteria, and giving students a say in this determination and control of their own affairs.

Taxation: The paper on taxation promised no more "taxes against the people," her term for sales and consumer-oriented taxes. She proposed a corporate profits tax as a source of new revenue, and if further increases were necessary, pledged to turn to other business taxes. She also pledged to not increase the sales tax or other consumer taxes. Other sections of her paper answered questions about a corporate profits tax hurting the business climate of the state, what the chances were of such a tax being passed on to the consumer, whether a personal income tax would follow a corporate profit tax, and what a fair rate would be. "The people of Texas know how I stand on taxes," the paper concluded, "and they know that I will stop putting high taxes on the consumer."

The Environment: The time has long since passed, began this paper, for politicians to run for office by pointing out the problems of our environment and merely promising to do something about it. Piecemeal, patchwork, and maze were the words she used to describe Texas's response to the crisis. Her knowledge in this area was firsthand, and the sentences reflected her frustrating attempts to deal with the agencies, boards, and commissions involved. The performance of the state agencies in pollution control is disappointing, at best, she stated, recalling that the Railroad Commission had never refused to grant a drilling permit for ecological reasons, and had never brought a polluting oil company to court. She proposed making the governor's office the focal point for ecological activities, promising to work in the Legislature for the necessary bills. She called for an

Environmental Protection Act which would grant legal standing to any citizen for the purpose of challenging decisions of the state agencies. She also wanted Texas to set up its own Environmental Protection Agency, to require environmental impact statements from all state and local programs, and to begin long-term planning in both land-use and water-management systems.

Public School Financing: This paper on the celebrated Rodriguez v. San Antonio Independent School District case was by far the most detailed of any of these "green-paper" reports. This decision, declaring Texas's public schools financing method unconstitutional, was only a few months old. She painstakingly explained what the decision did and did not do, what the alternatives might be if it were upheld, and what should be done anyway if the case were not upheld. Her proposals included having the state completely take over the burden of financing public school education without completely abandoning local control of the schools. She also wanted to correct the inequitable property tax situation by placing more of the burden on industrial and commercial interests.

Welfare Reform: This was the problem that took Sissy to Austin in the first place, and her uncommon knowledge of the subject literally jumped from the paper. It began by asking the governor to pay closer attention to the "goings on" in the giant Department of Public Welfare. Then she charged the governor with educating the public in the area of welfare. Too many self-serving politicians have helped maintain a number of welfare myths, she said. After laying bare a number of these myths and calling for attention to be paid to welfare-businessmen, too, she listed several proposals. These included appointing representatives of the state's minority groups to the Welfare Board, removing the constitutional ceiling on welfare spending, providing day-care centers, providing family planning information, and upgrading the nursing homes so they will not become "warehouses" for the forgotten.

The Arts and Humanities in Texas: A strong backing for the present Commission on the Arts and Humanities was pledged in this paper. More funding was necessary for it to expand the Touring Artist Program and to support Artists in Residence in Texas. Better co-ordination of cultural programs with existing agencies, and attempts to develop minority group cultural programs were also recommended.

These position papers are truly amazing political documents. In a land where a candidate usually ran on his last name, his friends' money, a handful of press releases, and a television and billboard image, here was one stepping forth with a platform so detailed it risked boring the reader. These papers represented a crash course in Texas government, and those who went through them would learn more about its problems and possibilities than they would in years and years of listening to political speeches. The readers would also know much more about this "candid-ate" than they would ever know about the others in the race.

The trouble with the papers, though, was that they *did* bore the reader. They never received much attention during the entire race, either from Sissy's opponents, her own supporters, or the press. They mostly were stuck in file drawers at her headquarters around the state, and promptly forgotten. And reporters looking for stories only had to ask her a question or two anyhow to elicit a juicy comment worthy of a lead, so they didn't pay much attention to them either.

Sissy also took many other stands during the campaign. The one which received the most attention was her "Texas Ranger" statement. It came early in the race and attracted little attention at the time, but later proved to be probably the most politically damaging statement Sissy made. Speaking in San Angelo to the directors of the American GI Forum, a Mexican-American organization, Sissy told them on Sunday March 26 that she was "in favor of disarming or disassembling" the Texas Rangers. "Maybe it's just that I was raised in South Texas, but I think the Texas Rangers are a festering sore." Her remarks brought a long, standing ovation from that crowd, but cost her many votes in North, East, and West Texas where the largely Anglo population still thought of the Rangers in the same way they thought of God, motherhood, and apple pie.

For days after the speech, rumors flew among her supporters that she was going to retract the statement, or explain it better, or do something. Later she did backtrack a little on the statement, saying that she had been "speaking in the context of South Texas." "I am for upgrading law enforcement every way we can," she said, "and the Rangers have provided beneficial services in some areas of Texas." One of her great-granduncles, Urban Bluntzer, even served as a Ranger long years ago, and she didn't mean to disparage the Rangers, she told one crowd, but where you see them today is in South Texas where Chicanos are legally, peacefully protesting.

No amount of backtracking could clear away all the damage, however, and the remark unfortunately became a smoke-screen hiding her carefully prepared position papers from the voters. Her opponents and enemies would talk about her as "that woman who wants to disband the Rangers," and all matters of substance would become irrelevant. Since this affair was good copy, the press concentrated on it, keeping it in the public mind at the expense of other, more weighty matters. Sissy remained rather philosophical about the flap, making one of her "that's the way I felt and that's it" commentaries after it was all over.

Another issue that created trouble for Sissy was busing. The forced busing bogeyman was tracking down candidates for all positions all over the state, regardless of what the office they sought could do about it.

Sometimes called plain busing, sometimes called busing to achieve integration, and sometimes called massive forced busing to achieve racial balance, it was an issue that stirred the people up so much that it was difficult to talk in any rational manner. The issue had come to Texas in the form of federal court-ordered busing in several cities, including Corpus Christi, Austin, and Fort Worth. The Nixon Administration's wavering on the issue in 1971 had given many anti-busing and anti-integration advocates fresh hopes of avoiding the orders and injected the issue into all state races. The fact that there was little state officials could do about an issue already in the federal courts was somehow ignored.

Sissy had already been branded a "liberal" by the press, and her opponents, notably Preston Smith, were charging her with being for busing. She chose Tyler, in conservative East Texas, to speak at length about the issue. "Busing is not the overriding issue," she said. "The issue is the quality of our schools. No one is particularly happy with busing, but I'll not say I'm against forced busing and then ask the support of those who have suffered from the dual school system. Let us seek solutions . . . . The Supreme Court has held that busing is one of the tools of integration—a last resort. I'm for following the Supreme Court. If other means [of achieving integration] are available—drawing of new boundaries or closing obsolete schools—they can be used."

This was obviously not a strong, die-hard stand against forced busing, and although she simply took the position of obeying the law, many anti-busing people were not pleased by the stand. A busing referendum had been placed on the primary ballot, and the expected large turnout of anti-busing voters caused some concern in the Farenthold camp. Her opponents continued to charge her with being for forced busing, at best a misrepresentation of her position.

Sissy's votes on the infamous Sharpstown Bills created a bit of a stir during the campaign. She had voted no on one of the two bills and yes on the other as they passed the House. Some attention was called to the yes vote in order to tarnish her reform halo. After all she had said about Mutscher and Sharp, this stunt defied credibility. Her explanation of the yes vote as one cast without a good understanding of the bill (a commonplace occurrence in the Texas House) didn't satisfy these critics and invited repercussions about responsible voting.

Sissy was a long-time supporter of Senator George McGovern's presidential candidacy. She had attended a meeting with him in Houston back in 1971, before most people even knew who he was, and had been committed to him ever since. Many politicians will ignore commitments of that sort during their own campaigns, but she freely discussed it when asked about it. With the exception of Preston Smith's last-minute endorsement of Hubert Humphrey, it was the only presidential endorsement made by any of the gubernatorial candidates.

Other stands Sissy took during the campaign included reducing the charge for a first-offense possession of marijuana from a felony to a misdemeanor, creation of a statewide public utility regulatory commission, and leaving abortion decisions up to the conscience of the woman involved. The abortion stand drew criticism from a number of Catholics, and in some places priests warned their parishoners against voting for her. Her reply that she personally opposed abortion but refused to force her views on others did not help very much among those for whom abortion was the key issue.

From the first the Farenthold campaign was plagued by money worries and disorganization, but before long it was evident that she had caught the attention of the public. Sissy's newsworthiness helped keep the attention. From the very first blow of the affray, the filing statement where she called the others "two contaminated candidates and a legislator from the fifties," it was clear that her reactions would have to be considered before the other candidates did anything.

Soon after filing, for example, Barnes challenged the other candidates to a debate. That's fine with me, Sissy shot back, as long as you pay for it. Ben was her chief target during the first primary. As he traveled around on his train trip she made almost as much news as he did by staying home and suggesting topics for him to explain during his travels. Some variation of her Barnes Bread Tax story came out in almost every speech she made over the state. When Ben promised something to someone, Sissy jumped in to challenge his plan. She carried with her a red notebook called her "Ben Barnes file," information compiled by Madelin Olds, a Del Mar College instructor, and she studied it every chance she got.

Preston Smith did not incur much of her wrath. She referred to him usually as "mediocre," but did not say much about him.

Dolph Briscoe did not draw much of her fire, either, at the first of the campaign. As it progressed, however, she began grappling with him. In one of the campaign's more memorable utterances, she referred to him as a "bowl of pablum," and reminded a reporter about to travel with him to take a "bib and spoon." The quip brought laughs as she campaigned, but reflected the same frustration Barnes found when he tried to cope with Briscoe's issue-less campaign. She ended up as Barnes did, wondering what Briscoe stood for but unable to coax him out of hiding. Shortly before the election she told a Dallas crowd the choice was between a wheeler-dealer from Brownwood, a political bowl of pablum from Uvalde, and "me, with all my shortcomings." "We'll leave the governor alone," she added; "I have shown an incredible amount of forbearance with the governor."

Most of the lumps Sissy took during the race centered on the Texas Ranger statement, the busing issue, nepotism, and an income tax. The nepotism probe (see Chapter 2) touched slightly on everyone in the race except Briscoe. The *Houston Chronicle* told (on April 1 in a page one story) about Sissy's four children working on the state payrolls. They had all worked a few months as pages or office workers, and Sissy said her inquiries about the legality of the work brought replies of "it's traditional" from the legislative authorities. If she had any indication the practice was illegal, she would not have allowed it, she told the *Chronicle*. When the investigation revealed that some of Barnes's children had also worked a short period of time on the state payroll, Preston suggested that maybe Ben and Sissy should withdraw from the race. A news story the next day chastised him, though, reminding him that he had engaged in the practice earlier in his legislative career.

She was also charged with favoring an income tax by her opponents. This oversimplification of her proposal of a corporate profits tax came most often from Preston Smith. Sissy did not favor a personal income tax for the state, and the broad use of the term "income tax" did not accurately reflect her position.

Toward election day, reporters began describing Sissy's campaign as the "Farenthold Phenomenon." Hers was a loose, broadly-based coalition of students, minority groups, laborers, stalwarts of society, and just plain Texans. People who attended Farenthold rallies fascinated the political observers, and themselves were the subject of some political reporting.

Sissy usually preferred the phrase "people's phenomenon" in place of "Farenthold phenomenon." She predicted a people's uprising in Texas similar to the uprising which killed the Barnes Bread Tax. An "ever-growing band of insurgents," she called her followers as she planned her coup.

The crowds loved her. They brought her cakes, cookies, sandwiches, tamales, and on one occasion, a box supper of crab mousse, ambrosia with cointreau, and a chilled bottle of wine. They wrote songs for her, changing the lyrics of familiar tunes and sometimes producing original lyrics and music to honor their lady. They wore her bumper stickers on their cars, their bicycles, their clothes, their bags, and one young Chicano in a small South Texas hamlet put one on the horse he had ridden to a Farenthold rally. One woman in Fort Worth brought her a mason jar with $29 worth of dimes, pennies and nickels, and told her it would have been more but her husband had been laid off. One youthful Mexican-American contributed a handful of pesos to her campaign. Sissy's financial reports listed over 4,000 individual contributors, proving how broad her appeal was. At a Dallas fund-raising dinner, she was endorsed by Stanley Marcus of Neiman-Marcus fame, and by young Blacks and Mexican-Americans. Bra-less girls, tennis-shoed little old ladies, young lawyers and engineers, grizzled old Mexican-American civil rights workers, and Afro-coiffed young Blacks all worked side by side to elect her.

Labor's Roy Evans said in April he expected most of labor's support to be for Sissy, and that if he had known in March how quickly her campaign would catch on, he would have recommended endorsing her at the COPE Convention. Even without the COPE endorsement she got significant help from locals and councils all over the state.

Texas's sizable Black and Mexican-American population were naturals for Farentholdian appeals. There were problems with both groups, however. This was the year that La Raza Unida was struggling to get on the ballot statewide, and, to do this, they had to persuade over 23,000 people to sign their petitions and stay out of the Democratic primary. Their drive undoubtedly cut into Sissy's support, since almost all of those votes would have been cast for her had they participated in the Democratic primary. The habit of voting Democratic proved to be so ingrained, though, that large numbers of Mexican-Americans stayed in the party, and she did run well in these areas. Dr. Hector P. Garcia and Paul Montemayor of Corpus Christi, and State Senator Joe Bernal of San Antonio helped with the campaign in South Texas.

The Black voters presented a different problem for Sissy, one of becoming known. Barnes had kept good ties with the more established Black leaders, and his name was far more familiar to the average Black voter. Sissy realized this, and with the help of her hometown NAACP president Irvin Brown, Houston's State Senator Barbara Jordan, and Dallas's State Representative Zan Holmes, a fellow Dirty Thirtian, she set out to become better known and to capture the vote from Barnes.

Her Houston headquarters made that city's ghetto area the target for a 75,000-piece direct mail campaign and then just kept their fingers crossed. "We know we're up against a male cultural block with Black men who just won't vote for a woman," said one of the workers. Sissy traveled in the ghetto areas when she could, and attended a rally for Mickey Leland, a young Black legislative candidate.

Students all over the state proved to be another source of Farenthold support. She won poll after poll at almost every college campus in Texas. At one point in the campaign, when it appeared that Sissy might have to give up the old DC-3 she barnstormed in because of money problems, a number of student body presidents organized a "Keep Sissy Flying" movement among college students to raise the necessary funds. Student leaders at The University of Texas at Austin, Southern Methodist University and Baylor University were joined in the successful effort by Richard Moore, a young Black University of Texas Law School student who had just recently been named Texas's first student regent by Governor Preston Smith.

Anywhere Sissy went, she knew there would be large turnouts of students. She had an empathy with them that no other candidate could match. Barnes and Briscoe both had youthful followers, but Sissy's race really caught fire on the state's campuses, and "Sissy's Kiddie Corps" grew into a large force.

The only negative note from this youthful following proved to be the reaction of the more sedate voters to the number of "longhairs" working for Sissy. One day-long caravan she made through East Texas attracted many hirsute students, and in some of the smaller, more conservative towns the negative reaction to the showing of hair probably offset the positive reaction to Sissy's speeches.

This then was truly a people's campaign that Sissy began to build to a climax as she entered the last hectic week. It had begun late, struggled fitfully through organizational difficulties, money problems, and staff headaches, and finally sputtered to life as a full-fledged political phenomenon. Along the way it attracted one of the state's best-known mechandisers, a brother of former Governor John Connally (Golfrey, a junior college teacher in San Antonio), a brother of former President Lyndon Johnson (Sam Houston, who placed a Farenthold poster over his bed in Corpus Christi), various personalities, politicians, and public figures, and throngs of just plain people. May 6 would have to come and go before anyone could accurately tell whether Sissy's predictions of another "people's uprising" would come to pass.

The Briscoe Campaign

Dolph Briscoe's political fire had been smoldering for a long time in the brush country in South Texas. The bit-player role assigned to him herein should not be interpreted to mean he wasn't a major force in the race, for he was. From the very start he was considered by most political observers to have a runoff berth in the bag. While he was a strong candidate, he was a quiet campaigner.

In sharp contrast to Farenthold's numerous and detailed position papers, and Barnes's reams of rhetoric on everything, Briscoe only put out two brochures during the entire race, one about him and one about his wife.

Dolph's brochure was a slick-paper, full-color foldout with pictures of him, his family, a "short biographical sketch, and his platform." The platform was a conglomeration of generalities and broad statements detailing Dolph's position on any number of issues. "Legislative Reform," for example, was considered important enough to warrant three whole sentences. "Tax Reform," "Pollution," "Insurance," and "Drug Abuse" likewise were disposed of in three sentences; "Busing," "Equal Opportunity," and "Vocational Technical Education" in two; "Our Youth" and "Mass Transportation" in four, "Economic Development" and "Tourism" in five, and "Education" in seven:

Education: The crisis we now face in our school system could have been avoided, but the leadership in Texas failed to act. I strongly support the concept of local government and local people deciding the kind of services they want. The state leadership, however, must develop a quality standard to assure all students the same level educational opportunities, with the general operations under direct control of the local community. Nothing should be spared to assure each child, wherever he lives, the best education the state can provide . . . .

Busing: I oppose the concept of forced busing to achieve racial balance, because busing is a hardship to our little children. Busing would also be a heavy financial burden to our educational system and would not help achieve our primary goal of providing quality education for all children.

Legislative Reform: We must break up the power base to allow our Legislature to be more responsive to the people. There is a concentration of power in the hands of a few people who can pass or kill a bill regardless of its value without a public hearing . . . .

Tax Reform: The economic growth of the state will provide additional revenues in the coming year. This, plus the savings that can be effected by efficiency, will go a long way toward solving the state's financial problems. If the savings effected and the increased revenues from economic growth cannot provide the services that are essential, I would not hesitate to provide the alternatives to the people.

Pollution: Our laws must be enforced to insure protection and maintenance of the abundant natural resources and beauty that abound in our state. New industrial growth will provide new and better jobs, but not at the expense of clean air and clean water. Our valuable natural resources must be preserved for future generations.

Economic Development: Texas's future economic development depends upon the successes of our efforts in a number of other areas . . . . It depends upon our ability to protect our environment and to provide responsive, co-operative government at local and state levels. Good management of our resources also requires sound and aggressive promotion. I will work to persuade the nation's business that we have the best place for their business operation, and they will offer our people better job opportunities.

Drug Abuse: It is, unfortunately, a growing problem in our state, and we must not degenerate into a drug society. Therefore, there will be no coddling of drug pushers and addicts. We must work with the first offenders to help them understand the problem . . . but the hardened criminal must be prosecuted to the fullest extent of the law.

Our Youth: I have great confidence in our youth. The vast majority is smarter, they're honest, they talk straight, but they really care. The challenge we face is . . . what kind of example are we providing?

Mass Transportation: Public transportation is a serious problem for the cities of Texas. It is a greater burden for the low income . . . . I will propose legislation to allow a city . . . to issue revenue bonds to build a system, with the state guaranteeing up to 30% payment.

Reporters were able to sound him out a little more, and Dolph took on the coloring of a "status quo" candidate calling for honesty and integrity.

He did not want to strengthen the powers of the governor, he said, he was running for the office "as it is now." He did not favor any statewide public utility regulations, because local governments were best able to deal with the situation. He promised to veto any bill that didn't get a public hearing, and when one observer remarked that would mean very few bills would get passed, he replied that would be fine since they were passing too many bills anyway. He did not favor annual sessions of the legislature, either.

Dolph told a press conference in pollution-conscious Houston he thought the existing pollution control laws were adequate, and we just needed to enforce them. He told college students in Houston he did not favor reducing the first-offense marijuana possession charge to a misdemeanor. A quantitative approach to the problem should be used, he said, and those with small amounts should get lower penalties, but it should remain a felony charge.

Aside from these revelations, however, Dolph refused to talk much about the issues, choosing to run instead a low-key, television and billboard campaign. Newsmen traveling with Briscoe were forced to practice press-release journalism, and not too infrequently their grumblings found their way into their interpretive articles.

The Dallas Morning News's Stewart Davis described one instance where Briscoe answered a question about land use regulation with, "I haven't made any proposals on that." When the question was rephrased, Briscoe replied he would need time to think about his answer. "He was still thinking at week's end," said Davis in his April 23 interpretive. A week later in another article Davis wrote, "Briscoe stymied and frustrated newsmen with his failure to answer questions about what they consider to be valid state government issues. Most times, he passed off such queries with the remark that he hasn't taken a position on that or that it isn't in his program. This reporter's question about land use regulation, posed nearly two weeks ago, was never answered."

The newsmen were puzzled and dismayed by the shallowness of Dolph's answers, and some wrote he must be trying to keep from alienating supporters for other candidates so he could win them over in the runoff. Ben Barnes and Sissy Farenthold, as has already been noted, shared these frustrations and were doing their best to "smoke out" Briscoe on these issues.

But, if Ben and Sissy and the reporters were frustrated, Dolph was not, and the grumblings didn't seem to bother his campaign very much. His country-boy image was making many friends in the rural areas of Texas, and he was counting on lots of campaigning to help him in the big cities. He wore his cowboy boots wherever he went, saying he would need them to wade in and clean up the mess in Austin. An American flag pin always adorned the lapel of his conservative, dark suit, and Briscoe never unbuttoned the coat or tried to appear informal when he was out in public.

Uvalde was strongly involved in the race of its home-town boy. Busloads of Uvaldeans went on caravans all over the state, stopping in the towns to distribute literature and bumper stickers. Some of them traveled with Dolph himself, trying to help out his paid staffers. Dolph's personal friends across the state were helping, too, usually forming the base for the local campaign. People who introduced him at rallies were generally old friends, and they would warmly speak of Dolph, Sr., and young Dolph.

In Dallas, where he had gotten only 8,800 votes in 1968, his organization boasted of having that many workers now. They had recruited their own bunch of Dallas Cowboys to offset Barnes's use of Bob Lilly and Walt Garrison. In Houston, where he had gotten only 6,200 votes in 1968, his people were making the same boast as in Dallas. Dolph evidently felt more at home in the rural areas, however, for that is where his campaign was concentrated. His style was more their style, and he felt more at home asking them for their support.

Briscoe considered Ben Barnes to be his major foe, and when he talked about his opponents (which was not very often), Barnes was often his target. Even then, Dolph usually did not mention names but talked instead of integrity, honesty, and restoring pride and confidence in state government. Once during the campaign one of Ben's computers went haywire and sent a money-raising form letter to Briscoe. Dolph used it in his own speeches for a while, telling his followers he'd be glad to help spread the story of Ben Barnes over the state.

Dolph's relations with Mexican-American voters were not bad, and he was hoping to pick up many votes there, especially in his own South Texas area. A number of Mexican-American volunteers were working in his campaign. His saturation advertising blitz would make his name known by election day, and he expected to do well in South Texas.

He faced more of a problem in Black areas, however. Like Farenthold, he was unknown. Barnes was the favorite because of his name identification, and a cowboy-booted rancher just did not appeal to very many Blacks. Dolph could try, though, and he made a few campaign sorties into Black areas; he was even introduced to one crowd as "a sort of John F. Kennedy in cowboy boots." But about all he could hope for here was enough votes to prevent a large victory for Barnes.

Dull, plodding, drifting, issue-less, low-key, no matter what you called it, Briscoe's campaign was gaining ground, and as he went into the last week, he was predicting a first-ballot victory. Others were not sure about that, but they agreed that he was in a good position to win a runoff spot.

The Smith Campaign

The other bit player in the 1972 election year drama, incumbent Governor Preston Smith, was really not drifting with the election tides so much as he was ignoring them. He was traveling around the state, shaking hands with all in sight, and telling of the accomplishments of his four years as governor. The state now had three more medical schools and several more branch institutions of state universities than it had had when he took office. He had held the line in taxes, also, he told his listeners. Most of his campaign speeches touched heavily on taxes, as he evidently felt it to be the key issue this year.

Smith's only major policy statement of the entire campaign concerned taxes, and came in the form of a thirty-minute, nineteen-station television show on April 19. "There will be no new taxes signed into law by Preston Smith during the next special session. This is a commitment to you and a friendly warning to the Legislature," he explained. "No new taxes will be acceptable and no new taxes will be signed into law." The special session Smith mentioned was an upcoming budget session, one made necessary by his veto of the entire second year of the Sixty-second Legislature's two-year budget.

Preston also used the telecast to bad-mouth his opponents. Barnes came under fire for those two oft-mentioned Senate-passed tax hikes, the one on food and the other on gasoline. Sissy drew jibes from Smith because she had "suggested that Texans should start paying income taxes." Barnes and Farenthold "differ only with regard to those whose taxes should be raised." Briscoe, continued Smith, "has said almost nothing about the vital issues which face this state. His brief record in state government . . . reveals even less about what he might do as governor."

Preston continued mentioning his "No new taxes" proposal as he campaigned, but other than that and a recitation of what the State had done in the last four years, he just asked for support. His campaign became as issue-less and low-key as Briscoe's.

It was clear from the outset that he was concentrating his fire on the young lieutenant-governor. They had never gotten along especially well, and many observers felt Smith wanted to take Barnes down with him if he should lose. The bit about the gasoline tax and food tax became almost as constant in his speeches as they were in Farenthold's. Preston denied a plan to take Barnes down with him when he was asked about it, saying that Ben was the only candidate with a record on the big issues, and thus the only one he could talk about.

Preston's optimism had never been greater, and he predicted he would lead the ticket with around 35% of the vote. His optimism flew in the face of every poll taken during the race, however, and a funereal air pervaded Smith's effort. The polls he could laugh at, for they had never really been an accurate measure of his strength. "I've never done well in polls, but I've done well in elections," he claimed, dismissing the polls entirely. He could not ignore, though, the number of past supporters who were backing someone else. Or the past supporters who were only going through the motions for him this time. Like Ben Barnes, he could not avoid the taint of Sharpstown. Ben tried, and Ben had reason to try, but by now everyone in the state knew about the $62,500 profit Smith had made on National Bankers Life stock, and there was no way Preston could fight that. All the rhetoric in the world about honest investments and banking bill vetoes wouldn't make the people forget about that money. That $62,500 dogged every step he took on the political trail as surely as if each dollar bill of it had been tied in a long string and connected to his Stetson hat. "I don't see why he is even trying this time," his people kept saying, but Preston kept gamely on.

The Role of the Media

As usually happens in Texas political races, a hue and cry went up early for a statewide television debate. And as usually happens, after the hue and cry died down, there was no debate. Very early in the race, Barnes challenged the other candidates to a debate. The only immediately response came from Sissy, who was willing if Ben would foot the bill.

Then, realizing the benefit to be gotten from such a production, she changed her mind and agreed to pay her share. Dolph then piped up that he was willing to come to the party if everyone else came (meaning Preston). Preston reacted as an incumbent might be expected to react and said why, of course not, he'd never subject the governor's office to the circus atmosphere which a so-called debate would produce. "It would be about the same as President Nixon debating Shirley Chisholm," he said with a straight face. At this, Briscoe hesitated, saying if all four were not on the program he was not sure he wanted to fool with it. Then Ben flaked off, saying that if Briscoe wasn't on it he wasn't sure he wanted to be on it. Sissy said she was still ready, willing to meet any candidate anytime, anyplace. From there on, it got confusing.

Charges of not returning phone calls flashed from camp to camp. Sissy's campaign manager said he couldn't get through to Briscoe's manager. Briscoe said his man was waiting for more information about the format. Barnes said his man was waiting for Sissy and Dolph to get the details worked out. By the second week of April, it was clear that there would be no debate.

There was still some hope for a joint appearance, if not a debate. Dallas educational television station KERA had invited all gubernatorial candidates of both parties to appear in a marathon question and answer session on the night of April 26.

One by one, the responses came in, and on that night, five Democrats and six Republicans showed up to answer questions from a panel. It was strictly a question answering session and there was no debate. The only thing really newsworthy about the affair was that it took place at all. The program was carried to most areas of the state by an educational television network, but the program's length, the difficulty in some places of quality reception of educational television stations, and the generalities used in most of the replies cast some doubt on the program's value.

Before the appearance, many observers felt that Mrs. Farenthold stood to gain the most and Briscoe to lose the most, but the three major Democrats (Preston didn't show) all played to a draw.

KERA's regular viewers also benefitted from the appearance of numerous candidates on its regular news show "Newsroom," the only real oasis in the vast desert of Texas television news. Extensive questioning by the "Newsroom" staff plus telephone calls from listeners usually helped cut through a candidate's political rhetoric, allowing the viewers a good look at the campaigner.

Most Texas newspapers, reflecting the large degree of "establishment" support behind Ben Barnes, endorsed the young Lieutenant Governor. Dolph received the endorsement of the *Austin American Statesman*, *The Port Arthur News* and a few other scattered small town papers. Sissy got the nod from her home-town *Corpus Christi Caller-Times* (whose publisher also kicked in $500 to her campaign), *The Texas City Sun*, the *Texas Observer*, and Nacogdoches' weekly *Redland Herald*.

Preston found only his hometown *Lubbock Avalanche-Journal* and the *El Paso Times* in his corner. Barnes was the favorite of the *Fort Worth Star-Telegram*, the *Houston Chronicle* (both of which endorsed him in January, before the filing deadline), *The Dallas Morning News*, the *Dallas Times-Herald*, the *San Antonio Light*, the *San Angelo Standard-Times*, the *Abilene Reporter-News*, the *Kilgore News-Herald*, the *Huntsville Item*, and other daily and weekly small-town newspapers.

Most of these newspapers made their selections early and touted them loudly and clearly up to election day. *The Dallas Morning News*, possessor of impeccable establishment credentials, waited until April 23 to endorse Barnes. It explained later that it had talked at length with three of the four major candidates and the choice boiled down to "somebody who does not equivocate" or "somebody who evades and shows virtually no knowledge about the job he seeks," an obvious slap at Dolph. And the *News* had been poking fun at Sissy for some time, especially since her Texas Ranger speech. "Will Slip of the Lip Sink Sissy's Ship?" asked one poetic headline over a column of editorial comment from other newspapers. "Texas Rangers 1, Sissy Farenthold 1" said a box-score headline over the letters-to-the-editor column one morning early in April. Perhaps its strangest editorial position of the election year was an April 18 editorial endorsing "barriers" to voting. It came only about three weeks after their veteran political writer Richard Morehead had fumed in one of his columns about the obstacles to the act of voting. "We wonder how many citizens share our feeling," he asked, "that the system presents an obstacle course to the conscientious, faceless citizen who likes to feel that he has a voice in running this republic." Evidently the editorial writers on his own newspaper didn't share his feelings. They took the position that the government shouldn't do much "nursemaiding" or "wetnursing" of voters. "If the want of a little exertion is going to keep millions of us from the polls, we aren't fighting very hard to get there in the first place," they intoned.

Three Texas newspapers also provided their readers with polls during the election; *The Dallas Morning News*, the *Fort Worth Star-Telegram*, and the *Houston Chronicle*. Only one of the papers made any pretense about following scientific polling procedures, the *Star-Telegram*, which hired a political research firm, Danny Parrish Associates, to do the work for them. All of the polls wound up proving little except that polling in Texas remains an "inexact science."

The *Chronicle* was the first to come out with a survey, predicting in its March 19 edition that Barnes would come in first (33%), Briscoe second (29%), Smith third (a "fading third" with 21% is how his campaign was described) and Sissy last (a "fast-charging fourth" with 17%). The survey, called a "cross section of expert political opinion at the local level" by the *Chronicle*, came during the Abilene trial, and found the stock fraud scandal to be the overwhelming issue of the day.

Two Sundays later, *The Dallas Morning News* published its "Mood of Texas" survey. Their talented pack of political reporters were sent around the state to listen and question. The consensus of their reports was that Barnes was ahead of Briscoe "only slightly," and that Preston was about to "pay for all the wrongs—real, imagined, and collected over the years since Sam Houston himself—in state government." Sissy Farenthold's campaign was on the rise and had already gone beyond Smith in some areas, said the report, without attempting to assign percentages to any of the candidates.

The next Sunday, April 9, the *Star-Telegram* published the first of its two Parrish polls. The 2,000-person sampling predicted about the same finish as had the other two polls: Barnes, 27%; Briscoe, 25%; Farenthold, 14%; and Smith, 11%; others 3%; undecided 20%. After three more weeks of campaigning, though, the poll predicted a reverse in the first and second place finishes and a much tighter over-all race: Briscoe, 28%; Barnes, 24%; Farenthold, 20%; Smith, 11%; others 2%; and undecided 15%. Sissy had made the biggest jump, from 14% to 20%, and, with a few votes from the undecided, she could really throw the race into a tight finish.

A new survey published by the *Chronicle* on April 30, the day Parrish's second poll was released, agreed that Farenthold had risen several percentage points, but still had Barnes in first place by a whisker. Ben would get 31.6% of the votes, according to the *Chronicle*, and Dolph would be right behind with 31.1%. Sissy's 22% was quite a gain over the first poll, but she "seems unlikely to close the gap on Barnes and

Briscoe," concluded the paper. Preston wound up in the basement with a 15.3% rating.

The only really accurate poll of the entire campaign came not from newspapers but from the politics-oriented Austin firm Executive Services, Inc. Their poll of 1,450 private citizens showed that 43.7% would vote for Briscoe, 28.1% for Sissy, 12.7% for Barnes, and 5.3% for Smith. It was released on May 1, and at first was discounted by political observers. The ESI people got the last laugh, however, after the votes were in, for they came quite close to predicting the outcome of one of Texas's most difficult-to-call political battles.

The Last Week

The last week of the campaign brought on a tremendous rush of activity by all of the candidates aimed at shoring up their support in what they considered their areas of strength. Barnes, hoping to do well among the state's more sophisticated urban voters, spent the entire week campaigning in large cities. It had been an expensive campaign for him, with later financial reports showing he had spent $1,073,216 and received donations of $933,962. This left a deficit of about $140,000 for the De Leon peanut farmer whose net worth was earlier reported to be $83,000.

He began the week by confidently talking about how he was the second choice of most of Farenthold's and Smith's supporters, and how this would put him over the top in the expected runoff with Briscoe. Monday he helicoptered over the Fort Worth-Dallas area, winding up the day with a rally at Dallas's Market Hall. He made a brief stop in Laredo Tuesday morning before flying on to San Antonio where he stumped well into the night and all day Wednesday. A riverside rally for him Tuesday night was highlighted by a fireworks display showing the initials BB superimposed on a large map of Texas. Wednesday was spent in a mad rush around San Antonio's west side. Eager volunteer workers had Ben's full-time staff members a bit confused by the day's end. One of the professionals remarked to a newsman later that the volunteers interpreted his request for an itinerary as a request to see a farm-worker. On to Houston that night Ben flew, appearing on a 30-minute television show. Thursday was a whirlwind: Houston in the morning (I'm against busing"); Beaumont in the afternoon ("little bit tired," he said); Austin in the evening ("glad to be at a sit-down dinner"). By now it was all a blur, and a worried Barnes was noticeably tired. Back to Houston on Friday he went, then back to Austin Friday night. After voting in De Leon Saturday morning, he made one last swing to San Antonio, then flew to Austin to await the verdict.

Sissy's last week was spent primarily in appearances before labor groups, minorities, and youth groups. She had been outspent badly by the other candidates, but she was now a major force in the race, and her breath was hot on the neck of Ben and Dolph. Her expenses, $325,666, were exceeded slightly by contributions of $337,793, leaving her a tiny nest egg in case she made the runoff. The lack of money had kept her from making any statewide television broadcasts as all of her opponents had done. Hers was almost entirely a traveling, speaking, hand-shaking race.

The last Monday of the campaign found her hitting the Houston ship channel docks at 4:00 a.m. to shake hands with Black longshoremen ("I never realized the hardship of life on the docks until I shook hands with so many men with missing fingers.") Later in the day she flew to McAllen in the Rio Grande Valley for a quick hand-shaking stop, and then doubled back to her hometown for an open-air rally on its beautiful bayfront. ("We are an ever-growing band of insurgents," she told the cheering crowd.) Tuesday she again hit the Texas Gulf Coast, stopping in Victoria and Port Lavaca, and climaxing the day with a rally in Houston's Hermann Park. An enthusiastic crowd of almost 10,000 cheered as she said the political coup of the decade was within their grasp. On Wednesday she blitzed the Dallas-Fort Worth area, shaking hands with union members and working in the Black areas. An endorsement of her by Rev. Ralph David Abernathy of the Southern Christian Leadership Conference was being played on Black radio stations in the area and she was hoping to cut into Barnes's support here. On a tour of a Black housing project, she stopped to remove a splinter from the foot of a little squalling Black girl (maybe we can charge her with practicing medicine without a license, thought one of her envious opponents).

On Thursday she made a flying stop at all-Black Prairie View College near Hempstead, and then went on to San Antonio for a series of stops in its Mexican-American and Black neighborhoods. She amplified her pablum statement about Briscoe for her Mexican-American audiences by saying he was like *atole* (a Mexican breakfast dish), "smooth, sweet, and without substance." By now her campaign was a blur, too. Friday she went back to Houston; Saturday she went to Corpus Christi to vote, then made stops in San Antonio and Houston, then went back to Corpus Christi to attend her precinct convention, and then flew to Austin to await the returns.

Dolph Briscoe's staggering television bills gave him the distinction of having the most expensive campaign. His expenses were reported at $1,126,693, and contributions of only $785,344 left him with a large deficit of $341,349. But all that money spent on television helped him do something in last campaign week that astounded many political watchers: ignore the big cities. He felt his strength was in the rural areas, and after much debate among his advisers, he decided to spend the first three days of the week talking to the rural voters. So he town-hopped, holding airport rallies in several dozen small towns in the Panhandle, North Texas, Central Texas, and East Texas.

While Ben and Sissy were concentrating on Houston, Dallas, Fort Worth, and San Antonio, Dolph was speaking in such places as Albany, Quanah, Dumas, Borger, Daingerfield, and Atlanta. And his speeches, about such things as fire ants, brush control, and agricultural tax rates, were not likely to turn on the urban voters very much. His thirty-minute television shows were put on stations in metropolitan areas of the state during that last week, however. Dolph hoped to run strong in the rural areas and hold his own in the cities. He did come in out of the woods on Thursday, for his last big day of working. He put in a long nineteen hours in Houston, beginning at 6:00 a.m. with a hand-shaking tour of the police station during a shift change, and ending with a reception late that night at his West Houston headquarters. In between he shook countless hands in shopping centers and downtown Houston.

Saturday morning Dolph and Janey went to vote in Uvalde and then retired to the ranch to rest. They had planned to fly in to Austin that night to the state headquarters, but bad weather socked them in and they remained on the ranch.

As the last week began, it was difficult to pinpoint Preston Smith's area of strength. Before 1972 he had always run well in the rural areas, but this year Briscoe had him on the ropes out there. And in the cities, well, he had never had that much appeal to city voters in the urban areas, occasionally making a foray into a nearby small town. He didn't spend nearly as much money as Ben and Dolph but he was still able to come up with more than Sissy. His reported expenses were $566,868, and his contributions $506,908, giving him a deficit of about $60,000. He did choose to have a state-wide television show in the last week, and on Thursday night he introduced a new concept in advertising—the political re-run. He ran his April 19 "no new taxes" speech again, hoping a money-conscious public would pay attention. Tuesday and Wednesday he spent in the Houston-Galveston area, shaking hands, drinking coffee, and talking about Barnes. Thursday and Friday he shifted his campaign to the Dallas-Fort Worth area, and at the Dallas Press Club "hot seat" luncheon, he ran into some sharp questions about his role in the food tax he was blasting Barnes with. "We have never been on record as having said we stopped the tax on groceries," *The Dallas Morning News* quoted him as saying, in an article that appeared on the same page as one of his ads telling the voters, "For you, Preston Smith stopped the Sales Tax on food and medicine."

On Friday, another of his ads came under fire. Newspapers in at least two cities published what appeared to be a normal ad with names of persons endorsing Smith. They were well-known names, and many of them were prominently and vocally supporting other candidates. Another look at the ad showed it to be a list of people Preston had appointed to various positions during his four years in office, but the ad's misleading appearance drew some fire in news stories.

From Fort Worth, Preston flew back to Austin Friday night for a rally, and then flew to Lubbock Saturday to vote and wait for the results to come in.

Election Saturday was a fairly normal May Saturday. There was some scattered bad weather around the state, but the lines of voters grew long in many places. Almost 2.3 million Texans went to vote that day, and as the first returns began to trickle in after the polls closed, it was evident that the voters had unleased their anger for the Year of Frank Sharp. The polling places were as jury boxes, and the voters were not so much people choosing among politicians as they were jurors pronouncing their verdict upon the Sharpstown Scandal. And the verdict for anyone connected with it (justly or unjustly) was guilty.

The early returns that night were from the rural areas; they were strong for The Man Texans Could Believe In, the only candidate who had not been in office during the Year of Frank Sharp. The 8:00, 9:00, and 10:00 p.m. figures from the Texas Election Bureau showed Briscoe far ahead with over 50% of the votes. It was clear by 10:00 p.m. that something exciting had happened, that young Ben Barnes, groomed by John Connally and anointed by Lyndon Johnson, was going down to defeat. The atmosphere of the night was not one of excitement, rather it was one of disbelief. Stunned reporters found themselves groping for words to explain the demise of Barnes, and kept repeating the words angry, mad, and Sharpstown.

The only exciting question of the night involved the runoff, or whether there would be one. As big city returns started coming in, Briscoe's percentage fell steadily. By 11:30 p.m., it had dropped to 48%, and a runoff became necessary. The cities didn't go for Barnes, though; they went for Farenthold. She began the night in second place, and wound up in the runoff. Barnes and Smith finished third and fourth, respectively. As the county-by-county totals were completed, the immensity of their defeat became staggering.

Shortly before midnight, Preston issued a statement of concession, indicating his "firm belief that history will prove that we've done a good job for Texas." His defeat was the worst ever suffered by an incumbent governor. He did not win a single one of Texas's 254 counties, and finished with less than 9% of the total vote. Lubbock, his home county, went for Briscoe, and Preston's second-place finish was only a few hundred votes ahead of Sissy. (See Appendix A for complete regional totals.) He finished last in every region of Texas, with his best showing coming from East Texas where he got 15% of the vote. His urban showing was extremely poor, averaging around 5%. Speaking to newsmen a few days later, he said, "the people just wanted a change." "I think we conducted the best campaign we ever conducted—and with the least results." The big problem any incumbent faced was "the fact that there had been so much adverse publicity about state government . . . I believe the press can change anything they want to. I believe the power of the press is tremendous."

Shortly after midnight, Barnes conceded, speaking to a large group of tearful supporters in his Austin headquarters. "Those of you in this room have done so much work that I can never find enough ways to thank you but I am only 34 years old and I'm going to be around for a long time and I'm going to find a lot of ways to thank you because you're my friends," he told them after he congratulated Briscoe on his showing. He still felt like the luckiest young man in Texas because of the twelve years of public service he had provided Texas, he added.

His defeat was much harder to figure out than Smith's pre-ordained failure. The complete returns gave him 17% of the total vote, and a first-place finish in only five counties. In one of these, his home county of Comanche, he was tied for first with Dolph Briscoe. In the other four, Brown, where he won his first legislative race, and Webb, Duval, and Maverick, all South Texas machine-oriented counties, he finished all alone in the top position. His regional showing was not much better. In only two of the nine geographical regions did he rise as high as second place, the Panhandle (24%) and West Texas (17%), and in both, Briscoe swept to an absolute majority. The sophiticated urban voters who were supposed to be his strength apparently never got the message, either. In the state's top four counties, where he concentrated his last week's effort, Briscoe and Sissy together took almost three-fourths of the votes, and Ben finished with a disappointing 21%.

Over at the Farenthold headquarters things were not nearly as gloomy as they were at the Barnes and Smith camps. After a couple of apprehensive hours when Dolph's totals were over 50%, the city returns caused him to slip below the majority point. Then it was clear that Sissy was in the runoff and Barnes was not. Jubilation took over and Sissy came in to tell her ever-growing band of insurgents that they had formed "a coalition that's thrown all the old tags and labels away." From now on, you could "disregard the cliches of so-called consensus politics and speak of the concerns and needs of this state. That's what this candidacy is about . . . ."

The jubilation that night was for a hard-fought victory and was clearly deserved. It was to be a long, uphill battle in the runoff, however, and the joy of her supporters might have been tempered a bit that night had they realized the immensity of the task before them. Statewide she had racked up over 600,000 votes, about 28% of the total. She ran first in only 14 counties, though. Nine of her counties were along the Texas coast, beginning with Orange County next to Louisiana, and going down the coastline to her home county of Nueces. This was organized labor's strongest area, and their support helped get her 42% of this region's vote. But it was the only one of the state's nine regions that she carried, and her six second-place percentages were pretty far behind Briscoe's percentages.

Sissy's concentration on the Houston area had paid handsome dividends, as she amassed over 125,000 votes there (that was almost one-fifth of her statewide total). Her concentration on minorities and youth paid off, too. In Dallas's Black precincts, she was not able to completely sidetrack Barnes, but she cut into his support deeply, and finished a strong second. In precincts around the state laden with students and young voters she also ran well. In Precinct Two in Nacogdoches County, for example, the voting place for many Stephen F. Austin State University students, she gathered over 1,000 votes, compared to 800 for her nearest competitor, Briscoe. Travis County, the voting place for most University of Texas at Austin students, gave her almost 40,000 votes, 45% of its output. Her strongest county was labor- and minority-conscious Galveston, where she took 53%, the only county in which she had an absolute majority.

Briscoe's party in Austin that night had to do without the candidate, who was weathered in at his Uvalde ranch, but that was about the only bad spot of the night. Dolph's share of the statewide vote finally firmed up at 45% (of the total vote for the four major candidates). He was in first place in all regions of Texas except the Gulf Coast, and he was only 7% behind Farenthold there. In four of those nine regions, he not only won, but he won a majority of the votes. His strength in rural areas was amazing. Small county after small county across the state gave him 50%, 60%, even 70% of the vote. And though he lost the state's most populous county to Sissy, he carried the next three in line, Dallas, Bexar, and Tarrant, and wound up just about even with her in the totals for the state's twelve most populous counties. It was, all in all, a remarkable showing, and from here on Dolph should have had nothing more than a waltz all the way to the governor's mansion.

Chapter 4

THE RUNOFF

After a day of voting frenzy, the tired voters needed a rest. They collectively leaned back, loosed a sigh of relief and began trying to grasp the immensity of the task they had performed.

By far the most amazing deed of the day had been the snuffing out of Ben Barnes's shooting star. He was a young man, and there was plenty of time for a political comeback, but it was hard to believe that the heir of a machine once strong enough to control the Presidency, the governor's mansion, both houses of the Legislature, and the attorney-general, would be so completely rebuffed by the voters. The man who had smothered opponents in previous statewide races, the man thought to be the next Texan to occupy the White House, the man who would rescue the national Democratic Party from the Eastern radicals, the man anointed by Lyndon himself was not able to persuade even one of every five Texans that he was the man. There were other problems of course (his rhetoric was too glib, his image too managed, his rise had been too fast), but the seeds of Ben's downfall that night had been sown by the cultivators of Frank Sharp's empire. Texas voters were madder that day than they ever had been, and Ben was just too much a part of the way things had always been done.

His true believers had a hard time understanding this, and many reacted the same way as a young man in Barnes's headquarters election night who muttered disconsolately, "Ben Barnes is too good for the people of Texas." A letter to the *Houston Post* later proclaimed: "When I clean house, I do not throw out my good china with a few of the everyday cracked dishes. Long live Ben Barnes and shame on the Texas voters." The *Dallas Times-Herald*'s Felix McKnight solemnly intoned that a "young white knight" had fallen because of the electorate's "kick the rascals out" mood.

Wonder at the voters' deeds also came from afar. These results were quite puzzling to observers in Washington and the rest of the nation. Most of them had never even heard of Briscoe or Farenthold. They had long ago fallen victim to the publicity surrounding young Ben, and they were hard put to assess his defeat now. Most of them had been too far removed from Texas during the year of Frank Sharp to understand just how seared the voters' sensibilities were. They had heard about the scandal, all right, but not on a day-in, day-out basis for fifteen months. So now, Ben's defeat was chalked up by many to some vague restlessness on the part of the voters, and incumbents everywhere were told to beware. One story even made the rounds that a nationally known columnist had told Ben shortly before the election that he had a good press, that he was known around the country, that he had a good image everywhere, *and* that he was going to lose, because this just wasn't a good year for incumbents.

Ben's personal setback was matched by the setback of the Connally-Johnson forces in Texas Democratic Party politics. Precinct conventions around the state the night of May 6 were captured by supporters of George McGovern, Hubert Humphrey, and George Wallace. Many of the leaders of these movements were brand-new in the game of precinct politics, but their zeal and sheer numbers helped them control most of the conventions in the state. Long-time conservative Democrats of the Connally-Johnson ilk had no one to rally around, and many of them found themselves on the losing side that night, excluded from the delegate selection process for the county, district and state conventions.

The voters releasing the sighs had few second thoughts about Preston. His poor finish surprised only a few.

The next week his wife told United Press International's Michael Wester, "It hurts. There's no reason to say it doesn't. We are still trying to figure it out." She also had some relief in her voice when she said, "I'm glad Preston is finally out of it. I think he has aged a lot during the last year just over the stock issue. Politics is not like it was—not even ten years ago. There are too many factions, too many critical of the top officials."

One of the more complimentary articles about Preston appeared in one of the most unlikely places, the *Texas Observer*. Molly Ivins summed up his last campaign:

> *If it hadn't been for Preston Smith, his last campaign would have been a sad one. There is a smell, a feel about losing political campaigns that is depressingly poignant: the gay banners, the brave talk, the thin crowds. Some form of invisible but actual buzzard circles overhead, waiting. But Smith's campaign was almost jolly. True, the crowds were thin, but they were loyal. And Smith's incredible optimism overcame even reality—until the votes were counted. The power of positive thinking is infectious: no political reporter who traveled with Smith was ready to write him off completely. They all went away, shaking their heads and quoting the polls and then adding, "But Preston could surprise us. Preston always surprises us."*
>
> *Publicly, he said he'd win without a runoff. Privately, he said it would be a runoff; first with Barnes, later with Briscoe. He really*

believed that for a long time. But they said he knew on election night before the votes started to come in. They said the only thing that upset him was losing Lubbock.

His wind-up campaign rally was in Austin. You know who gave him the big intro? Elmer Baum. And after Baum got through, Smith thanked him and went on about how Elmer was his good friend and had always been so loyal and true and helpful through the years. If Smith were a sharp pol, you would have gasped at the gall of it. But he isn't, so it was touching. Do you think that if some friend of Ben Barnes's had gotten him into a mess like the one Baum got Smith into, Barnes would have ever spoken to the guy again? Even been seen with him anywhere, much less stand up and thank him?

Funny, that issue, the issue, Sharpstown, disappeared toward the end of the campaign. Oh, the press asked him about it. The press always asked him about it. But his people didn't. When he announced this year, he said he would make it a major issue in his race and he talked about it all the time, almost compulsively.

When the Sharpstown scandal broke last year, Smith was desperately unhappy and defensive for at least six months. He avoided reporters as though they were vampire bats and when he did meet them he was curt, harsh, uncooperative and terribly, terribly defensive. You see, it hurt him, hurt him deeply and personally that anyone would question his honesty. He could not understand it. He was convinced there must be malicious motivation behind it. The motivation, of course, was $62,500. But he explained that. And they still kept after him. He thought if he explained it again and again, people would understand. But sixty-two/five from a man like Frank Sharp is not easy to swallow. It is a credit to Preston Smith as a man that the people who know him do swallow that sixty-two/five. Some of them assume a cynical posture—course Ol' Preston is dumb enough to have gotten into it without knowing it was a payoff. Others say it was all Baum. Still others just say, if you know Preston, you just know he wouldn't do a thing like that.

But Smith's campaign this year was an effort to make millions of people who don't know him personally swallow that sixty-two/five. And they wouldn't.

In Houston one night, as we were coming in from the airport, the cabbie tuned into our political conversation and suddenly volunteered, in a gravel voice, "I thought that Preston Smith was honest. But he turned out to be just as big a crook as all them others."

Earlier the same night, Smith had said, "Briscoe might buy this election yet. But you know something? Briscoe doesn't like people. He just wants to be governor. I like people. I relate to 'em. I talk to 'em. I could win this election if I could do like I did in '68 and visit *every little place. If I could just talk to the people. But I don't have time . . . ."*

One foreign observer of Texas affairs, the *Louisville* (Kentucky) *Courier-Journal* asked editorially a week after the election, "Democracy in Texas? Is no place safe?" The editorial examined the primary returns and concluded that "Texas's orthodox political faith, corrupt conservatism" had lost out in the election:

> *It's unheard of for Texas voters to turn up their noses at a Pedernales-baptized politician, whether his freedom from the law's clutches is attributable to moral purity or political-financial wizardry. It's also unheard of for Texans to vote for—of all things—a woman for such high office . . .*
>
> *Does this presage a new day in Texas Democratic politics? Probably not. Now that they've thrown the incumbent rascals out, the voters will probably go for Mrs. Farenthold's opponent in the June 3 gubernatorial runoff—Dolph Briscoe, a wealthy rancher with the charisma of a gallon of yogurt, who said practically nothing during the primary and whose chief qualification is that he's had nothing to do with state government for a dozen years . . .*
>
> *But if the [Saturday] madness continues—if that uppity woman gets the gubernatorial nomination . . . then the shock waves will extend beyond the Pedernales, beyond the Red and the Sabine, perhaps to the Potomac itself, where the Establishment might also tremble.*
>
> *For if democracy can break out in Texas, it can break out anywhere.*

Leaning back for a rest along with the voters were the two candidates still in the race, Dolph and Sissy. At this point, both were pleased with their showings, Dolph because he came so close to winning outright, and Sissy because she came from nowhere to make the runoff.

When the weather around Uvalde finally cleared, Dolph flew in to Austin on Sunday to meet with his happy supporters and plan his runoff campaign strategy. He predicted a hard campaign, but most of his workers didn't take him too seriously on that count because of his immense lead and the fact that his opponent was a woman.

Dolph told reporters that day he thought he would get a very high percent of voters from people who had supported Barnes and Smith in the May 6 election. "The people of Texas have responded to my positive platform," and have "approved of the high level campaign we have conducted and the results of this election confirm it." He also said he would not make many changes in his campaign style since it had proved to be so successful.

He was happy that day. "We had a doubly good day—when you get a good vote and a good rain," he said. The turning point of the campaign, he teased his wife, came on January 10 when Janey made her first speech for him in San Antonio. The group of cheerful supporters present applauded loudly as he proclaimed confidently, "I don't believe there is any doubt about where we are going from here."

Sissy spent that Sunday after election day telephoning her supporters around the state. In spite of the overwhelming odds against her, she declared the race "winnable."

"Who would have thought, when I announced for governor on February 6, that I was even going to be in the runoff? Every race I have ever had has been a hard one and I'm planning to win this one, too." Her enthusiasm was shared by her workers, as was her confidence although many of them had taken long, sobering looks at the returns by now, and were beginning to hedge their predictions with comments such as, "Well, no matter what happens from here on out, at least we got rid of Barnes." Creekmore Fath, her campaign manager, presented her a small bag full of pennies, marbles and chalk early Sunday morning after the runoff position was assured. It was a symbolic gesture, aimed at Lyndon Johnson's past endorsement of Ben Barnes all the way, "money, marbles, and chalk." It was, really, a sweet and satisfying victory for Sissy.

Her first strategical move was to renew her challenge to Dolph for a debate. From her position as a distant second-place finisher, a debate would make sense politically. It was the first in a number of moves aimed at smoking Briscoe out of hiding; she had high hopes at this moment that his elusive performance of the first primary would not be repeated.

The debate request was quickly rejected by Briscoe. Fath wrote a letter to Calvin Guest, Briscoe's campaign manager, proposing three one-hour debates on statewide television, and offering to pay one-half of the costs. "We must respectfully decline," Guest replied. "It is Mr. Briscoe's sincere belief that Texas faces a great challenge in restoring unity and a spirit of co-operation in the Democratic Party. . . .

"Since it is also his sincere belief that argumentative and publicity-oriented exchanges will not serve to stimulate the unity and spirit of co-operation Mr. Briscoe's campaign is striving to achieve, we feel that these broadcasts would contribute to further divisiveness and bitterness and would not be in the best interests of the people of Texas."

In addition to Guest's rhetorical reply, Bill Gardner of Briscoe's staff made some comments getting at the heart of the matter. "We're not going to get into that hassle again," he said. "I don't see why we should [consent to debate]. . . .We're some 24 percentage points ahead—why would we be wanting to get involved in something like that?"

Politically, Briscoe's answer made good sense, at this point. He was far ahead of Sissy, she needed the statewide attention far more than he did, and most observers felt he would come away second best in any sort of debate. Fath replied caustically, as expected, "I'm amazed that he won't take the people of Texas into his confidence. He is not willing to trust the people."

Sissy was not yet through with Dolph on this issue. It was a good one to use in her speeches, and it began to catch on with the public. On Monday, May 15, she got more mileage out of it by issuing a debate ultimatum to Dolph: "I am asking Mr. Briscoe to spend from now through May 20 searching his conscience and reconsidering his decision not to debate me . . . .

"By the end of that time, if he still refuses to meet me in a televised debate, I will go out and find him! If necessary, I will follow him into every corner of this state. If necessary, we will hold our debate on street corners. But I will do everything in my power to bring about the debate on street corners that the voters expect and that the people of Texas certainly deserve.

"I believe the people of this state are sick and tired of political candidates who make vague promises and avoid the crucial issues of the day . . . . if Dolph Briscoe truly believes the reform image he has fashioned for himself, he will stop running away from the voters, from the issues, and from me."

She was becoming again, as she had been during the first primary, a lead player in the election drama. At the moment, she was the one determining the site and the weapons for the contest. Briscoe's silence was giving her a good club to swing at him with, and there was enough sentiment being expressed across the state by voters for one to realize that the issue was hurting Dolph here in the early days of the runoff campaign.

The Dallas Morning News's Stewart Davis wrote on May 13 that Dolph could not be faulted for the decision politically, but that philosophically he could be faulted, because he got into the runoff by claiming to be The Man Texans Can Believe In. "How can they believe in a man who ducks a fight?"

Sissy was given another bludgeon to use against Dolph on May 13, when the *Houston Chronicle*'s George Kuempel reported that Briscoe had received strong individual endorsements during a secret meeting of about 75-100 of the state's most powerful lobbyists. According to Kuempel, former State Senator G.C. Morris, now lobbyist for Automotive Wholesalers of Texas, endorsed Briscoe in a speech before the group, and gave out letters for other lobbyists to use in urging members of their groups to support Briscoe. There were no speeches in behalf of Sissy, reported Kuempel.

Sissy also failed to get an endorsement this second time around from the Texas AFL-CIO, although there were several speeches made in her behalf. According to her supporters in the labor movement, the villain was the state AFL-CIO president Roy Evans. The struggle in Galveston back in March had been between the Barnes and Farenthold people, and Sissy had emerged without a recommendation, but with a "commendation."

On Tuesday May 9, the COPE Executive Board met to decide on recommendations for the runoff. Some labor people now wanted to completely endorse her, but Evans had already stated his opposition to that. "She's got the same problem Don Yarborough had in 1968 when nobody was mad at Preston Smith. I like Dolph—he's a progressive person," Evans commented to Ernest Stromberger of the *Dallas Times-Herald*. He also remarked Dolph was coming on strong with union members during the first primary "because they didn't see anything to fear from him," and "our people are pretty pragmatic" about endorsements. Besides, he indicated, Briscoe could probably help Texas go Democratic in November better than Farenthold, anyhow.

The best reporting about the May 9 meeting was carried in the *Texas Observer*. Molly Ivins reported that Farenthold's regulars had decided the night before not to fight for an endorsement, but to try to reject any move to commend Briscoe.

The next morning, Evans backed a motion to commend Dolph and lost by 18-10 on a roll-call vote. "It was the first time in anyone's memory that an AFL-CIO president had been beaten by his own executive board," reported Ivins.

Thus labor's official position was left as it had been after the Galveston convention—a commendation of Sissy. Some of her labor people felt that they should have pressed for an outright endorsement. There were some newspaper reports that labor's rank-and-file around the state was angry with Evans over his role in the meeting. Individual locals were left on their own again, and some of the locals that had endorsed Barnes switched to Briscoe, but Sissy still had the overwhelming support of most Texas union members.

The middle of May came and went, and suddenly there were only a couple of weeks to go to election day. So far the runoff had been nothing but an instant replay of the first campaign. Both Sissy and Dolph were maintaining the same type of campaign that had brought them this far. With two candidates gone from the race, the size of the spotlight focused on the remaining ones was increased, and more people were wanting to know who these two upstarts were.

Dolph's tremendous lead easily made him the favorite. But it also created some problems, for the accompanying demand for information about him and his positions sorely taxed a campaign style built around personal friends, hand-shaking tours, and bland, issue-less advertising. His refusal to debate Sissy compounded the problem, and his campaign began to bog down.

On Sunday May 14, he emerged from a week's rest on his ranch and announced his travel schedule for the rest of the campaign. The plan for each of his campaign stops was similar—a day of hand-shaking tours followed by a fund-raising banquet or rally each night. Most of the banquets were priced at $25 a couple, for which the guests would receive a good meal and a speech carefully prepared by Briscoe's staff. This would begin in Tyler on May 16, and take Dolph to 16 cities before the June 3 election day. The election-eve dinner was tentatively scheduled for Corpus Christi, Sissy's home town. A Briscoe win here would be highly embarrassing to Sissy, but Dolph's planners evidently decided Nueces County was hopelessly lost and the dinner was later scratched.

As this series of rallies began, Dolph's speeches revolved around the theme of unity. The greatest issue in this runoff, he said, "is the question of which candidate can do the best job of pulling Texas together." He also told the 1,000 Tylerites that there had been too much bitterness, division, and political factionalism, and that he was concerned over a trend toward confrontation politics in Texas. This attempt to rhetorically avoid a debate had perhaps a bit more credibility here because only the day before Alabama Governor George Wallace had been shot down in a Laurel, Maryland, shopping-center parking lot as he campaigned for the Democratic presidential nomination.

The next night in McAllen, he repeated this theme, ignoring a few long-haired pickets who showed up with signs urging him to "Face Sissy."

On Thursday, the city was El Paso; on Friday, the city was Beaumont; in both places the theme was unity. The same remarks were made, along with a few statements for the local supporters.

In Amarillo the following Monday Dolph gave a speech fairly representative of his remarks during this phase of the campaign:

> *Our state faces tremendous challenges and nearly overwhelming problems in a variety of complex and demanding fields.*
>
> *In education, transportation, environmental protection, and in stimulating new economic opportunities for everyone. We must be able to establish a set of realistic goals and construct a program which will help us reach them.*
>
> *To succeed in meeting these challenges, we are going to have to make some major changes in state government.*
>
> *On May 6th, the people of Texas made it abundantly clear that they favor major change in state government.*
>
> *This determination to change the course of leadership in state government came about for a variety of reasons, but, in my opinion, the greatest of those reasons is that people are convinced that state government has not been responsive to the people.*
>
> *By their votes in the primary election, the people of Texas indicated that they want someone in the governor's office who can make state government work.*
>
> *It isn't simply enough to be against bad government or ineffective government. It isn't simply enough to take things apart.*
>
> *We must have a governor who is capable of putting together a program which will work. We must have someone who can return this*

state to a time of effective leadership.

We must have a governor who can restore the confidence of the people in state government.

To do this, we are going to have to generate a new sense of unity and a new spirit of cooperation in Texas, and we are going to have to do it soon.

During the last few months I have spoken repeatedly of the necessity for pulling together the people of Texas so that we can work together in harmony and a spirit of mutual understanding for genuine improvement in the quality of life which is available to us now and which will be available to our children.

Our country has seen much too much bitterness and too much divisiveness. I think that our state has seen too much mistrust and too much working apart between various groups in recent years.

I believe that the great issue in this runoff election is the question of who can do the best job of pulling Texas together.

To achieve this, we must have an administration which is completely fair and open and honest, one that is completely independent of any special interest.

It must also be an administration which enjoys broad based support and one which is not dominated by any particular faction.

I think that my record both in public office and in business and civic affairs illustrates that I can and will be the kind of governor Texas needs, that I can and will put together the programs which will be of benefit to all Texans.

It is my conviction that the governor of Texas must be actively involved in cooperating with each region of Texas on projects which will be both good for those regions and for the state as a whole.

I am strongly in favor of developing a workable Texas water plan which will bring from sources outside Texas water to our water deficit areas.

I am also interested in seeing Texas emerge as the number one agricultural producing state in the nation.

California is currently ahead of Texas in agricultural production, and I believe that Texas can and should be the leader in this field.

This is not to say that I am more interested in rural goals than in urban ones. On the contrary, I believe that the only way we are going to achieve the maximum balance of opportunities in Texas is to make the most of both our rural and our urban resources. The fact that California, which is clearly an urban state, now out produces us agriculturally should be a clear example of the fact that it is possible to achieve this balance. And I think we can do a better job of it than our neighbor to the west has done.

I will also seek to establish a system of regional branch offices of *the governor's office so that we can begin work immediately toward striking this balance of opportunities.*

The regional branches of the governor's office will propose as their responsibility the job of seeing to it that communications between state government and the people reach the point so that you know what is going on in state government and government knows what is going on with the people.

I will also propose for state government a state budget commission which will have as its responsibility the job of creating better financial controls over the taxpayer's investment.

Sound financial management of state government is perhaps the greatest single task facing us today, and I believe that we must have in the governor's office someone who is capable of getting the most in government services for the taxpayer's investment.

Sound financial management of state government is perhaps the greatest single task facing us today, and I believe that we must have in the governor's office someone who is capable of getting the most in government services for the taxpayer's dollar.

I believe I am the only candidate who can bring to Texas an immediate return of trust and confidence in state government.

I believe I am the only candidate who can bring sound financial management to the governor's office.

I believe that I can help get this state moving again so that each and every citizen of Texas has the opportunity to make a better life for himself and his family.

The vote which you helped give me in the May 6th election illustrates that you want these characteristics in your next governor.

Now I am asking for your help again.

And when this election is over, I'll need your help too. I'll need your help in pulling the people of Texas together and closing ranks behind this movement to make state government a force for a better way of life.

With your help, I know we will be successful in both undertakings.

The Briscoe dinners were gala affairs for all concerned. Everything from the food to the decorations to the speech was carefully planned. The programs and posters were usually colorfully and professionally printed. The food served was usually high above normal political banquet fare. This is not to say that the dinners were dull, because for Briscoe's loyal supporters, they were not. Their enthusiasm would most likely be shown through polite applause and self-conscious singing, however, in contrast to Sissy's raucous rallies. No matter what part of the state the dinner was in, Briscoe's people all had a sameness of quality. The crowds would be full of obviously prosperous, middle-aged Anglos. Very few Blacks and Mexican Americans were present, and those who were, normally were the older establishment types. (An exception to this would be some of Briscoe's South Texas gatherings, which did have more than a smattering of Mexican Americans.) The Anglos came dressed in the latest double knit suits, and if they had on cowboy boots, they usually were the more expensive hand-tooled kind. There were usually some young people present, too, but not very many. They were also dressed up in their finest, their hair was on the short side, and they usually accompanied their parents. And someone, before the night was over, would get up and talk about "all these young people, and what a fine job they've done."

Dolph's relations with the working press did not get any better during the runoff. The grumblings that erupted during the first primary race grew louder and louder. There were several reasons for this.

For one thing, Dolph's campaign was highly media-oriented, but only toward bought media time and space. It was a slick, conscious effort at image building, and the questions and snooping of reporters were a bother. Thus a sort of mutual suspicion grew up between the candidate and the reporters.

Another problem was Dolph's inherent shyness. Various words and phrases were used describing him: recluse, aloof, reluctant to answer, playing hide-and-seek with newsmen. His friends and aides (many were the stories quoting a "Briscoe aide" about something or other) were quick to explain this as a part of Dolph's "cowman ethics." There's just a code of ethics among ranchers wherein one doesn't come out and ask another flatly how much land or how many cattle he owns. Even long-time friends don't do this, they said. And a rancher telling about his ranch is apt to use terms such as "little spread," "few acres," or "couple head." Thus his natural reluctance to discuss such things as his personal wealth or how many acres he controlled.

He was also accustomed to being taken at his word. Because if a cowman said he'd do something, by gosh, he'd do it. So when Dolph said he'd veto every bill that didn't get a legislative hearing, perhaps he got a bit irked at reporters who kept asking how and what and when. And when he said the State would live within its income, why did the reporters start asking questions about whether he would prefer increasing the sales tax or installing a corporate profits tax?

After one rather hostile news conference in Houston, his aides said he was just used to one-on-one situations in dealing with people, and was not accustomed to facing large groups of reporters asking questions rapidly. Then they would say, "if he really told you how he felt, he would never get elected." He is undoubtedly a sincere man. The many friends and aides who would swear to his complete integrity and honesty showed a deep trust in their candidate.

The Briscoe campaign organization also created some trouble spots for the candidate. A multitude of mixups, scheduling problems, and missed deadlines did nothing to help his press relations. Since most of his speeches came at night, reporters with late afternoon deadlines needed advance copies to write their stories, but most of the time they got copies shortly before the banquet began. There was usually a separate plane for press people, even though Dolph's plane (nicknamed the "Janey B") had room for them. They sometimes stayed in separate motels, and, on one memorable occasion, the press plane wound up in Houston while the candidate was speaking in Wichita Falls. On some days about all the reporters got from him was a good-morning handshake as he left for a round of private meetings. "Doesn't he understand," griped one reporter, "all I want is a lead for my story? I'm not trying to get him."

Once, as the candidate's entourage walked into a private club in Dallas for a luncheon with a number of important bankers who had supported Barnes earlier, the reporters found themselves stopped at the door. Briscoe's aides, at first open-mouthed and then red-faced, discovered the club did not permit women inside, and one of the reporters happened to be a woman. Appeals to higher authorities to bend the rules failed, and finally the embarrassed Briscoe men, one of whom muttered softly he was beginning to understand Sissy's determination, tried to smooth over the press's ruffled feelings by buying them steaks at a plush restaurant nearby.

Occasionally, there would be a thaw, and for a flight or two the reporters would be with the candidate, but such thaws were short-lived. Then the freeze was on again and the reporters were left to their own devices to ferret out the man behind the image.

One week of traveling like this caused Ann Atterberry of *The Dallas Morning News* to begin her Sunday analysis: "For a reporter, traveling the campaign trail with Dolph Briscoe is an incredibly bad trip." The press and the candidate, she said, "are spooking each other badly, and it's a vicious circle. As Briscoe becomes more evasive, the press becomes more hostile and aggressive . . . . the lack of communication between Briscoe and the press is unfortunate for both sides." Her stories that week had turned up instances of Briscoe meeting privately with Austin lobbyists for the vending machine and nursing home industries, and a "Godfather" scene in a Houston hotel where deputy sheriffs refused to let persons off the elevator on Dolph's floor unless their name was on a list given to them.

Other reporters also phrased their frustrations into their analytical pieces. One wondered if "Briscoe realized fully how crafty the crafty lobbyists are, how complex and interrelated the problems are, and how really weak our Constitution has rendered our governor." One spoke of Dolph's rural expertise but asked, "How will he learn of the urban screwworms?" (Dolph's reply that big cities didn't have different problems from small towns, just bigger ones, didn't satisfy the scribe, Henry Holcomb of the *Houston Post*.) They also wondered about Janey and her influence on her taciturn husband. She was by Dolph's side almost every mile of the campaign trail, smiling, helping, shaking hands, and occasionally taking her shy husband by the hand and leading him into groups of possible supporters. The inevitable remarks that "You'll get a woman governor no matter who you vote for this time," and "Sure I'm for Briscoe, Janey'll be a fine governor" were duly noted and recorded.

Perhaps the final reason that Dolph's problems with the press continued is the fact that his opponent's relations were so good. His campaign was not much different from that of many a Texas politician, and in another time, with another opponent, he might not have seemed so close-mouthed. But the contrast between his race and Sissy's was so immense and so apparent that the reporters forgot that he was only doing what many candidates had done. It was also what many candidates had won with, and Dolph was clearly playing with a winning hand here.

In the meantime, Sissy's bunch of volunteers was dreaming the impossible dream. A runoff spot had once seemed to be an impossible dream for her, and she had made it, but to win the runoff, she would have to almost double the support she got in the first primary. The coalition of labor, students, and minority groups by itself would not be enough to win. In fact, the student vote, which had clearly been overwhelmingly for Sissy, was causing some concern for her now because of calendar problems. Since the voter registration drives early in the year had come while they were in school, most of them had registered to vote in their college towns. But the June 3 runoff would come after their schools had dismissed for the summer vacation, and they would either have to vote absentee, or drive back to their college towns on June 3. Both the alternatives presented hassles, and Sissy would be lucky to retain the degree of support in the runoff that she had received in the primary.

Her problem, the, was to hold together the 600,000 votes she got in the May 6 election, and to capture enough additional votes from the Barnes and Smith voters, plus the defectors from Dolph's camp, to put her across the majority mark.

In the last days of the first primary, Sissy had been noticeably weary, so the first thing she did was to take a well-deserved week's rest at the Greenhouse, a health spa in Grand Prairie. Creekmore Fath, meanwhile, called together the young state headquarters staff and told them that a lot of VIP's would be coming in since they had made the runoff so from now on a new headquarters rule would be established: all the workers would have to wear shoes. It was a sacrifice they appeared willing to make.

Not all of the organizational problems were solved quite so easily. Money, for one thing, remained in short supply. Without it very little radio and television advertising could be done. Workers and organizers in the rural areas were badly needed. Part of this might be solved by the student workers who went home for the summer, but this was Dolph's area of strength, and she needed badly to make some inroads here. Her organization did expand tremendously during June, but these small town voters were the ones hardest to reach. She had had only 35 county chairmen on May 6, but the list grew to 221 in the runoff campaign. As in any campaign, but especially a poorly-financed, volunteer run race, there were the usual internal squabbles and hassles. The acerbic Fath himself ruffled a good many feathers, and local workers trying to get bumper stickers and buttons from Austin were often left muttering to themselves and wondering if things could get screwed up any worse. "Every vote she got, she got by herself," said her daughter after the election, and many people around the state who had tried to deal with her staff were inclined to agree. "It was the first time I'd ever seen a staff pull a candidate down," exclaimed one incredulous observer during the early days of the first primary battle.

Once during the runoff, a frantic call from the state headquarters came for Sissy while she was speaking to a reception in a small Gulf Coast town. They wanted her to cancel her plans for the next day and return to Austin for a Capitol press conference in response to some charge or other that Briscoe had made. She thought it would be foolish to do so, and argued with them for a while, then handed the phone to an aide. "I am the candidate," she proclaimed witheringly, "I may not be much else, but I *am* the candidate. If I had listened to everyone, I wouldn't even be here now." She went on with her plans for the next day.

Sissy's relations with the press, meanwhile, were good all through the runoff campaign. It was a necessity for her, since a campaign not relying on bought media time and space needed all the free time and space it could get. She did manage to come up with some good television spots toward the end of the runoff. Enough money came in for her to hire Charles Guggenheim, a nationally known image-maker. Guggenheim had made the award-winning film on Robert Kennedy that had produced an emotion-packed, spontaneous singing of the "Battle Hymn of the Republic" when it was shown at the 1968 Democratic National Convention. He was also handling Senator George McGovern's television ads in McGovern's quest for the Presidency in 1972. Guggenheim brought a crew down and filmed a question and answer session with a rested and relaxed Sissy facing a small studio audience. The resulting one- and five-minute spots were extremely good. Sissy didn't have enough money to put on a thirty-minute statewide television show, but the spots were shown in a good many Texas cities.

The working press continued to travel on the same plane with Sissy as they had done in the primary. It was a large, old, green-and-white DC-3, nicknamed the "Sissy plane." She was available to them on the plane for instant interviews, and they could also observe the workings of the young staff members traveling with her. Jamie Anderson, an ex-aide to Senator Ralph Yarborough, was her constant right-hand man; Francie Barnard, a Washington reporter, came to Texas to work as a press aide; and Harvey Katz, author of the controversial *Shadow On the Alamo*, came back to Texas to write speeches for her.

There was usually a good contingent of press people with Sissy. Reporters for the big city dailies in Texas were fixtures in her campaign now, and many national publications sent their representatives down to travel a day or two with her. A woman in the Texas gubernatorial runoff was quite notable, and she was mentioned in articles in the *Wall Street Journal*, *Nation*, several Washington and New York papers, and several national newsmagazines. Sometimes these national reporters got carried away with this "different" candidate, and their oversimplifications caused Sissy some problems. *Time*, for example, described her as an "advocate of busing, liberalized abortion and marijuana laws, a state tax on corporate profits, [and] elimination of the Texas Rangers . . ." This capsule description was good copy for *Time*, and no doubt provided a laugh for their readers in the other 49 states, but the gross simplifications of her positions caused problems for Sissy. This quote from *Time* soon began to appear in campaign literature opposing her.

Sissy's campaign trips were fun for all concerned. There were no strained, tense relations such as those in the Briscoe camp. Her crowds were noisy, cheering, and full of adulation for their candidate. A campaign run on a shoestring like hers did not have charcoaled steaks like Dolph's, but it surely did have more enthusiasm, and the people attending came from extreme cross-sections of society. Not all of them had been for her in the first primary, either. It was clear she was getting some converts. One of Preston Smith's county chairmen in the Gulf Coast area showed up at a Sissy rally; one of his El Paso contributors announced his support of Sissy; people turned off by Dolph's campaign style began to switch. She also had many supporters in another anti-establishment movement: that of George Wallace. The fiery Alabama governor had made a quick plane trip to Texas shortly before the first primary, exhorting his people to get to the polls and then back to the precinct conventions to support his Presidential ambitions. At an airport rally in Corpus Christi, many cars bearing "Wallace for President" bumper stickers also were sporting "Farenthold for Governor" signs. At first glance, the alliance seemed unlikely, but, considering the economic policies and anti-incumbent nature of the two, the support was not surprising.

There are many other examples of Sissy's variegated support. In Galveston, she was introduced to a woman who had toted her kids around in her arms while she worked her precinct for Sissy. As the woman left, another worker whispered to Sissy that the woman was blind. A crotchety, old, well-known liberal leader showed up at another rally, and a wealthy matron driving a brand new luxury car informed the people around her that if he wasn't one, he sure had some friends who were card-carryin' communists. In Dallas, a man who was the president of a "quite large" engineering company and a warden in the Episcopal Church said he was planning to vote for her. "What about her position on a corporate profits tax?" he was asked. Well, this didn't bother him too much, he said, because it was going to come anyway, and, at least with her, it'll be an honest and fair tax. In Houston, the daughter of a former Texas governor helped host a reception for Sissy. This lady had been for Briscoe earlier, and had even given him some money, but now she had switched.

In Houston, some youthful supporters, minding Sissy's self-imposed ban on billboards, patiently held long banners with "Farenthold" printed on them aloft on grassy knolls near freeways during rush hours. In Dallas, the candidate was carried around in a mobile-home-van nicknamed the "Sissymobile"; drivers in cars around the van often flashed "V" signs at its occupants, and chased it down to ask for bumper stickers. And once, in Dallas, while Sissy spoke to members of the junior bar association, a call went to the local organization for some literature, and pretty young sandal-shod girls dressed in blue jean cutoffs and a sweater sans bra quickly showed up to give out pamphlets to the startled young lawyers.

Most of Sissy's speeches were off-the-cuff jobs. She sometimes had note cards, but she never used a completely prepared text. She had not been noted for her speech making in the Legislature, but she surprised some of her longtime observers by becoming an effective campaign orator. She got better as the campaign went on, and she was at her best when she faced a friendly audience. She and the crowd both seemed to feed on each other's enthusiasm, and the rally would become not so much a word-communication event as a mutual-love happening.

Since her speeches were spontaneous, their content varied slightly from town to town, but a common theme emerged during the first part of the runoff. Sissy herself had trouble expressing it and communicating it to the voters; it involved public government versus private government. She explained it to a Victoria rally:

I went to Austin thinking that I, in some small part, could participate in the lawmaking process. I'm a lawyer, by training as well as tradition. I went there knowing that the Mexican American had not been represented in state government. I went there knowing that the Blacks had not been represented in state government. But what I learned was that most Texans had not been represented in state government. And this is what my concern has been. I had wanted to move us away from the kind of victimizing that is done to just plain Texans. Let me tell you about the kind of private government, the kind of victimizing government.

We had an appropriations bill last year. For the first time in people couldn't say how many years, there was a fight on the floor of the House of Representatives trying to put some humanizing appropriations in there and taking some pork-barreling ones out. That fight just didn't happen. A group of us took that appropriations bill and worked

*four days and four nights. That's all the time we had to do it in. Well,
we came up with eighty amendments or questions. Well, the
proponents of that appropriations bill got the message when we put
those eighty proposed amendments up on the speaker's desk.*

*There was an amendment to allocate $400,000 so the State could
help hospitals buy kidney machines that would save Texan's lives.
That's all—just the human factor in our state. It was voted down. At
the same time that that was voted down, the same day, a million
dollars was appropriated to the LBJ State Park, the most
over-developed park in this state, a park that the Parks and Wildlife
Commission had only asked $100,000 for, but the Legislature saw fit
to give $1,000,000.*

*Let me give you another example. Bills can look very plausible. We
had one on traffic safety, and we're all for traffic safety, and the
sponsor of that bill got up and said we need this to fulfill some federal
requirement on safety. Well, if any of you or your friends live in the
country you know about the trailer brake law. It was sponsored by
lobbyists and it was simply to prevent the small farmer from moving
his own produce. That's what I call victimized government. It
affects just ordinary Texans. Now it's up to the people of this state
what kind of government they want, whether they want this
continuation of private government with its recitation of platitudes or
if they want public government—public decisions made in public—
that's what my candidacy is about.*

Sissy's campaign addresses usually contained a mention of several other
subjects, too. Among the topics mentioned most frequently were taxation,
the Texas Rangers, marijuana, and a public utility commission. Typical
remarks on these issues follow:

Taxation (to a Victoria gathering):

*I've made some proposals. I've made them because I think they're
rational and I think they're reasonable and plausible. I can only
present them to you. We will need additional taxation because of the
very fact of the built-in programs we already have. I'm committed to a
teachers' pay raise and have been ever since I voted for one in 1969. I
don't know where my opponent is on it or if he even knows about it.
But we will need additional revenue. That's indicated by the Texas
Research League of which my opponent is a member. Now where's it
going to come from? We can extend or increase the sales tax. And
what does that mean? The ordinary Texan victimized again. We can
go to a personal income tax, and mark my words, you will see the big
corporations pushing for a personal income tax before a corporate
profits tax against these massive corporations that are so much a part
of this private government. All I am asking is that the powerful pay
their fair share. That's all!*

Texas Rangers (in a Dallas television interview):

Let's not confuse the Ranger situation with law enforcement. I have made statements time and time again for modernization of our police, for additional training, for additional salaries, for fringe benefits for them. I'm a great respecter of the law, and I'm not going get pushed back into the corner that I'm not. But when I speak of the Rangers, and I call this a nation-state that we live in, I speak in the context of South Texas—an area that I'm from. And I don't really think Mr. Briscoe is familiar with the history, perhaps, of the Rangers. They have been, in the past years, a private police force. They've been used for strike-breaking in South Texas, and as long ago as 1902, John Nance Garner asked that they be moved out of South Texas. I want to see a peaceful, humane state. I see a lot of trouble brewing in many places and I feel very deeply it would serve everyone's purpose for the Rangers not to be in South Texas. I've been there and frequently they've come for civil demonstrations— peaceful ones. And there's just such a history in South Texas that I think it would be better for them not to be there. I feel that very deeply... I don't disparage the Rangers. You know, I actually had a great-granduncle, Urban Bluntzer, that was a Ranger. My traditions go back in that direction, too, but I want to see this a peaceful state.

Marijuana (also in the Dallas television interview):

I introduced legislation in the 62nd Session to reduce the possession of marijuana to a misdemeanor. It really first came to my attention in the 61st Session. A district judge from Corpus Christi called me and said, "Please, can't you do something about this? I'm under law sending people to prison—it's just not justice." It was impossible to do anything then, and I introduced legislation in the 62nd Session. All I did was track the Nebraska statute making it a misdemeanor for the possession of marijuana. Since then the Board of Directors of the State Bar of Texas, the Texas Medical Association, and a lot of groups have asked the governor to open the call [of a special session for such legislation]. Well, here Mr. Briscoe is coming out with something that by implication I'm proposing the legalization of marijuana. [He should know better, she said the next day.]

Public Utility Regulation (in Victoria):

"I am proposing a public utilities commission. That sounds far off and long away, and maybe unecessary. But let's look at the facts. Let's look at the fact that Texas is the only, the only state that doesn't regulate telephone rates. Let's look at the increases that have been asked—28.6% in Houston, 44% in Texarkana, and whatever the situations in the cities are, the rates are higher in the rural areas. The same goes for electricity and gas. The average income for utility companies is double in this state what it is anyplace else. And is there *any safer return that when you have a monopoly? I'll tell you where the balance in Austin, Texas, is. There are 117 utility lobbyists that are registered. I don't know how many others there are. And that brings me to a third point I want to make. I say let's relegate the lobbyists to petitioners. Under our system of government, everyone has the right to petition the government and I'm just saying let's put them back where they belong.*

As can be seen here, Sissy's words and phrases left a little bit to be desired, but her audiences rarely seemed to mind. A professional political public relations man would have winced at phrases such as "relegate the lobbyists to the role of petitioners," and words such as "nation-state."

Sissy's mind was sometimes too legalistic, and she occasionally assumed too much knowledge of the governmental process on the part of her listeners. And for all of her fulminating about public and private government, many of her supporters went away not quite understanding what she meant. Too often she did not tie her arguments up neatly; the ends were left floating around, even with friendly interviewers. If they didn't understand a word she used, they still loved her, and if a phrase she used left them slightly puzzled, they still cheered, for they knew she was getting after the boys who had been controlling things all these years.

The Runoff--Phase Two

The candidate who took the lead in delivering the runoff into phase two was Briscoe. It was really the first agressive move he had made all year, but he needed to do something to shore up his sagging campaign. The move came in a speech at a $50-a-plate dinner in Houston on May 24. It was undoubtedly a result of Sissy's momentum. Her open, candid candidacy was becoming more and more distinct when compared to his, and the debate issue in particular was yipping at his heels like a tiny chihuahua, too small to kick, but too shrill to ignore.

Oh, he had told a press conference that very afternoon that he had found no great demand for a debate, but only the day before he had been almost lectured to about the issue by the editors of one of the Dallas newspapers in an editorial conference. It was no secret they were planning to endorse him and they were concerned about his refusal to debate. Buy the time yourself, one of them urged him, and let her get on the air and make a fool of herself.

Actually, it is difficult to understand why Dolph did not do this. By now he was good enough at fielding questions that he could have made some sort of appearance without being humiliated. And by doing this, he could successfully defuse the big issue that Sissy kept throwing at him. He could easily have held his own in a question and answer session with newsmen asking the questions. If nothing else, he could have appeared on the KERA-TV program again. The Dallas station had invited them both to participate in another "joint appearance" on Wednesday, May 31. He had handled that before without many problems, and surely could have again.

"We're trying to work that into our schedule," he told newsmen, but he never did, and he went to Lubbock that night for another dinner.

Something had to be done, though, because "we are feeling Frances Farenthold breathing hot air down our back," said George Lowrance, a Briscoe adviser. And if a debate was out of the question, then the next best thing would be to begin hitting at Sissy as hard as possible.

So, that night in Houston, Dolph lashed out at Sissy for the first time. "My opponent favors a radical upheaval in nearly every aspect of the entire governmental and political spectrum. I am offering diligent and effective leadership which will bring us progressive and balanced change."

This was the key to his campaign from that point to election day. His opponent, whose name he still did not mention, was pictured as a radical, an extremist, a frantic rabble-rouser. Dolph was presented as the sensible, reliable candidate who would bring about orderly and responsible change.

Dolph went on television on election eve, Friday, June 2, with a thirty-minute statewide bradcast summing this up:

> *Announcer:*
> *Tomorrow, Texas voters will decide the direction state government will take for many years to come. You have already made it clear that you want a change from the old politics. You stated on May 6 that you want sensible, reliable leadership and sound, responsible organization in government. You have now narrowed our options to two. One option is for radical, revolutionary upheaval. The other is for orderly, sensible change . . . .*
>
> *To any Texan who has even been aware of the race for the governor's office, it is clear that the two candidates agree about very few issues, even though both have been called reform candidates. Briscoe's approach has been one of cautious, deliberate change in the way Texas government functions. His primary concern is for the manner in which state government relates to the people it is supposed to serve. Briscoe has appeared as the problem solver in this race. Clearly, he is the more practical of the two candidates . . . .*
>
> *In contrast to his opponent, Dolph Briscoe is a moderate, sensible man who prefers to speak directly to the issues. He generally ignores the attacks of his opponent, but occasionally will deliver a reasoned reply to the glaring errors often found in those frantic attacks.*
>
> *Briscoe's voice:*
> *One issue I would like to clear up concerns a statement made by the other candidate that I will not work for pollution abatement. I would*

like to call attention to the fact that I've been actively involved in conservation practices and the ranching business for over a period of many years and before ecology was of special concern to many people I was practicing proper land management and natural resources conservation . . . I've stated throughout this campaign that I will, as governor, do whatever is necessary to not only stop the deterioration of our natural environment, I'll work to see that active restoration gets underway. . . .

Announcer:

It is interesting comparing the records of the two candidates in this campaign in the field of ecology, that Dolph Briscoe's opponent would even raise the subject. One could guess, in view of the radical campaign of Dolph Briscoe's opponent, that desperation is the reason for so many exaggerations and unreasonable accusations . . . .

Briscoe:

Texas clearly faces a crisis of epidemic proportions in the abuse of drugs by men, women, and children of all ages . . . The other candidate seems to think of this tremendous problem only in terms of a simple solution, discussing it only in terms of making the laws more permissive . . . My opponent's only suggestion has been to simply reduce the penalty. It has been implied that she favors legalizing the sale of marijuana . . . .

Announcer:

Education is costly. It's a complex procedure, but it is so vital to the future of our children and our state that we must increase our resolve to improve it every day. Yet it's a subject that has been clouded and hampered by the furor over busing . . . .

Briscoe:

My opponent has said that she approves of forced busing. I think that this position indicates very clearly that my opponent is out of touch with the real problem. It is easy to say that busing is a useful tool: so would be helicoptering children across town or carrying them by any means of conveyance . . . .

I'm 100% committed for the goal of making education, and I mean a real practical education, not only the birthright of every Texan, but I want to make it work . . . .

Announcer:

. . . There comes a time and that time is here and now when state government must learn to live within its income and learn to be effective without the constant addition of new taxes. Here again the two candidates differ drastically.

Briscoe:

. . . it is misleading, I think, for a candidate to stand up and say 'Don't worry about new taxes affecting you because we're just going to tax business.' I submit to you that when you tax a business that

bakes bread, you're taxing bread itself. When you tax the business in the fields of medicine, you're taxing medicine itself. The cost of bread and medicine and every other consumer item in service is going to increase and the people of Texas are going to feel it and they're going to pay for it.

Announcer:

... it has become more and more difficult to guarantee safety for our people and freedom from crime in the streets and even in our homes. It is an age in which we must, for our own safety and security, provide increased protection and better law enforcement.

Briscoe:

My opponent has advocated the abolishing of the Texas Rangers, and I don't think this time in which we live is a time in which we should think of reducing any of our law enforcement agencies. I think this is a time that we need to upgrade and improve law enforcement here in our state....

Briscoe again, summing up:

I'd like to remind you that I'm opposed to forced busing, legalization of marijuana, abolition of the Texas Rangers, and fiscal irresponsibility in government because my opponent and I disagree entirely on these issues.

Dolph's approach in this phase two of the runoff campaign, as summarized in the above broadcast, was devastatingly effective. That it was also a blatant misrepresentation of Sissy's positions was either overlooked or ignored by the voters. For the first time in the entire campaign, she became not the prime mover, not the initiator, but the defender. And the four issues that Briscoe chose to concentrate on in the last days were the four most inflammatory issues of the race, the four that were the hardest to rationally explain.

Dolph's statement that Sissy implied she favored legalizing marijuana was simply not true, but explanations of her position proved to be difficult to communicate. His characterization of her position on crime and the Texas Rangers was a bold misrepresentation of the position of one who had long worked for the upgrading of the police profession.

His statement on busing hit at probably the most inflammatory issue of the primary, and the one about which statewide candidates could do the least. Briscoe and some of his supporters misrepresented her position on it, also. A full page ad, sponsored by San Antonio Briscoe backers, on the day before the election proclaimed that Sissy favored "complete busing," an out and out lie. Any attempt to talk about busing in a rational manner was doomed to defeat, however, and Sissy's explanations were futile. The last issue on which he hammered, fiscal irresponsibility, brought forth some Briscoe rhetoric about taxing bread and medicine that completely obscured the real fiscal issue Sissy was concerned with, the issue of public versus private government.

In spite of its fairness or unfairness, though, Dolph's approach threw Sissy's campaign off balance, and she clearly had a hard time trying to get it righted.

The last week of the runoff brought more of the same for the two exhausted candidates. Briscoe spent the first four days of the week in the urban areas of Dallas, Austin and Lubbock, and then took to the "boonies" again on Friday, traveling through a number of East Texas piney-woods towns.

On Monday, he picked up the support of the controversial State Democratic Executive Committee Chairman, Roy Orr of De Soto. Orr's endorsement was a ringing criticism of Sissy, and helped emphasize the radical tag Briscoe was trying to pin on Sissy's campaign. "I don't know of a thing Mrs. Farenthold would do for this state other than be good for the long-haired radicals," Orr said. It was unusual for a state party chairman to take sides in a primary battle, Orr admitted, but he hopped in anyway.

Briscoe himself kept hammering away with variations on the radical theme. Late in the week he began pinning a "machine" label along the "radical" label on Sissy. She wishes to replace one machine with another machine with herself and the Washington liberals at the controls, he charged. "Those who have participated in the division of the spoils," he claimed, should not be given a chance to govern. The law books purchased through her contingent expense account, the children on the state payroll, and the Washington, D.C., publicity man (Guggenheim) were given as the factual basis for these charges.

A curiously-timed federal investigation into Briscoe's alleged hiring of illegal aliens ("wetbacks") came into the news in the latter part of the week. Originating in Illinois U.S. Senator Adlai Stevenson III's office, the charges were quickly dismissed by Dolph as something trumped up by Sissy's "Washington, D.C., public relations firm."

The last week of the campaign for Sissy began in El Paso. She also concentrated on the urban areas, spending time in Lubbock, Houston, Dallas, and San Antonio before winding up the campaign in Houston again. Sissy's entourage had now become a cavalcade of stars, but the biggest star of them all was Sissy. The crowds surged forward now after her speeches, thrusting posters, campaign literature and everything else at her for her autograph. She rarely refused to do this, staying as long as it took to make the people happy, though her schedule-concerned staff often became frantic. At one time or another during the week, she was joined in her travels by Liz Carpenter, former press secretary to Mrs. Lyndon B. Johnson and now author of *Ruffles and Flourishes*; movie actress Shirley MacLaine; Marlo Thomas, star of television's *That Girl* (That Girl endorses That Lady . . .); U.S. Senator Fred Harris of Oklahoma; and blues singer Lightnin' Hopkins.

The largest crowds any candidate had drawn attended rallies for her in Houston's Astrohall Tuesday night, and in Dallas on Wednesday night. In Dallas she also accepted KERA-TV's invitation to a "joint appearance" with Dolph, and sat next to an empty chair that had been reserved for him. He was in Lubbock that night speaking to another of those $25 dinners, and he had stopped by KERA earlier in the week to "tape" answers for the Wednesday night program. The previous Saturday in Fort Worth, the two candidates had come together face-to-face after addressing the Texas State Network Convention. Sissy took advantage of the situation to politely step forth, shake hands with Dolph, and ask for a debate to clarify some of the issues. Dolph just as politely refused to debate, telling her that he had already taken clear stands on the issues. So, Sissy faced the empty chair in Dallas on Wednesday. (That night, 17-year-old Emilie Farenthold flew to Lubbock, and while Dolph spoke at his $25 rally, attended a 25-cent beans and cornbread dinner with the Farenthold supporters.)

On to San Antonio and Houston Sissy went on Thursday and Friday, winding up her campaign. Mr. Briscoe was a secret candidate, she charged, who "thumbs his nose at the people while holding hands with the lobbyists."

"He lives on a vast empire. He doesn't know our problems, our needs, our dreams. He is one of the richest landowners in Texas. He has never felt the burden of high telephone and utility bills . . . He is a relic from the past, a product from a shameful era of Texas politics. He doesn't know what it means to give the citizens a real voice in their government. He is a friend of the big lobbyist in Austin. He doesn't know the meaning of public government," concluded Sissy.

Referring to Dolph's campaign, she said, "Texans have lived too long with packaged candidates who hide behind their public relations men . . . [but] I have news for you, Mr. Briscoe. The governor's office is not for sale this year."

This was about the strongest attack made by Sissy in the campaign, but it didn't strike home the way Dolph's attacks were hitting. Her charges are harder to assess, also. That Dolph was the favorite candidate of the lobbyists is undeniably true. He was not in the first primary, but they flocked to him in the runoff. Whether this was because his philosophy matched theirs or was simply an anyone-but-Sissy movement is more difficult to tell.

Many of Dolph's long-time personal friends resented these pokes at his integrity, but the type of media-oriented campaign he was running left Sissy little choice but to do this. It was a novel development, for no one had ever been held responsible before in Texas politics for keeping his mouth shut. Dolph was doing the same thing that countless Texas politicians had done to get elected, and he never did quite comprehend why he was being criticized so.

From a money standpoint, the runoff was more even, though Dolph still outspent Sissy by over $100,000. His report showed expenses of $364,000 and contributions of $468,000 and the $100,000 excess was presumably applied to his huge deficit from the first battle. Sissy went into debt in the runoff, spending $254,000 and receiving $166,000. The difference was financed through a $100,000 loan from J.M. Parten and Robert Lanier of Houston, and Bernard Rapoport of Waco, well-known names in liberal Democratic circles in Texas.

Saturday, June 3, brought the Sharpstown jury a second chance to visit the polls, and almost 1,990,000 of them did, slightly less than the nearly 2,160,000 who had gone the first time. Those statistics that had sobered up the Farenthold voters after the first primary held the key to the whole election, and it was clear from the very first returns to trickle in that Dolph Briscoe had won. It was also clear that Sissy had come up remarkably from her 28% finish in the first primary, and they wound up splitting the runoff by a 55%-45% margin.

Sissy's main area of strength again proved to be the Gulf Coast, where most of the 17 counties she carried were located. She captured 58% of the vote in that area, but was able to carry only one other geographical region, Southwest Texas, where El Paso's votes gave her a slim margin.

The other seven regions were Briscoe country, however, as Dolph wound up carrying 237 counties. His best returns came again from rural counties where he usually got 60% of the vote. He held his own again in the cities, losing Houston by a whopping 80,000 votes but getting small wins in Dallas, Fort Worth, and San Antonio. The figures for the twelve most populous Texas counties showed Dolph with 48% of the vote.

Sissy ran surprisingly well in Dallas County, losing by roughly 10,000 votes (90,000-80,000). That she came so close is a credit to her campaign manager Zan Holmes, a fellow Dirty Thirtian. Without the complications brought on by the Texas Ranger statement and the marijuana stand, Holmes said later, she probably would have won in Dallas.

Sissy carried most of the Black vote across the state, getting about 90% of the vote in Houston's Black precincts, and 80% in Dallas. She also made a good showing in most Mexican-American areas statewide, rolling up 75-80% majorities in many precincts.

Students and young people also voted for her strongly, but, as expected, their turnout was hampered because so many were away from the county where they were registered. That Precinct Two in Nacogdoches County for example, where she had won by 1029 to 851 for Dolph in the first primary, she lost this time 781-673.

She lost 356 votes in that precinct alone. Some of them voted absentee, no doubt, because the absentee total for Nacogdoches County increased by 400 in the runoff, but many more than 400 students had left town. In Austin's Precinct 435, where she won 1699 out of a total 2071 votes on May 6, the June 3 totals were 889-141 in her favor, a decrease of 810 votes for her. In fact she lost Travis County to Dolph in the runoff by

44,408 to 41,915. And, although 4200 more absentee votes were cast in the runoff than had been cast in the first primary, there were 28,500 students registered in Travis County, so a good many of them did not take the trouble of voting in the runoff.

By 9 p.m. that Saturday night, United Press International had declared Dolph the winner, and a couple of hours later, he flew into Austin from Uvalde to issue a victory statement. "I am going to do everything within my power as a human being and utilize every resource of the governor's office to see that ours is a government which is responsive to the people," he told a late-night press conference.

Over at the Farenthold headquarters, the atmosphere was considerably gloomier than it had been on May 6. As it became evident what had happened, Sissy declared she would not give up her fight for a public government. Telegrams deluged her that night urging either a write-in race or a 1974 race. She rejected immediately the write-in suggestions, and left her options open for 1974. "Believe me, there are interims before 1974, and let's not forget that. Call it tenacity or stubborness, we will prevail because you and I and thousands of others in this state have had enough."

After Dolph's victory, the press began treating him as the governor-elect, even though he still had a general election gauntlet to run in November. They could hardly be blamed, for he seemed unbeatable at this point, and the Republican nominee was not being taken too seriously by anyone, even the Republicans. (Later events would change things considerably, however.) And so these reporters, who, along with Ben and Sissy, had been trying to get a line on Dolph for months, began speculating on the rule of Governor Briscoe.

Their speculations are worth noting here, then, as the first thoughts of some veteran political observers on the man who was the beneficiary of the fallout from Sharpstown.

Jon Ford, of the Harte-Hanks newspaper chain wrote:

> At a time when 'restoring confidence in state government' is Chapter One in the politician's things-to-do book, Briscoe appears to have adequate credentials for presiding over a reform movement. He is too rich to be tempted by questionable deals, and has long enjoyed a reputation for conscientious honesty in his business and personal life. He received second choice backing of the major business lobby (after Lieutenant-Governor Ben Barnes and Governor Preston Smith fell in the first primary), but he denies any strings or commitments . . . .

> Briscoe also is a man of genuine warmth, kindness and good-will-to-most. The fact apparently was projected more clearly to rank-and-file voters than to those who watched his campaign clinically and found it unrevealing, sometimes contrived and often frustrating in a curious mix of over-eager amateurishness and over-slick professionalism.

A comfortable man is heading for the governor's office in uncomfortable times. On balance, he has about a 50-50 chance of coming out looking better than when he went in.

The *Houston Chronicle*'s Austin bureau chief Bo Byers asked himself "What Kind of Governor Would Dolph Briscoe Make?" The answers would not be simple, Byers said. "They call him a conservative, and he sounds like one—most of the time. Perhaps he is, but many labor leaders like him, and oldtime liberals and conservatives remember him as a progressive, often pro-labor, pro-liberal state representative . . . ."

Byers also mentioned as pluses his financial independence, along with his careful, cautious attitude, his ability to bring in outside talent, his many personal friends, and his outgoing, enthusiastic wife. He also noted that Briscoe was a warm, kind man, and warned him, prophetically, of the tough decisions just ahead in party politics.

Henry Holcomb, a young Austin reporter for the *Houston Post*, penned one of the finest essays of the entire election year on June 11 when he reminded Dolph of the difference between Uvalde and Houston. Plaintive, yet hopeful, it represented the feelings of many urban area dwellers about the rich, cowboy-boot wearing rancher. Recalling Dolph's insistence during the race that the problems of Houston and Uvalde were different only is size, Holcomb wrote:

Well, Mr. Briscoe, those of us who have lived in both the big and the small cities disagree, some of us respectfully, others angrily.

And if you're going to succeed as governor, you'd better hear us out, because the cities we live in won't go away because a lot of rural people think we're crazy to live in them. They won't go away, but they will become disaster areas, maybe even the downfall of our system, if things don't change fast.

We, in the big cities, noodle along our expressways at 10 or 20 miles an hour, bumper-to-bumper, each morning, our vision obscured by a cloud of fumes from the cars with us and the industries that directly or indirectly employ us, then search for a place where we can pay maybe an hour's wages to park, knowing our fenders may get banged or worse.

Then we walk to our jobs, hoping our pockets won't get picked and that some economy wave isn't closing in on our job. Also hoping some thief won't back up to our house or apartment with a truck and move our things out, and that our schoolchildren will learn something today besides racial prejudice and fighting.

Hoping. Hoping.

You have confidence in your county commissioners. You said so. We don't have confidence in ours. Even the ones we elected to clean things up, build roads to nowhere, buy expensive trash cans that grind up what they throw away and make shady deals with used voting machine salesmen.

You've known your city councilmen all their lives. We haven't. We've read about them in the paper and seen them on television and it seems they just want to peddle real estate on the side and push our city to grow like there was no tomorrow.

You think the Legislature was responsive back when you served in it during the 1950s. You said so more than once. Well, maybe it attacked your screwworms and put concrete over your muddy roads—which is good—but we in the city cannot find much evidence that it has been responsive—ever—to our problems. Come look for yourself.

When we go home at night we find the landlord who is so nervous about collecting our rent on time ($248 and rising, by the way) is still pretty relaxed about the crack that has developed in our wall. We begin to get some slight notion of what the Blacks have been putting up with for years.

We get pretty nervous about the Blacks, by the way. Too many of them live in rotten neighborhoods and find the same high prices in their neighborhood stores that we pay, but lower quality goods.

They have the highest unemployment and the worst schools.

You ought to hear a big-city Black church congregation sing "Beautiful Hope." They sing it like it was all they have . . . .

The sturdy house with a dozen trees in the private yard, central air, three bedrooms, two baths—real nice—a working man could buy for $115 a month (tax, insurance included) six years ago in the small city, doesn't exist today in the Big City.

It's elbow to elbow in a big apartment complex.

Please don't get me wrong, Mr. Briscoe. There's a lot we love in our city, a lot we think our city has over Uvalde. We're proud of our city, as you are proud of Uvalde.

We're just worried. You obviously understand rural transportation programs; the Colson-Briscoe Farm-to-Market Road Act suggests that.

But if you think our transportation problems are like Uvalde's, only bigger, you are mistaken. We don't have screwworms but we do have other problems that sap our vitality.

We hope you will face up to this pretty soon. We need help.

Chapter 5

THE GREAT LEGISLATIVE HOUSECLEANING

The Sixty-second Texas Legislature produced one of the largest membership turnovers in Texas legislative history. Of the 150 members of the House of Representatives on March 15, 1971, when the vote on Sissy Farenthold's resolution created the Dirty Thirty, only 73 would show up to take the oath of office when the Sixty-third Legislature began. Over in the Senate, where things did not get as tumultuous, there was a large-scale change also; of the 31 senators who sat across the rotunda and watched while the Dirty Thirty battled the Mutscherites, only 16 would be returning to Austin again as a senator.

The purpose of this chapter is to measure the effect that the Sharpstown Scandal had upon the re-election hopes of the representatives and senators involved in the turmoil of that Sixty-second Legislature. It is, frankly, a task that cannot be done with much certainty, for legislative races are complex mixes of state and local issues, personal and regional jealousies, business and social relationships, and occasionally, just plain irrelevant and intangible considerations. It is, however, a necessary task if one is studying political change in Texas in 1972.

We shall also take a quick look at one other agent of change in 1972, the single-member legislative district. Long sought by liberals and Republicans, they were created for Houston by the Legislature, and for Dallas and San Antonio by federal court orders. In practical terms, it meant that the 53 representatives (over one-third of the total) from these cities would not be running city-wide or state-oriented contests any more. From now on they would be involved in personal, hand-shaking type contests in small neighborhood areas. It also meant that only 14 of these 53 representatives would return to Austin to take the oath of office for the Sixty-third Legislature.

Sharpstown and the House

More than anything else, the Sharpstown Scandal created an atmosphere around the spring election days that damaged the hopes of the incumbents who ran for re-election. The atmosphere was as apparent as an early morning fog, and several veteran legislators chose to retire gracefully or to run for other positions because they felt that fog had too seriously dampened their re-election chances.

Fifteen of the 150 House members did not run for anything. Some of these were paired with other representatives, some were victims of the new single-member districts in the cities, and some were much too old to face a difficult race in this year when incumbents already had one strike against them.

Thirty-five of the representatives set out to win higher offices. Many of these races were serious, well-planned attempts to move up the political ladder, but some were undoubtedly seeking other fields because either the Sharpstown fallout or the new single-member districts had made a re-election try too difficult.

The Role of the Dirty Thirty

The 100 members of the House who offered themselves for re-election found an unexpected and unusual development in the political cards: an organization of their fellow House members that publicly graded all representatives' reform voting records, and endorsed their opponents if they appeared to be more reform minded.

The Dirty Thirty had gone establishment, complete with steering committees, strategy sessions, and even a letterhead. The rag-tag group of liberal Democrats and conservative Republicans began looking for a way to keep the specter of corruption prominent in the minds of the voters. Periodic planning meetings produced the idea of selecting a number of key reform votes during the session, and compiling a list of "reform votes" and "non-reform votes" for each legislator. This was duly done, with 19 key votes being selected for the ratings, and after the session a complete list of the voting record of each representative on these key votes was released. (This information is in Appendix B.)

It is difficult to determine which of the Thirty provided most of the leadership for the group, but the names Lane Denton, Sissy Farenthold, Dick Reed, Charles Patterson, and Tom Moore appeared often in press releases.

The group kept meeting, and later in the political year (during Mutscher's trial, to be exact) they announced that they would take a good look at each of the about 600 announced candidates in the House races and endorse the ones they thought would be the most reform-minded candidates. There was some infighting in the group before this decision was made. One faction wanted to publicly endorse candidates in all legislative races, and one wanted to endorse only those candidates who sought the endorsement. The latter alternative was finally chosen, and questionnaires were sent out to all candidates.

Replies were received from about one-half the candidates, and, after sorting through the answers, Lane Denton announced on April 26 that the group was endorsing 51 Democrats and 26 Republicans. Later, after the fierce primary dust had settled, the group met again and endorsed 38 Democrats and eight Republicans in runoff contests.

Any attempt to measure the success of the Dirty Thirty's endorsements quickly runs into difficulties. Some endorsees welcomed the pat on the back and used it extensively in their campaigns; some seemed almost embarrassed by it and did not use it at all. In some areas, public knowledge of the group was almost non-existent. The group had no money to give to its endorsees, and in the crucible of the next legislative session, an endorsement of questionable value from a group mostly forgotten might easily be ignored.

At any rate, a study of the 150 winners of the legislative races showed that 56 members of the Sixty-third Legislature should have a favorable image of the Dirty Thirty's survivors. This number includes 51 winners who were publicly endorsed by the group, and five winners who returned their questionnaire with favorable answers but did not ask for their endorsement.

Since 29 winners of legislative races defeated an opponent who was endorsed by the Dirty Thirty, there will also be a group of representatives present whose image of the group is less than favorable.

There was, of course, during the entire session and the following campaign, much discussion of the pros and cons of the Dirty Thirty. Their goals, their tactics, their honor and even their ancestry were subject to much questioning. At first, they were pretty much a group of white-hat wearers. Campaign counterattacks and countercharges by non-Dirty Thirty representatives smudged many of the hats considerably, though, by the time the first primary rolled around.

Dirty Thirty members are "as dangerous as a rattlesnake," declared Representative Neal Solomon one afternoon in a Capitol interview. They are a bunch of ultraliberal McGovernites, he said, who are in favor of laws that hurt people who desire a better way of life. The liberals would like to tax and take from those who are attaining and who are desirous of a better way of life, and give to those who are not helping themselves. And that's just not right. You can give some people a million dollars and they won't have a penny tomorrow.

His sentiments were echoed by Representative Steve Burgess, an establishment-oriented conservative from Nacogdoches. "They're a group of militant liberals, and not a one of them is for good government." Most of the House, the other 120, was not with them at all, he added.

"Demagogues, that's all they are, a bunch of radical demagogues," complained Wichita Falls Representative Vernon Stewart, a veteran member who lost a re-election bid to a Dirty Thirtian. "To beat them, you've got to get down and demagogue on their own level. The people are going to wake up in two years."

These charges are open to interpretation, of course, much as many of the Dirty Thirty's were. Solomon's view of "laws that hurt people," Burgess's view of "good government," and Stewart's definition of "radical demagogues" would have to be ascertained before the statements could be meaningfully measured. The charges were quite common, though, in re-election bids in the spring of 1972, as non-Dirty Thirty representatives attempted to discredit and darken the white-hat image that the Thirty had gotten during their fight.

One of the more eloquent Dirty Thirty spokesmen was Dallas Representative Dick Reed. Without the Sharpstown Scandal, Reed said during an interview, the Dirty Thirty would have been just that—an obnoxious group of petty troublemakers. "Most of us who made up the Dirty Thirty were, shall we say, anti-Mutscher in the 61st Session. We periodically challenged his power in a somewhat unorganized fashion and little note was taken of our challenges by the media or anyone else. By and large we were regarded as somewhat disorganized and somewhat ill-guided legislators. I think that would have been even more true for our efforts in the 62nd Session . . . I think that the efforts we put forth would have been passed off as the efforts of a disenchanted group of people who were merely bent on calling public attention to the fact that they were there." But, he said, "the fact that the Speaker of the House and his key people were involved in this scandal dignified our efforts in a way that we couldn't have dignified them ourselves."

Reed felt that a "near clear majority" of the next legislature would be composed of people who held the Dirty Thirty reform views. He was also concerned that the group might have failed to communicate the key issues to the public. "I think that our great failure, if we had a failure, was in communicating with the public the need for overall reform. I'm aware that the public does see the need for reform but I fear that they felt the real changes needed were the changes in personnel, and I fear that, inasmuch as these changes in personnel have now taken place, the public may feel that the problem has been attended to."

He hoped that the public did not take the position that the fight was between 30 good guys and a somewhat corrupt leadership. This ignores the really key issue, that being the powers of the presiding officers. Regardless of who presides over the House or the Senate, the powers that they have can lend themselves to the kind of dealing that produced the Sharpstown mess. Unless the powers of the presiding officers are changed, he thought, we will be confronted with similar situations in the future.

Reed's arguments are open to the same interpretations that were applied to those of Solomon, Burgess, and Stewart. His idea of reform is certainly much different from those of many of the legislators who usually voted with the establishment team. For many of them, reform was a word to be tied to the level of taxation. Representative Ray Lemmon, a Houston conservative who lost a Senate battle to Dirty Thirtian Bob

Gammage, said in an interview that, during the campaign, a member of a Chamber of Commerce group he was addressing asked him about the issue of reform. "I told them that we were now 48th lowest among the states in our level of taxation, and that if they wanted to 'reform' Texas to the number one spot, then go after it." He referred to his opponent as a "so-called reform" candidate.

Running Against Mutscher

Former Speaker Gus Mutscher himself became an issue in many races, even where the Dirty Thirty did not. In districts where the Thirty was either unknown or had too liberal an image, many contenders tried to tie Mutscher around the neck of the incumbent. In many of the races it was quite effective.

Representative Fred Orr, a Dallas legislator who had voted with the Speaker, found himself being labeled a "Mutscher man wearing the Mutscher brand" by Ron Clower, who defeated him in a Senate race. A Fort Worth representative, Mike Moncrief, lost a Senate race to Republican Betty Andujar who asked voters in her ads, "Why fire the ventriloquist [Mutscher] and keep the dummy [Moncrief]?" In the Wichita Falls battle between team member Vernon Stewart and Dirty Thirtian Dave Allred, Allred called attention to Stewart's Mutscher connections by dramatizing his opponent's signing of a scroll praising Mutscher on the Speaker's Day celebration. Lindsey Rodriguez, a Rio Grande Valley Dirty Thirtian who was "paired" by redistricting with non-Dirty Thirty member A.C. Atwood, charged in his ads that Atwood had voted six times to protect Mutscher while he had voted six times "to investigate Gus Mutscher and the Atwood gang." Tommy Shannon of Fort Worth, one of Mutscher's co-defendants in Abilene, and Charles Jungmichel of La Grange, one of Mutscher's committee chairmen, both were tagged by hard-fighting opponents as Mutscher men, and both went down to defeat.

Questionnaires mailed out to all incumbents who ran for re-election produced replies that indicate most of them found the Mutscher issue being used against them to some extent. Thirteen of the eighteen non-Dirty Thirty representatives who replied said their opponent had tried to link them to Mutscher's "team." Most of the replies indicated that it hurt their campaign to some extent, also, although many of them won re-election in spite of the charges. Some were quite bitter about these charges. One incumbent who lost to an opponent who had made much of his loyalty to Mutscher said, "I am no criminal because I had confidence in the administration. I am certainly not ashamed of loyalty." This incumbent, who had 18 non-reform votes out of 19 according to the grading of the Dirty Thirty, also had some unkind remarks about this group. "This kind of filth [their grading] is not worthy of an answer. I have no respect for this type of crap. The Dirty Thirty wanted publicity,

not clean government or reform, and the press gave them full opportunity
. . . . What shape would our state government have been in if we had
followed the Siren Cry of the Dirty Thirty all the way?"

Battles in the Boondocks: A Look at Some
Individual Confrontations

The two House races which attracted the most statewide attention in
1972 were the re-election bids of former Speaker Gus Mutscher and his
successor Rayford Price. Mutscher had astonished most Texans when he
filed for re-election. He and Donna had been trying to pick up the pieces
of their life ever since their stroll on the front page of the state's
newspapers. He had resigned his speakership position shortly before a
special legislative session which took place after the Abilene trial. His
lawyers had begun the long appeals process, and if the Abilene verdict
was finally upheld, he, as a convicted felon, would be barred from holding
any office. But that would be in the future, and now he was trying to keep
his flickering political fires from being completely extinguished. So, back
home he went, to get ready for the hardest fight of his political life. The
39-year-old ex-Speaker had been born during the Depression to a farming
family in the tiny German-American community of William Penn in
Washington County. His family later moved to nearby Brenham, and Gus
graduated from high school there in 1950. After two years at Blinn
College in Brenham, where he was a popular student body president, he
went on to Austin to attend The University of Texas. He earned a
Bachelor of Business Administration degree in 1956, and began a
business career with bright promise in the Houston area. In 1960 he went
back to Brenham, defeated an incumbent representative, and began his
legislative career. He parlayed a chairmanship appointment of the House
Redistricting Committee (by Ben Barnes) into the Speaker's job in 1969,
and ruled almost unchallenged until the SEC suit was filed in January of
1971. Now it was not Speaker Mutscher anymore, and there was not any
concern, or good wishes, or contributions from the state's important
people anymore. It was just Gus and Donna now, running a poorboy
campaign, hoping to prove correct the billboards which informed
travelers around Brenham that "This Is Still Gus Mutscher Country."

Gus drew two opponents this time, the first serious opposition he had
had since that first race in 1960. Two lawyers, Hulon Hall and Latham
Boone III, both were trying to unseat him. Boone was the biggest threat
to Gus. A 32-year-old Grimes County native, he came from an old family
that had contributed one attorney-general to the state, and any number of
officials to Grimes County and Navasota. Boone's father, for example,
had been both sheriff and county judge in Grimes County. This was
young Latham's first race, but his family ties, his law degree, and his

Marine Corps service in Vietnam made him a strong contender. Describing himself as a "populist," he came out strong for honesty in government.

Gus ran on a "what I have done for my district" platform, emphasizing his seniority and experience. As Preston Smith did in the governor's race, Gus took credit for killing the sales tax on groceries in that 1969 special session. This exercise in sophistry caused much chuckling among Capitol hands who remembered the arm-twisting done by Mutscher's lieutenants in behalf of the bill.

Many people were surprised when Gus finished in first place on May 6, the night Preston, Ben, and Crawford got theirs. He got 40% of the vote to Boone's 38%, while Hall came up with a little over 20%. Campaigning steadily and quietly in the runoff, Boone was able to swing almost all of Hall's support his way, and on June 3 won by 11,119 to 8,614 for Mutscher. Gus's flickering flame was probably permanently snuffed out by that defeat.

Meanwhile, to the north and east of Brenham, up in the East Texas piney woods, Rayford Price and Fred Head were doing battle in one of the hottest races of the year. The 35-year-old Price, a Palestine lawyer, was from an old Anderson County family. He had gone to the House in 1960, the year that Mutscher arrived, and the two had become close friends. Rayford had even served as the best man in 1969 when Gus took Donna Axum, the former Miss America, as his bride. Price had helped Gus capture the speakership, but, when Price started campaigning for himself for speaker, the friendship was broken. Price campaigned openly in the Sixty-second Legislature as Gus's troubles mounted.

After the Abilene verdict, he threw himself whole-heartedly into the leadership race, and when the next special session convened, he won a narrow victory over DeWitt Hale of Corpus Christi and replaced his one-time friend as speaker. The time he spent concentrating on that race, however, caused him to neglect his own district, and when he returned to fight his re-election battle, he found himself in deep trouble.

Fred Head, 33, and also a lawyer, was a native of Troup, in Smith County. He was elected to the Legislature in 1966, and was living at Henderson, in Rusk County a few miles east of Troup. Since Head and Representative Ben Grant of Marshall were both members of the Dirty Thirty and thus thorns in Speaker Mutscher's side in the Sixty-second Legislature, they found themselves redistricted into one district by the vengeful Mutscherites. Head decided that, instead of running against Grant, he would move the few miles back to Troup and challenge Price. So he did this late in 1972, and he and his wife, both tremendous campaigners, began working Price's district in November, while Rayford's actions were directed toward the speaker's race. Rayford was, of course, successful there, but when the newly-crowned speaker came back home to Palestine, he was five months behind in his race with only four weeks until election day. And his new title, he found, didn't impress the voters the way he had thought it would.

There was a third candidate in this race, too: Bill Green, a young Palestinian who was a student at the University of Houston law school. On May 6, he finished in third place, but he drew enough votes to force a runoff. The big surprise, however, was Head's 45% first-place finish. Speaker Price found that the cost of ignoring his district for so long was high. His 32% showing put him in the runoff, but he clearly had a long, uphill pull if he was to survive.

Head had been making hay with his Dirty Thirty credentials, and Price's desperation now caused him to mount probably the strongest, unfairest, and most vicious attack on that group that the state would observe in 1972. Working with Danny Parrish, a young political consultant from Fort Worth, Price devised a telephone and handbill operation attacking Head and the Dirty Thirty. As recorded by the *Houston Chronicle*'s Bo Byers in an excellent May 28 article, the handbill asks "What Does the Dirty Thirty Really Stand For?" "Here's some examples of the type of legislation members of the Dirty Thirty have supported," the handbill answers:

Legalization of marijuana
Abolish the Texas Rangers
Registration of all firearms
Repeal of the right-to-work law
Liquor by the drink
Abolish the farm-to-market road program
Authorize drivers' licenses for convicted drunk drivers
Legalize abortion.

The handbill closes "Fred Head says he's proud to be a part of the Dirty Thirty. Is this the kind of representation you want in Austin?" The telephoning was quite similar. Operators told the listeners: "I'm a volunteer for Rayford Price. I want to tell you why I'm supporting Rayford Price. His opponent, Fred Head, is a member of the Dirty Thirty. The Dirty Thirty is for liquor by the drink, legalized marijuana, and legalized abortion. We don't think that's the kind of men we need representing us in this district." If the listener responded properly, he would be sent a copy of the handbill.

A few hours after word of this new move reached the Heads, Mrs. Head confronted Rayford on the Courthouse square in Athens. Their brief exchange was recorded by Byers: "Rayford," said Mrs. Head, "are you ready for a slander suit? You've got people telephoning that Fred is for legalization of abortion and marijuana. You know that's not true."

"It's true," Price said.

"It's not and you know it," Mrs. Head replied, and Rayford turned and walked away.

The attack was similar, of course, to the one Dolph Briscoe was currently using on Sissy Farenthold in the governor's race, and Head, like Sissy, found himself on the defensive. His months of campaigning paid off, though, with a narrow 309-vote win on June 3. The vote totals were 10,935 to 10,626.

In addition to the above two races, there were others that attracted attention. The collective luck of the Dirty Thirty members, for example, drew some interest. As it turned out, when they ran for re-election, they were almost invincible, winning 17 of 18 races. When they ran for other offices, however, they took their lumps, and only 4 of the 12 who tried were successful.

The first hitch in collecting these statistics is deciding just who is in the Dirty Thirty. For purposes of these measurements, the top 34 names on the group's "reform voting analysis" were chosen. This includes all legislators who had more "reform" votes than "non-reform" votes. This obviously takes in the "hard-core" members as well as some considered to be on the "fringe" of the Dirty Thirty.

Of these 34 representatives, three bowed gracefully out of politics, one because Mutscher's redistricting ax had chopped off the favorable counties of his district, one because he wanted to devote more time to his job, and one because of personal and family reasons. That left 31, and 18 of these filed for re-election while 13 announced for other offices. As mentioned in the preceding paragraph, 17 of the 18 running for re-election were successful, a good track record in anyone's league. It is enhanced by the fact that the only one who lost, Charles Patterson of Taylor, went down to defeat at the hands of Dan Kubiak of Rockdale, a fellow Dirty Thirtian, in another race brought on by Mutscher's vindictive redistricting bill.

Seven of the 13 who ran for other offices tried for the state Senate (three of these, Houston Republicans, against each other in a bloodletting that saw Walter "Mad Dog" Mengden emerge victorious). The only other victor, aside from Mengden, was Bob Gammage, a Houston Democrat who won a bitter race against Ray Lemmon, a non-Dirty Thirty representative. The losers here included Edmund Jones and Will Lee in Mengden's victory; Rex Braun, who lost to incumbent Chet Brooks in another Houston battle; Tom Moore, Jr. of Waco, who was barely defeated by Grant Jones, an Abilene representative in a curiously drawn district that meandered from Central Texas out through the West Texas "Big Country"; and Paul Moreno, who was taken by Tati Santiesteban in an El Paso clash. Two members tried for county commissioner posts, Tom Bass successfully and Dick Reed unsuccessfully. Bass defeated an incumbent in a Harris County race, and Reed lost a Dallas County race to Roy Orr, the Dallas establishment-backed incumbent. Dirty Thirtians also made unsuccessful attempts at Congress (Curtis Graves, losing in Houston to State Senator Barbara Jordan), at state treasurer (Maurice

Angly, losing a close November race to incumbent Jesse James), and at governor (Sissy Farenthold, losing the runoff to Dolph Briscoe). A successful fight for Angelina County district attorney was made by John Hannah of Lufkin.

Members of the Dirty Thirty had pretty good luck with their endorsements. Of the 150 winners after all three election nights were history, 51 were candidates who had been openly endorsed by the Dirty Thirty, and five more had returned their questionnaires with favorable answers but had not requested an endorsement. On the other side of the ledger, 29 winners had defeated Dirty Thirty-endorsed candidates, and would probably have an unfavorable image of the group's successors in the Sixth-third Legislature. Waco Representative Lane Denton, one of the group's sparkplugs, said he was pleased with the results of the endorsements. He hoped a "reform caucus" of 70 to 80 members could be organized in the Sixty-third Legislature. Generally, these endorsements proved to be of more value in urban areas, possibly because, Dick Reed said, the rural areas are "really not convinced that there's any need for reform. They do not see the role of government as we see it in our population centers."

There were six direct confrontations between Dirty Thirtians and "team" members. Three were for House seats (all brought about by Mutscher's redistricting bill) and three were for Senate positions. The three House clashes, all won by the Dirty Thirtians, included the Rayford Price – Fred Head struggle mentioned above and the Lindsey Rodriguez – A.C. Atwood bout in South Texas and the Wichita Falls fight between Dave Allred and Vernon Stewart. Both Rodriguez and Allred tried hard to tie their opponents to the Mutscherites. Rodriguez had lost twice to his opponent in previous races, but he was able to overcome him this time by an approximate 1,500-vote margin out of almost 25,000 votes. Allred's opponent, a ten-term veteran, tried to make Dave into a Mutscher man because they (Dave and Gus) had both voted for the same man in the speaker's race after Gus's resignation. This logic-defying act was also tried in a few other races around the state. Allred survived it, however, defeating Stewart by 6,490 to 5,205.

The three confrontations for Senate seats did not turn out as favorably for the Dirty Thirty, since they won only one of them. These battles, mentioned above, were the Houston race of Ray Lemmon and Bob Gammage, the El Paso fight between Paul Moreno and Tati Santiesteban, and the Central-West Texas struggle between Tom Moore and Grant Jones. The only successful candidate from a Dirty Thirty standpoint was Gammage. Lemmon tried to turn the race into a liberal-conservative contest, calling himself a constructive conservative and Gammage an ultraliberal. Lemmon heavily outspent Gammage, but his association with Mutscher and Gammage's hard work ("He's one ferocious campaigner," Lemmon admitted later) helped send Bob over the top on election day. Gammage was a rarity in Texas politics in 1972, a candidate who didn't turn tail and run when the busing issue was mentioned. He once called the Houston anti-busing group, Citizens for Neighborhood Schools, a "group of discredited racists more concerned about integration than busing. If I've got enough bigots in my district to defeat me, then I don't want to win, because I couldn't represent them properly. They should elect my opponent if they want a bigot."

While almost all of the Dirty Thirty members who made re-election bids were successful, a good many of Mutscher's friends and supporters saw their careers wrecked (or at least derailed) after the votes were counted. About two dozen House members who had voted with the ex-Speaker were turned into lame ducks by the voters.

Among those who lost out was Tommy Shannon, the Fort Worth legislator who was found guilty along with Gus at Abilene. Several of Mutscher's committee chairmen were also defeated, including Neal Solomon of Mount Vernon, chairman of the Banks and Banking Committee; Charles Jungmichel of La Grange, chairman of the Education Committee; Delwin Jones of Lubbock, chairman of the Redistricting Committee and architect of that cruel and unusual punishment known as Mutscher's Redistricting Bill; Clyde Haynes of Vidor, chairman of the Labor Committee; Jake Johnson of San Antonio, chairman of the Military Affairs Committee; and Bill Swanson of Houston, chairman of the Oil, Gas, and Mining Committee.

Other Mutscher supporters turned out to pasture were Forrest Harding of San Angelo, Rufus Kilpatrick of Beaumont, Cordell Hull of Fort Worth, J.E. Ward of Glen Rose, Aubry Moore of Hillsboro, J.A. Garcia, Jr. of Raymondville, Steve Burgess of Nacogdoches, James Lovell of Grapeland, Harold Davis of Austin, Paul Silber and Guy Floyd of San Antonio, and Sam Coats and John Boyle of Dallas. (Discussed already have been the losses of Vernon Stewart and A.C. Atwood.)

Many of these losers blamed their poor showings on the state's press. Those reporters "created an atmosphere that cost many good people their jobs," complained Neal Solomon during an interview. "The press runs this state," he added. All the publicity about Sharpstown and the other scandals, the argument went, made it tough on all incumbents anywhere, no matter how clean their hands might have been. "The fallout from Sharpstown is what beat me, there's no doubt about it," agreed Steve Burgess. There's no doubt, either, but what that Sharpstown affair was a serious, if not mortal, wound for many of these, but there were always other things to be considered.

The three who probably suffered the most because of their Mutscher loyalty were Shannon, Solomon, and Jungmichel. The Abilene verdict itself pretty well destroyed Shannon. He went on campaigning as though nothing had happened and finished a poor third in a four-man race. Then he watched from the sidelines as the seat he had held for 16 years went to

24-year-old Tom Schieffer, a recent master's degree (in government) graduate of The University of Texas at Austin. Solomon had chaired the committee through which those infamous Sharpstown bills had traveled, and his opponent, former Representative George Preston of Paris, used a picture of the bill with Solomon's signature in his campaigning. (Solomon said later he thought those bills were good bills, that he'd vote for them again, and that what really defeated him was the union support Preston received.) Jungmichel, who was defeated by John Wilson, a young La Grange rancher, was a close friend of Gus Mutscher. This association, plus a vote for an unpopular trailer-brake law, proved to be too heavy a burden for Jungmichel to bear.

Others in the list of losers suffered, too, and, as it has been in this entire chapter, it is quite difficult to say exactly how much effect the Mutscher ties had. According to one veteran Capitol hand, Aubry Moore, Steve Burgess, and J.E. Ward all were just too old, had been around too long, and were easy targets for a fresh new face. Jake Johnson and Rufus Kilpatrick, according to the same source, just happened to be in races with better campaigners. In a Dallas race, Representative Sam Coats lost to Jim Mattox, a liberal with a Dirty Thirty endorsement. Mattox used the Mutscher issue extensively, but there was another strong issue in this race, the fact that Coats didn't live in the district, and those two issues combined were enough to send Coats to the showers.

Several Mutscher-men tried to advance to the Senate, and two of them found the other chamber an impossible place to get to. Fred Orr of Dallas and Mike Moncrief of Fort Worth both discovered one of the problems in their losses to be their ties to the Mutscher regime.

Other Mutschermen didn't find the way to the Senate so rocky. As Stewart Davis pointed out in *The Dallas Morning News* on December 31, 1972, "one of the puzzling events of 1972 politics is the way voters threw out scores of public officials, particularly state representatives, in the aftermath of the Sharpstown Scandal, while apparently unknowingly promoting eight of these (Mutscherites) to seats in the Senate." These eight were Don Adams of Jasper, Bill Braecklein of Dallas, Grant Jones of Abilene, Raul Longoria of Edinburg, H. Tati Santiesteban of El Paso, John Traeger of Seguin, Jack Ogg of Houston, and Nelson Wolff of San Antonio.

Perhaps Mutscher's closest ally to survive was Ben "Jumbo" Atwell, the colorful Dallas conservative who chaired the important Revenue and Taxation Committee. The new single-member districts made him get out and work this year instead of relying on the usual advertising blitz of the Dallas establishment slate of candidates. He had some opponents, but they were never able or willing to go after Atwell effectively and dramatize his ties with Mutscher, so Ben polished them off in the first primary.

In spite of these occasional successes, however, it was not a good year for the Mutscherites, and Jon Ford's prediction back in the Sixty-second Session must have haunted the dreams of some of them for awhile.

Single-Member Districts: The Big Boys
Lose A Round

Ever since time began, it seems, the Texas Legislature has been dominated by a curious amalgam commonly referred to as "the establishment." Occasionally adjectives such as rural, conservative, and business have been thrown in, and together the small-town conservative and the big-city business interests have kept a tight rein over the irregular bands of populists, labor liberals, Mexican Americans, Blacks, and assorted bleeding hearts that have opposed them.

When you dominate the political game, you can also make your own rules, and the establishment has used any number of specially-devised rules, both constitutional and statutory, to maintain its degree of control over the years. The control has been particularly notable and the rules especially effective in the House.

For years, there was not much the irregulars could do about this, being outnumbered in the Legislature. Federal courts were no help, either, because of a 1946 U.S. Supreme Court decision saying that judges had no business messing around in this political thicket. This rather unrealistic decision was overruled in 1962, however, by the historic *Baker v. Carr* decision of the Warren Court, and the federal court machetes began hacking away at the political thickets all over the country.

Texas was no exception, and the first federal court challenge of Texas's legislative apportionment was filed in 1963 by a group of Houston liberals. It is not too much an overstatement to say that, almost constantly since that day in 1963, the vagaries of Texas legislative districts have been of interest to many federal judges and justices, and to many more lawyers and public officials. Without getting into a case-by-case study, it can be said that almost every trick seen by federal judges everywhere has shown up in Texas. Legislative Redistricting Committees, normally needed about once every ten years, have become permanent fixtures of the Legislature since 1965. Constitutional amendments, flotorial districts, gerrymandering, silent gerrymandering, and malapportionment: all have been challenged and have caused biennial redistricting to be almost automatic.

As 1972 began, about the only tool the establishment had left (aside from plain ol' gerrymandering, which will be hard for the courts to stop) was the large multi-member district. The unfairness of these might not be apparent at first glance, but a careful consideration of them will point out several problems. Used as boundary lines for densely populated areas that have enough people to qualify for several representatives, they allow all of the voters in the area to vote on all of the representatives. This means that all of the representatives will usually be the same politically, socially, and ethnically as the dominant majority of the area. It also makes it very expensive to run for office, and thus allows groups of well-to-do businessmen, who can put up and finance slates of candidates, more of a voice in the legislative process than they perhaps deserve.

This tool was probably most effective in Dallas, which was one huge district with 18 representatives who all ran at-large races. As a result, each representative had a constituency of over 1,000,000 people, more than 16 times the number of people the average rural legislator represented. A race in the entire city of Dallas is prohibitive financially, and only the more affluent could normally run.

This situation was made to order for the Dallas downtown establishment, and for years they controlled almost all of the area representatives through a group known as the Democratic Committee for Responsible Government. The DCRG would select a slate of candidates, one for each of the positions, and then would throw in enough money for the slate to run a strong media campaign. The candidates themselves wouldn't have to campaign personally very much; they could just let the media do the job for them. It worked like a charm, and the entire Dallas delegation was usually beholden to (and usually representative of) the white, downtown, conservative Democratic businessmen.

Dallas's sizable Black and Mexican-American population, and its large chunk of Republicans were never happy about this. They felt that the crumbs thrown to them by the DCRG slate (one Republican and one Black in 1970) were not enough, and that if the entire city was split up into 18 geographical districts of equal population they would do much better. As it was, the DCRG slate usually edged past the liberals in May (with Republican help), and then squeaked by the Republicans in November (with liberal and blue-collar help).

Similar situations existed in many of the state's urban areas, and when they lost a vote on single-member districts (for the umpteenth time) in Mutscher's House, the Dallas minorities took it to a federal court. (The Mutscherites had created single-member districts in Houston, because that city's delegation wanted them, so the Houston bunch did not join the battle.) Their case became one of the decisions in that unconstitutional month of January, 1972. The judges agreed with them that that red barn really was a red barn, and ordered single-member districts immediately for Dallas and Bexar (San Antonio) counties. They also instructed the next Legislature to eliminate other inequities they found, suggesting that single-member districts for the entire state might be a way to do this.*

The decision created instant turmoil in Dallas and San Antonio, and many veteran legislators found themselves running for their lives in small districts against brash young newcomers who could shake hands better than they could. Since the multi-member district tool had been most effective in Dallas, that city also was the best example of the political change brought about by the decision. After the elections had come and gone, Dallas Republicans were holding seven seats instead of one, liberals (both Black and white) had increased their representation from two to five, and the downtown establishment's conservative Democrats had slipped all the way from fifteen down to six out of the eighteen-member delegation. The once-powerful DCRG found itself de-fanged and de-clawed, and could only make endorsements in the individual races. And, like the Dirty Thirty, it found that endorsements sometimes helped, but sometimes they didn't help, too.

The total turnover figure was quite high, with only four of the eighteen Dallas representatives from the Mutscher House being elected. Most Dallas political observers felt this large-scale change was due more to the new single-member districts than to the Sharpstown fallout (three of the four returning legislators had been pro-Mutscher).

San Antonio's legislative delegation was also shaken up by the decision. Only four of its eleven representatives to the Sixty-second Legislature returned to take the oath of office when the Sixty-third Legislature convened.

The most notable loss was that of Bill Finck. A conservative, balding cigarmaker, he had been named chairman of the Appropriations Committee by Speaker Rayford Price. This was the most powerful committee in the House, and it was a bit incongruous to see the second most powerful man in the House out working so hard to win re-election. He survived the first primary, but went down in the runoff to Matt Garcia, a liberal, Dirty Thirty-liked lawyer. As in Dallas, the San Antonio establishment's power was cut dramatically by the decision, and the new legislative delegation changed, as Sam Kinch, Jr. wrote in *The Dallas Morning News*, "from an almost monolithically Anglo-style conservative

*On June 13, 1973, the United States Supreme Court spoke in reply to the state's appeal of this case. They ordered the single-member districts kept in Dallas and Bexar counties, but overturned the rest of the lower court's decision. Since the Sixty-third Legislature had adjourned two weeks earlier without taking any redistricting action, this left the boundary lines just as they were for the 1972 elections. The Court said the Dallas and Bexar county single-member districts were being retained because the multi-member districts there had been used in the past to discriminate against racial and ethnic minorities. This finding opened the door for challenges on similar grounds of some of the other multi-member districts in the state, so the battle for single-member districts continues.

delegation to a mixture of the conservative, the moderate, the liberal, the radical, the Republican, the Black, and the Mexican American."

In Houston the political change was not as dramatic or as unexpected as it was in Dallas and San Antonio. The Harris County delegation to the Sixty-second Legislature had wanted the single-member districts, and Mutscher's Redistricting Committee had reluctantly created them. Harris County had already been split into three multi-member districts, with two of them electing six representatives and the other electing seven. Formal state-oriented contests had disappeared already, and many of the Harris County legislators were known as political mavericks.

The change in Harris County was as large, though, if not as unexpected, as it was in Dallas and Bexar counties. The 24 Harris County members of the Sixty-third Legislature included 18 brand new faces. There were seven Republicans, an increase of three, and four Blacks, an increase of three. Liberals dominated the delegation, but almost all shades of both ends of the political spectrum were represented.

The total turnover for these three cities is quite impressive. Together they have 53 seats in the 150-member House, and 39 of these seats in the Sixty-third Legislature were occupied by legislators there for the first time. Clearly, then, that January federal court decision has to be ranked as one of the major forces of political change in Texas in 1972.

"The human wave of candidates has stunned and overwhelmed voters," opined the *San Antonio Express-News*. This year "has emerged as the year of the lone wolf candidate. The new districts have Chicano running against Chicano, Black running against Black, and conservative running against conservative. As a result it has been impossible to forge the old-style combinations."

Change in the Senate

The Senate's facelifting job in this political year of 1972 was unusually extensive. The Sharpstown fallout probably played a negligible role in this change, except for the general "throw the rascals out" atmosphere it created. Indeed, most of the change came about because three incumbent senators retired, and eight ran for other positions. Thus eleven vacancies were created by choice. This left twenty senators running for re-election, but nine of these had no opposition. In the eleven contested races where incumbents were trying for another term, four senators suffered defeats.

Many of those who ran for re-election or for other offices found their races a bit tighter because of the anti-incumbent mood, but only three of the senators had any charges hurled at them because of their actions in the Sharpstown affair.

There were at least a couple of reasons why most senators had less trouble with the Sharpstown fallout than, say, members of the House. For one thing, the bitter, session-long feud between the Mutscherites and the Dirty Thirty never really crossed the rotunda. Most senators watched the thrusts and parries in the lower chamber with both amazement and amusement, but they also stayed above or out of the fight as much as humanly possible, both individually and collectively. The attention of the public and the press was focused not on the Senate, then, but on Preston Smith, Gus Mutscher and the Dirty Thirty.

Too, senators run for re-election in much larger districts than representatives (the average senatorial district has roughly five times as many people as a House district). This means the races are less likely to be shoe leather and hand-shaking contests, and are more likely to be media-oriented affairs with large amounts of money and public relations talent thrown around. In a race of this sort, it is hard for one issue to make the difference. The bigger stakes attract more money and interest, and local and regional matters become more important. Many of these races are turned into television-oriented affairs, with both sides' public relations experts striving to create a more favorable image.

Of the three senators who faced some Sharpstown flak, only one came away laughing. He was Charles Wilson, a tall, skinny, flashily-attired East Texas liberal-populist who had edged toward the political center when he began planning a Congressional race. Back in those far-off days when the Sharpstown bills had slipped through the Senate, Charlie Wilson was chairman of the Senate Banking Committee. In that capacity he had shepherded the bills through the Senate when a personality clash between the original sponsor and another senator threatened to kill the bills. Wilson now was running for John Dowdy's old East Texas Congress seat, and his major opponent, Dowdy's wife J.D., kept reminding the voters of Wilson's actions. Perhaps trying to counter her own very considerable image problems, Mrs. Dowdy made a television commercial doing a take-off on the popular "I can't believe I ate the whole thing" Alka-Seltzer ad. "I can't believe he sponsored the whole thing," moaned the husband; "He did it, Ralph, Charlie Wilson sponsored them," retorted the wife. About all the ad did was provide a bit of humor, though, for Wilson won easily, taking almost 65% of the vote in the first primary.

The other two senators were Ralph Hall of Rockwall and Wayne Connally of Floresville. They had jumped into the crowded free-for-all for the lieutenant-governor's gavel being given up by Ben Barnes. Hall had been the chairman and Connally a member of the Senate committee that had rushed the Sharpstown bills through. (Some parliamentary maneuvering kept the bills out of Wilson's committee.) Both Hall and Connally had signed the floor report sending the bill out for a vote on the Senate floor. Various ones of their opponents took pride in pointing this out during the race. Hall, who had finished in fourth place in the first primary, was so embittered by some of the other candidates' embellishments of his record that he considered a libel suit for a time, but he never filed it. Connally, who made it into the runoff, came under fire from his opponent, Bill Hobby, for having a "business relationship with John Osorio and National Bankers Life at the same time the Senate had the Sharpstown bills under consideration." Connally shot back that it was a simple hunting-lease deal on a West Texas ranch of his, but Hobby was playing his cards (and his cash) right, and on June 3 the name Connally was struck from the list of Texas office-holders.

The Sharpstown issue weighed quite heavily in many other races to fill vacancies in the Senate, several of which have been discussed already. Two that haven't been are worth at least a brief mention here, one a Deep East Texas bout to replace Charlie Wilson, and the other a fight in a strange-looking district that encircles Harris County.

The East Texas jousters were Representative Don Adams of Jasper and J.C. Stallings, a Nacogdoches radio station owner. Adams, an establishment conservative, had voted down the line with the Mutscher team, and Stallings worked on that alliance in his campaign. It was a close race, and Adams squeaked by with a 4,000-vote margin in a 100,000-vote contest.

In the Harris County race, Republican Walter "Mad Dog" Mengden was pitted against Democrat Lee McElmore. Mengden, a stalwart Dirty Thirtian, had won the nomination over two other Dirty Thirty Republicans, Will Lee and Edmund Jones, and was favored to take it all in the Republican-leaning district. McElmore was a 17-year veteran Houston city councilman; both he and Mengden were conservatives. McElmore's only chance in this race was to get a good showing in the eastern part of the district, a liberal, labor-union-oriented area. The Democratic politicos in this area were not too sympathetic to his pleas, however, thinking Mengden, an "ideological conservative" who had voted against the Mutscherites, to be preferable to an "establishment conservative" who would likely join the hated "team." As a result they did not help McElmore much, and even quietly gave some aid to Mengden, so "Mad Dog" sent Lee down to defeat in November.

In a footnote to this discussion of Sharpstown's effect on the Senate, let it be noted that while it was the conservative Democratic establishment team that was responsible for the mess, it was the liberals who suffered the most electoral damage. Two liberals ran successful races for Congress, and both were replaced by conservatives; the four incumbent senators who were defeated were all vanquished by conservative foes. So the Senate in the 63rd Legislature was firmly controlled by establishment conservatives, and was the "death chamber" for lobby-opposed bills.

Sharpstown and the Legislature: A Summary

It is especially difficult to summarize a chapter plagued by inexact measurements. Yet it can be said that, in the Year of Frank Sharp, it was clearly detrimental to a candidate to have strong ties with either Gus Mutscher or the Mutscher team. And it was clearly an advantage to be a member of the Dirty Thirty, or at least to have their endorsement, if you were running for the Legislature.

As always, there are no hard and fast rules here, for neither the losses of the two dozen Mutscherites, nor the near-perfect record of the Dirty Thirty members who ran for re-election, can furnish any guidelines for all of the legislative contests. There are enough exceptions to destroy any formula.

There are those who agree with the veteran lobbyist who was queried about the number of legislators who were defeated by the Sharpstown fallout.

"Hell," he snorted, "it didn't beat any of them all by itself, except for maybe Shannon and Solomon. All it did was create an atmosphere that made it hard on incumbents. It was one issue among many. But, sometimes, if you hit a drowning man on the head with an English pea it's enough to push him under."

There are also those who would agree with Neal Solomon's contention that the press runs the state. They were the ones who always corrected the author's questions about the effect of the Sharpstown Scandal by asking, "Don't you mean the effect of the *publicity* about the Sharpstown Scandal?"

And there are those who would agree with Dick Reed that Sharpstown was the rule rather than the exception as far as doing business in the Legislature was concerned, and that, even with the publicity, not enough real change occurred.

Whatever your position, you'll have to agree that Gus Mutscher took a lot of men down with him.

Chapter 6

THE OTHER PRIMARIES

There are at least two other primary elections worthy of a close look in any examination of political change in 1972 in Texas. Neither was as important, nor had the long-range implications of the Farenthold-Briscoe battle, but both the lieutenant-governor's race and the attorney-general's race provided fresh new faces that are likely to stick around in Texas politics for quite some time. The other state-wide races, for land commissioner, agriculture commissioner, treasurer, and comptroller of public accounts, provided no change, and were significant only from the standpoint of the number of votes unheard-of candidates got running against incumbents. This, perhaps, was another indication of the voter's mood in this year.

But, back to the two major considerations of this section, the battle to replace Ben Barnes and the fight to unseat Crawford Martin.

Battling for Ben's Gavel

The Texas lieutenant-governor is a powerful man. Just how powerful he is remains a function of his own personality and leadership capabilities. The Texas Constitution declares him to be the presiding officer of the Senate, and the attendant power of a presiding officer to make committee assignments and recognize senators on the floor give the man a tremendous opportunity to influence legislation. Thus the office is of much more than passing interest to Texas politicians and political interests.

Ben Barnes's decision to run for governor in 1972 created a large-scale, wildly-swinging fight for his gavel. Three state senators, one well-known newspaper editor, one lesser-known businessman, and a couple of minor candidates provided a wide range of political philosophies and styles for the voters to choose from.

The two candidates with the best name-identification among the voters were Senator Wayne Connally and Bill Hobby, president and executive editor of the *Houston Post*. Both were known not so much for their own accomplishments as for what someone else in their family had done. Wayne, of course, was the younger brother of John Connally, who, after three terms as governor, had gained national prominence as President Nixon's mouthpiece in his Secretary of the Treasury job. Wayne Connally had been a staunchly conservative state senator for six years, but had never attained any statewide prominence there. He readily admitted that his last name was a very significant factor in the race, and that it opened a number of doors for him around the state. Hobby had never held public office before, but both his father and his mother had held high governmental positions. His father, William P. Hobby, Sr., had been governor of Texas, succeeding to the office from his lieutenant-governor's position in 1917 when Governor James E. Ferguson had been impeached, and then winning a term of his own in 1918. Bill's mother, Oveta Culp Hobby, served Republican President Eisenhower as Secretary of Health, Education, and Welfare.

The other two state senators in the race were very personable men with different political philosophies. One was Ralph Hall, a sophisticated rural conservative from Rockwall, a tiny place outside Dallas. The other was Joe Christie, an El Paso product who usually voted with the liberals in the Senate. The businessman who threw his hat into the ring was Odessa oil man Bill Jones, who said he planned to spend $250,000 of his own money in the quest. His campaign never got off the ground, in spite of his travels over the state, and many observers relegated him to the status of a minor candidate after the first glance.

Looking at the Individual Campaigns

Bill Hobby had at least three things going for him in 1972. He was not an incumbent, he had a good last name, and he had lots of money to spend. Add to this a not inconsiderable talent, and it is easy to see why he was a strong candidate from the moment he announced.

The major issue he raised in his campaigning all over the state was ethics. "Bill Hobby," his billboards soberly remarked, "will make you a good lieutenant-governor. Honestly." His literature and advertising described him as a concerned, decent, honest man who wanted to help clean up the mess. "The thing that most concerns everyone in the state is ethics, confidence in government," he said. He laughed out loud when the other major candidates tried to grab the ethics issue, reminding the voters that all three of them had voted for the Sharpstown bills, and that Hall and Connally had been on the committee that whisked them quickly out for a vote.

Reporters, analysts, and voters speculated all year long about Hobby's political philosophy. He resisted efforts to label his views, as many candidates do. "[I am a] moderate or progressive on social issues and a conservative on fiscal issues," he stated at one point. Some people tried to make him into a liberal. He had, after all, been chairman of the Texas Senate Interim Committee on Welfare Reform in 1969 and 1970.

That committee's report had taken many people to task for believing in the so-called welfare "myths." Too, he had spoken at a banquet honoring Sissy Farenthold in Corpus Christi, and she had ruled out running for lieutenant-governor, she said, because her friend Bill Hobby was planning to. But then, his newspaper had supported Richard Nixon for President in both 1960 and 1968, and Hobby himself had supported Republican George Bush over Democrat Lloyd Bentsen in their 1970 U.S. Senate clash. His positions on taxation would probably not please the more liberal members of the Senate, either. All this made it quite difficult to pin a philosophy tag on him, and a good many observers decided to just label him a "moderate."

While this was his first try at an elective position (after years of talking about it), he was really no stranger to Austin. In addition to his work on that interim committee, he had once served as parliamentarian of the Texas Senate, and he had served on the Texas Air Control Board, the University of Houston Board of Regents, and President Lyndon Johnson's Task Force on Suburban Problems.

His was very largely a media-oriented campaign. This suited his personality, since he was usually described as a shy, introspective man who did not care for handshaking or personal campaigning (Hobby overcame this, as many men do when they enter a political race; still annoyed by a stuttering problem when the race began, he was an accomplished public performer when it ended). Almost $800,000 went into his first primary efforts, most of it ($680,000) from his own resources. With that kind of money to throw around, he could forget about most of the hand-shaking tours, and let the television and billboards spread his gospel.

One of the stands he took during the campaign was the espousal of a new constitution for Texas providing a cabinet form of government. Under this system, the governor would appoint such officials as the state treasurer, rather than having them elected.

Hobby also came out for reducing marijuana charges to misdemeanors, with a mandatory probation for the first conviction. On another controversial issue, he favored making abortions a private matter between a woman and her physician. He ignored the busing issue, at least in the first primary, telling those who asked about it that the lieutenant-governor's authority over busing is "roughly the same as his authority of the Vietnam War."

His rhetoric on taxation was about as revealing as Dolph Briscoe's. "On the sales tax, we're at or near a practical ceiling," he said, but he made it perfectly clear that he didn't want either a personal or corporate income tax. He did suggest one different idea, levying the property tax "like it's supposed to be levied. Levy it on all property, not just real estate, stocks and bonds and bank accounts and other forms of wealth."

Hobby thought his most dangerous opponent was Connally and he directed his best attacks at him: "A senator who voted for the bread tax, against the 18-year-old vote, and signed the floor report recommending the Sharp bills forfeits his right to consideration for higher office." Also, he said, if his name were Wayne Smith instead of Wayne Connally, he wouldn't even be a serious candidate.

Wayne Connally like Bill Hobby had some things going his way from the very beginning: his last name and lots of money. Brother John did not actively campaign for Wayne, but at least one of the other candidates claimed John was making phone calls to his old money sources urging them to stay out of the race if they couldn't back Wayne. There was a slight resemblance between the two brothers, and Wayne undoubtedly hoped the voters would get him confused with his popular brother. Like Hobby, Connally also turned his campaign into a media-oriented one. He only spent about one-half the money Hobby did in the first primary, but it was still a considerable amount and his advertising covered the state. "Wayne Connally will do something about the state we're in," was his slogan, and it became familiar to television viewers and travelers. Unlike Hobby, Connally got almost all of his first primary money from contributions. Only $14,000 of the roughly $300,000 he reported spending came out of his own pocket.

Connally was the most conservative of the four major candidates, and much of the establishment support went for him. He campaigned hard and frankly as a conservative, and never worried too much about alienating non-conservative voters. "I'm not trying to build a political career," he said, "and I'm not trying to win a popularity contest, either."

His vote for the 1969 food tax, his support of sales taxes (the "fairest" tax), his strong anti-busing stand, his opposition to lower marijuana possession penalites, and his poor conservation voting record were all popular stands with conservative voters, but they got him into some trouble with the more moderate voters. His vote against the last session's ethics bill was particularly hard to explain this year, but he didn't seem to worry about it much. He voted against it, he said, because legislating morality just doesn't work. Such bills don't accomplish anything, and the best way to assure honest officials would be to raise their pay to a reasonable level, he said.

He talked a lot about leadership, too. "The Legislature has abdicated its responsibility to the cities and forced them to go straight to Washington for help. It's because we've played politics too often—our state leaders have felt many of the city problems have aspects that were too strong for them politically . . . . It is high time we had people give leadership and not be so all-concerned about politics."

He also urged quick action of some kind on the public school financing problem. The schools should be equalized educationally, he said, and if it isn't done soon, then people may well lose the local control of their schools.

Ralph Hall, the other establishment conservative in the race, did not have the ultra-conservative image that plagued Connally. He called himself a "true moderate" during the fight, and he could point to a few legislative actions that were not too "establishment," but he never did really shake off that establishment conservative tag. A lawyer-business-man, Hall had spent twelve years as Rockwall County Judge before coming to Austin. He had also served as president of the powerful Texas Association of County Judges and Commissioners, and he was counting heavily on his old courthouse friends from these years to help him build an organization over the state.

He was not a newcomer to the fight, having announced two years ago that he would be a candidate for lieutenant-governor as soon as Ben Barnes was not. His effort this time was a valiant one, and had Connally not entered the race, he probably would have made the runoff. But, although he was a more attractive candidate than Wayne, they were both going after the same votes and the same money, and the Connally name was just too much for Hall to overcome.

On the issues, Hall came out strongly for revising the Constitution, for annual legislative sessions, for higher pay for legislators and permanent professional staffs for legislative committees. He tried hard to grab the ethics issue from Hobby, too, saying that he was the one who had sponsored the ethics bill in the Senate during the last legislative session. Getting all the mileage out of it that he could, he went on to blame Connally and Christie for amending it to death.

Some of his campaign rhetoric on welfare must have surprised a few of his courthouse friends. Poor people, he said, are not "fat lazy people, but people who were born into that environment, and people who can't find a job." He also praised day-care centers, an extension of the Job Corps, and an increase in the minimum wage to help solve the problems of the poor, all distinctly un-establishment ideas.

Like Connally, Hall got some sharp questions about his role in passing the Sharpstown bills. In turn he tried to pass the blame on to Preston Smith because the governor had opened that special session call to too much legislation in too short a time period. He said his committee didn't look that closely at those bills because it had not had the time, and that the bills had never really been proved to be bad bills.

Another action that haunted both Hall and Connally was the vote for the food tax. Hall said now that his vote had been a big mistake. "I shouldn't have voted for the food tax. I wish I hadn't, and let me tell you, I slept alone and ate out for about six weeks after that." He was not ready to accept either a personal or a corporate income tax, however, and pledged to fight them both as long as he could. A corporate income tax would be "just the blocking back for a personal income tax."

Joe Christie, the other senator trying for a promotion, defied those who like to place labels on their candidates. He was clearly to the left of the other contestants on most issue, he had the endorsement of the Texas AFL-CIO, yet the tag "liberal" did not accurately define him. He was, for example, a longtime law-and-order advocate, and had even sponsored legislation providing for oral confessions. Most people didn't get so persnickety about their labels, though, and Christie was usually referred to as the liberal in the fight.

Speaking frankly on the taxation question, Christie came out foursquare for a corporate profits tax. "It's about time that the corporations began paying their share of the cost of state government." An earlier action on a tax matter caused Joe some problems, however. Back on that now-famous food tax vote he had voted "no," but earlier he and Ronald Bridges of Corpus Christi had left the Senate chamber for a few minutes on a pre-arranged deal with Ben Barnes. Their absence had allowed a liberal filibuster against the tax to be broken, and had infuriated a bunch of liberals. This "walk," as it was called, was the subject of many a question to Christie during the race and he always responded candidly, admitting the deal, and saying he thought it was a wise move because the bill had then been killed by the House.

In addition to the labor backing, he was endorsed by most liberal and minority organizations in the state, even the Harris County Democrats, a liberal group in Bill Hobby's town. He was also the darling of conservation groups, having sponsored bills creating several state parks and putting the Texas horned toad on the endangered species list. (This was a favorite campaign topic of his; it could usually warm up even the most lethargic crowd.)

Christie, like everyone else, talked a lot about cleaning up the mess in Austin. One of his committees released a report during the race charging that millions of dollars in sales tax money was being lost each year through the inefficiency of the state comptroller's office. He promised to support a good ethics bill, and he released a copy of his income tax return, showing an income of around $40,000 in 1970.

The First Primary

When this contest first shaped up many people saw it as essentially a regional battle with each of the four major candidates carrying his own home area. It didn't quite turn out that way, perhaps because of the money and the name identification of Hobby and Connally. The race was overshadowed most of the time by the gubernatorial contest, and all of the candidates had a hard time finding a campaign theme that grabbed the voters' attention. Hall and Christie both campaigned tirelessly, but their cries for attention were lost in the crowd and their advertising budget was puny compared to the two last-name boys.

Aside from the ethics and food tax votes, the first primary never really stirred up much excitement. Most of the polls predicted a Hobby-Connally runoff, and on the election night that's the way it wound up. Bill Hobby led the field with roughly 688,000 votes (35% of the total for the top four candidates. Connally came in with 598,000 (30%); Christie finished third with 374,000 (20%); and Hall fourth with 304,000 (15%). Both Hobby and Connally ran strong all over the state, with Hobby capturing five of the nine geographical regions (the Gulf Coast, East Texas, North Texas, West Texas, and Central Texas), and Connally taking three (his own South Texas, the German Hill Counties, and the Panhandle). Christie won his own Southwest Texas area, while Hall did not carry a single area, though he made a good showing in his North Texas home country. Hobby was clearly the urban candidate, winning all four of the state's most populous counties by an average 40% margin.

The Runoff

The runoff between Connally and Hobby turned into one of the bitterest, name-callingest brawls that Texas had seen in many years. The strategy at first seemed rather obvious. Hobby would go after Christie's votes and Connally would try for Hall's votes, and since the race was so close, whoever did the best job would probably win.

To carry this strategy out, Connally held a Capitol news conference on Thursday May 11 to declare that he considered the clash a classic liberal-conservative fight. Hobby had just received the Texas AFL-CIO's runoff endorsement and Connally said that proved his opponent was a liberal. He also lumped Hobby with Sissy Farenthold, and accused them of planning to take over the state. Hobby is a "multimillionaire liberal from Houston . . . who is willing to take the AFL-CIO's endorsement and join with Sissy Farenthold in their campaign to take over the state government of Texas."

At this point, Connally told reporters, he was not trying to pair himself up with Dolph Briscoe, but before much more time had elapsed, Connally was openly identifying with Briscoe. Later on, Sissy let it be known that she preferred Hobby over Connally, probably to Connally's delight, and both races began to have an effect on each other. Before long, Connally's rhetoric had escalated, and his "liberal" opponent became his "radical" opponent.

Like Briscoe, Connally charged his opponent with being for busing and legalization of marijuana. Hobby dealt with these charges more effectively than did Sissy, and his campaign never seemed to falter as hers did. To be sure, Hobby had more ammunition to fire back with than did Sissy. He began hitting harder and harder on Connally's food tax vote, on his vote against the ethics bill, and on his signing the floor report for the Sharpstown bills. Wayne gave him a little more ammunition by stating that he would be willing, and thought most Texans would be, to raise the sales tax to 11% if necessary to avoid any sort of an income tax. The strong endorsement of Connally by lobbyists at a meeting in Austin also was used by Hobby, as was Connally's acceptance of some corporate contributions to his campaign in violation of state law.

On Wednesday, May 24, Hobby came up with a brand new charge. Connally, he said, had been involved in a $3,000 business deal with John Osorio and National Bankers Life during the special session while the infamous Sharpstown bills were going through. Connally roared back that it was just a routine business deal involving a deer lease on a West Texas ranch of his, and Hobby retorted, "Yeah, that's the problem, there's been too many routine business deals in Austin already."

On Thursday, May 25, Connally came up with a charge of his own, Hobby, he said, had been charged in 1967 with aggravated assault on a minor. Hobby said yes, he had spanked an 11-year-old neighborhood bully who had hurt Hobby's 3-year-old son. The older boy's mother had then brought charges against Hobby, but the charges were later dropped. A spokesman for the Harris County District Attorney's office confirmed that the charges had been dropped, saying it was "not a meritorious case." "Speaking as a parent, either you or I might have done the same thing," he added. This didn't stop Connally from using the charges, and he told more than one audience that he had been working for good government while his opponent had been slapping kids around.

By this time, slander and smear charges were coming from both camps. Substantive issues had long ago left the campaign trail, and charges which generated heat but shed little light were now the main campaign weapons. On Wednesday, May 31, the two men met twice face-to-face in Dallas, once at the Dallas Press Club "Hot Seat" luncheon, and once on KERA's "Newsroom" show. Both confrontations were bitter name-calling affairs, and both settled absolutely nothing. It was almost a climactic day for the weary campaigners. A few more hurried remarks, a few more quick handshakes, a few more smiles and frowns, and the voters would settle the issue.

On June 3, the voters returned a verdict in favor of Bill Hobby. It was nearly a quarter of a million vote win. Connally took only two geographical areas, the German Hill Country counties and the Panhandle. Hobby took the other seven, even defeating Connally on his own home turf in South Texas. The totals were approximately 1,095,000 votes for Hobby (56%) and 857,000 votes for Connally (44%). Hobby really slaughtered his opponent in the urban areas, carrying 67% of Houston's vote, and taking 61% in the 12 most populous counties.

It is always difficult to try to assess the grand failures and triumphs in a race like this. Most voters probably had a hard time getting a handle on the struggle because there were so many candidates and other races clamoring for attention. It was a pretty gentlemanly contest until the runoff, and then it quickly developed into an ugly, vicious, mud-slinging brawl. Issues of substance, which struggled for attention in the first primary, were quickly forgotten for more publicity-getting charges about crooked deer lease deals and child beating. Surely one of the things that helped Hobby win the race was the fact that he was a new face, that he had not been in office during Sharpstown. He never actually proved any wrongdoing on Connally's part, but the voters didn't really need any proof. After all, Connally had been there, and in this year, that in itself was proof enough for the voters. Connally's own screams of "ultra-liberal" and "radical" were never effective (and also were not true).

Dolph got away with it, but then Dolph hadn't been in office as Connally had been. And so it came to pass, the name Connally disappeared from the roster of Texas politicians.

A New Lawyer for Texas

Way down in public visibility in the spring of 1972 was the election contest for attorney-general of Texas. A three-man race that was settled without a runoff, it was never able to grab the attention of the public in an election year crowded with candidates. It was a race in which the main issue was the diligence of the incumbent in bringing the Sharpstown characters to justice, and, in the final analysis, the anti-incumbent mood of the voters probably was the key to the fight.

The two major contenders were Crawford Martin, the 56-year-old incumbent who had held the post since 1967, and John Hill, a 48-year-old Houston trial lawyer. A third candidate, William Pate, an El Paso lawyer, never figured prominently in the campaigning until election night, when it appeared for awhile that he might siphon off enough votes to bring about a runoff.

Martin and Hill had many similarities. Both had come from the political stable of John Connally, both had been secretary of state for him, both were Navy veterans and University of Texas Law School graduates, both had lost statewide races to Preston Smith at one time, and Hill had even once represented Martin in a law suit involving an automobile accident that cost Martin his left eye.

Martin was a native of Hillsboro, and had been serving in the state Senate back in 1962 when he got ambitious and jumped into a big free-for-all lieutenant-governor's race. He lost that race and was rescued from political oblivion by John Connally, the man who had just won the governor's contest. Big John made him his secretary of state, and Crawford became a loyal supporter of Big John and, later, Ben Barnes. In 1960, he resigned as secretary of state to run for attorney-general. He successfully downed liberal Franklin Spears, and was sworn into office in January, 1967. His three terms had been relatively quiet and uneventful until the Sharpstown mess had broken, and his opinions were generally reflective of the establishment stand on most issues.

Hill, the challenger, had replaced Martin as secretary of state. He did not remain in the Connally stable, leaving it in 1968 to enter the wide-open governor's race. Connally's tacit support went that year to Eugene Locke, but neither Locke nor Hill nor anyone else could stop Preston Smith's hand-shaking juggernaut, and Hill became a working lawyer after finishing sixth place. Politics was still in his blood, though, and he announced his candidacy against Martin on the filing deadline day in February. Until Hill's entry, it appeared that Martin would escape any serious opposition, but Hill quickly showed that he couldn't be taken lightly. His television commercials began asking the Texas public, "When the Sharpstown scandal broke, where was the Attorney-General of Texas?" This was the major theme of Hill's campaign, a charge that Martin had not been aggressive enough in his investigation of Sharpstown.

Martin, no kid-glove man, fired back his own charges. When he had announced for an unprecedented fourth term, he said he was doing it because he hadn't finished cleaning up the stench from Sharpstown. Early in April, he urged the U.S. Senate to make a full investigation of the deal whereby Frank Sharp obtained his grant of immunity. "There remains a great deal of doubt as to why Mr. Sharp was not prosecuted for his part in the alleged conspiracy," said Martin.

Hill laughed out loud at this request. "If there ever was a case of closing the gate after the cows got away, it's Crawford Martin's suggestion that Congress investigate the granting of immunity to Frank Sharp." Then Hill referred to Martin's response shortly after Sharp had made his deal: "I don't attach much significance to it." Futhermore, Hill charged, a 1967 Martin ruling allowed Sharp to increase his bank's capitalization by 2,200%. "It was Crawford Martin's opinion that allowed Sharp to get his paper financial empire off the ground in the first place."

Martin exploded at these charges, and threw everything he could think of at Hill. His campaign, though, was completely off balance, and he found the voters' ears deaf to his explanations and protestations of innocence. Martin also found himself fighting Preston Smith's Secretary of State Bob Bullock. Bullock was Smith's political hatchet man, and he was working over Martin regularly. And U.S. Attorney Anthony J.P. Farris, who had arranged the Sharp immunity grant, was angered by Martin's apparent change of heart on the subject and publicly questioned Crawford's line of reasoning.

Martin's most serious charge against Hill was that the Hill effort had been planned by Preston Smith's office and financed by Galveston multimillionaire Shearn Moody, Jr., and some Texas "vending machine moguls." This, said Martin, was because of his investigation of Moody's affairs. Moody had sent threats to Martin "that he was going to run John Hill against me if I didn't suppress evidence on some of his questionable business and political activities." Martin could never come up with any concrete evidence on the charge, and it faded out as the election day approached.

On that election day, in another example of the voters' preferring a new face, Crawford Martin joined the long list of officials thrown out of their offices. Actually the race was extremely close, and was not finally decided for several days. Hill took a slim lead on election night, but the trickle of votes for Pate prevented him from having a majority until late Sunday. Still the counting was closely watched, and it was not until the final totals were announced on Saturday May 13 that Hill could count himself in. He had 995,057 votes to Martin's 892,801 and Pate's 98,137. Hill had avoided the runoff by taking 50.1% of the vote.

Chapter 7

NOVEMBER

The Republicans: The Way They Are Fighting You'd Think They Were Democrats

The Year of Frank Sharp was to have been the year of opportunity for Texas Republicans. They had been running around gleefully dreaming of victory ever since the SEC suit was filed. The more optimistic party leaders were already counting up the number of appointments the governor got to make, but they were so busy counting up the spoils of victory that they forgot to round up a good candidate. Oh, they had candidates, all right, especially in the gubernatorial race, but their failure to come up with an attractive, well-known, respected standard bearer proved to be the worst mistake they could possibly make. (In their defense it should be pointed out, however, that Republicans who meet these qualifications are extremely scarce in Texas.) After all three 1972 election nights were history, it was clear that the Republicans had blown their best chance since Reconstruction to control the State's highest office.

They had a surprisingly bitter fight in May and June for the gubernatorial nomination. Contested Republican primaries are still political curiosities in Texas, but the eye-gouging Democratic battles overshadowed them both. The Republican faithful were aware of the fight, but the average Texan probably knew little about the candidates or the issues.

Four major candidates and a couple of minor ones threw their hats into the ring, offering party voters a wide range of political philosophies —on the right end of the political spectrum. The moderate conservative in the battle was Dave Reagan, a 33-year-old college professor from Sherman; the ultra-conservative was State Senator Henry Grover of Houston, one of the two Republicans in the Texas Senate. Between these extremes were Houston's Albert Bel Fay, a long-time party loyalist, and Tom McElroy, a Dallas lawyer. Two other candidates joined the fight, Weatherford oilman John Hall and Dallas lawyer Joseph Jenkins, but neither of them was expected to be a serious contender.

The two best known names were Fay and Grover. Fay's long years of party service, his term as Texas's Republican National Committeeman, and his two races as the Republicans' nominee for state land commissioner (1962 and 1966) gave him a hard-to-match reputation with other Texas Republicans. A multimillionaire oilman, he also had the money to wage a serious campaign. Grover had been in public office for twelve years, but in only six of those had he been a Republican. A schoolteacher by profession, he had first run for the Texas House of Representatives in 1960 as a Democrat. He won re-election in 1962 and 1964 as a Democrat, but then switched parties in 1966 when he ran for a western Harris County Senate seat. During his years as a legislator, he built a reputation as a solidly conservative voter. His brash, independent actions alienated the other senators, and, at times, his own party leaders. Grover had been laying the foundation for his campaign for over a year, without much help from party officials, and his name identification plus his campaigning ability easily made him a good bet for the runoff.

Reagan, a University of Texas political science graduate, also was a top notch public speaker and campaigner. He quickly lined up a bunch of old-line GOP leaders on his side, including a number of key workers in George Bush's unsuccessful Senate race in 1970. New, fresh, dynamic, and a quick thinker, he was eyed warily by some of the Democratic contenders as the biggest threat in November.

McElroy, the other new face, was a graduate of the University of Texas School of Law. He had previously worked for such stalwart Republican candidates as Bush, Nixon, and John Tower, but he found his own Republicanism under fire in this race. When he admitted having voted in the Democratic primary in 1970, he really began to have trouble with the issue and all his talk about transforming the Republicans into a majority party didn't help much.

The four major candidates had similar views on the issues. All were conservatives, all were opposed to either a corporate profits tax or a personal income tax, and all wanted to cut down on spending and taxing. They all strongly opposed busing, called for welfare reform, and took a tough "law and order" stand. They all favored constitutional revision, but Grover wanted only minor changes while Reagan felt a cabinet-style government should be created. And each felt he was the only one who could win in November. This was an important point, for they all saw this year as the Republicans' golden opportunity, and each had his own reasons why he would be the best Republican nominee. Grover's selling point was his established campaign and his name identification; with Fay, it was money—he was the only candidate who would be able to finance the race, he said; with Reagan, it was statistics—he would be able to forge a coalition of Republicans, moderates, and dissatisfied Democrats that would bring victory.

With all these similarities, it is surprising that they found anything to disagree on. About all they came up with, in fact, were charges dealing with the other candidate's degree of Republicanism and conservatism. There was enough flak in this area to create some campaign excitement, however, and to completely shatter President Nixon's own command- ment, "Thou shalt not speak evil of a fellow Republican."

Dave Reagan began the questioning very early in the race when he leveled a broadside at Henry Grover. Appearing on the Austin television-radio program, "Capitol Eye," he said, "Many people feel that if Senator Grover were to receive the nomination that he would in effect set the party back eight years. He has a very narrow view of the party. He is not interested in broadening the base. He is a loner. He has the reputation of being an obstructionist and is what I would consider a professional 'aginner' . . . a negative candidate who cannot appeal to the youth vote or a large number of independent or conservative Democrats." These were strong charges, but Reagan was voicing the fears of a number of his party leaders. They had never been on very good terms with Grover, a man they considered too stubborn and too conservative.

Later in the campaign Grover fired his own blast at Reagan, charging him with being a liberal "Ralph Yarborough Democrat." In Republican circles this was something akin to a morals charge, and it shook Reagan's campaign. Dave, said Hank, was a "liberal college political science professor" who had a degree from Harvard, was a Fulbright scholar, and had lectured for the State Department during the Lyndon Johnson administration. "Furthermore, Waco Republicans were stunned when Professor Reagan filed as a Republican because they say that he and his father have been long-time Ralph Yarborough Democrats." Grover also sent out a picture showing Reagan wearing a button supporting Hubert Humphrey, a move that Reagan decried as a "smear." Reagan admitted supporting the Johnson-Humphrey ticket in 1964, and said the picture might have been taken that year. "I never made it any secret that I used to be a Democrat, just like Henry Grover," he replied, maintaining all the while that he was a true conservative, a "progressive conservative." Fay was the only candidate who escaped any serious questioning about his Republicanism; his twenty-year career in Texas Republican politics simply left no room for doubt.

After this spirited battle, the most exciting Republican primary since Reconstruction, approximately 113,000 voters trekked to the polls on the first election day. Hank Grover took about 37,000 of those and Fay got about 24,000; thus the two men were thrown into a runoff, the first runoff the Republicans had ever needed in Texas. Reagan and McElroy finished third and fourth, respectively, and both chose not to endorse anyone in the runoff.

With the Republicanism questions out of the way, Grover and Fay had to come up with something else to fight about in the second primary. Political philosophy was, again, out of the question, since the two agreed on most matters. After a few embarrassing moments when it appeared they would have nothing to battle over, they finally hit upon an issue—money. Henry Grover's first primary expense report, to be more exact, became the battle ground. It was, at best, a peculiar document. Newsmen had been unable to figure it out when it had first been filed, and Grover's aides were unable to shed any light on its strange accounting methods.

Fay brought all this up in the runoff, and threw out hints that he might bring some type of court action against his opponent. But it didn't seem to bother the front-running Grover. Toward the end of the runoff, Grover was so confident that he quit worrying about Fay, and started running against Dolph Briscoe, whom he saw as the Democratic winner. His confidence was justified when, on June 3, he buried Fay in a landslide, capturing 66% of the votes. This win was another example, commented the *Texas Observer*, of the fact that, in any given set of circumstances, the Texas Republican Party will do the stupidest thing possible.

During the summer, Hank tried to consolidate his support for the November battle. He did not get much help from the party officialdom, and he created a stir by asking that some of them be removed at the state convention in June. They, in turn, began concentrating all their attention and money on President Nixon and Senator John Tower. Grover limped confidently on toward November's battle, crying in the wind that Dolph Briscoe had better get ready to get it on. No one but the wind seemed to hear him, though.

La Raza Unida: The Silent Minority Awakens

For years, the Texas Democratic Party has known one thing for certain: the state's Mexican-American population would vote heavily for any Democrat on the ballot, whether it was to their best interests or not. Concentrated primarily in South and Southwest Texas, this vote had not been outlawed as the Black vote in East Texas had been; to the contrary, several efficient political machines in South Texas were built around a Mexican-American base. Pull *"la palanca"* (the big lever), they were told, and pull *"la palanca"* they did, out of fear and out of habit. Economic reprisals, physical pressure, and rewards for the faithful all worked to keep the bosses in power.

In the 1960s and early 1970s things began to change. The change was slow and painful, and the nation's interest seemed to be focused on the lot of Blacks in the South. The Mexican-American civil rights movement stayed several years behind the Black movement, although the conditions were more intolerable in parts of South Texas than in much of the South. A rising political awareness swept South Texas in this era, and Mexican-American leaders began to realize that they had the votes to control elections if only their people would use this ballot-box power. A 1963 election in the small town of Crystal City was the first dramatic breakthrough; the success of a Mexican-American slate attracted much statewide attention. A few years later, a young man named Jose Angel Gutierrez, possessor of a master's degree in political science, began organizing a Mexican-American Youth Organization out of this small town. The success of the MAYO's, as they were known, was mixed, and their more militant members quickly earned a "troublemakers" label for the group and its leader. In 1970, Gutierrez, with an eye toward the inherent but untapped Mexican-American political power in South Texas, began organizing a political party. La Raza Unida, it was called, and it managed to frighten, at the same time, both the conservative and the liberal wings of the Texas Democratic Party. The conservatives were afraid of what would happen in November without those votes, and the liberals were worried about the May and June primaries.

Gutierrez was just worried about getting the party on the ballot, however, and getting the long, tedious organizing process underway. The Texas laws concerning third parties are somewhat restrictive, and La Raza Unida was unable to get on the ballot for the November 1970 elections. Their candidates who attempted write-in campaigns had little success, and they all set their sights on 1972. Plans were in the works for a full slate of candidates for statewide offices, and for as many legislative and county candidates as they could muster. The seemingly insurmountable problems they faced—finding candidates, raising money, getting enough signatures to get on the ballot—would have demoralized many a group. But this one went on, trusting that the problems would somehow be overcome.

One of the major problems, finding candidates, was solved by Ramsey Muniz, a young lawyer who joined the movement. He became the party's gubernatorial candidate and proved himself in the heat of battle many times before the race was over. People were found also to fill the other positions on the statewide slate, but the articulate Ramsey was the only candidate taken seriously by the public, the press, and even the La Raza Unida workers.

Ramsey was a Corpus Christi native, born into a union family and a political environment. Politicking, passing out literature, block work, all the nitty-gritty stuff, was old hat to him when he was high school age. He was a football player, and his 1960 Corpus Christi Roy Miller High School team went all the way to a state championship. Ramsey's play attracted both all-state honors and a scholarship offer from Baylor University.

Injuries interfered with his football career at Baylor, but he still earned three letters and a degree (in history and physical education) which he took in 1966. Then he enrolled in their law school, and got that degree in 1971. There was a noticeable difference, he felt, in Muniz the athlete and Muniz the law student. As an athlete, he enjoyed immediate acceptance on the largely Anglo campus. As a law student, though, things were different. "When other students talked to me, I wanted to talk about the law and politics. They wanted to talk about Mexican food and Mexican whorehouses in the border towns. I never felt I was accepted for anything other than a Mexican."

It was not the first time Ramsey had confronted these problems. In grade school he had done poorly because of a speech impediment that made it difficult for him to speak either English or Spanish. "None of the teachers would believe I had a speech problem. They thought I was just a dumb Mexican who couldn't speak English. It wasn't until the seventh grade that I had a teacher who was understanding enough to know I had a problem."

Ramsey the campaigner was a flashy, emotional man who loved to make his speeches into windmill-chasing affairs. He was capable of a fiery, eloquent speech and also of enough humor, changes of pace, and hells and damns to keep a crowd laughing, interested, and listening far longer than the average politician.

On the issues, he took a strong liberal position. A corporate profits tax and utility regulation were both needed, more help for the poor was a necessity, stronger environmental protections should be established, and an abortion decision should be between the woman and her doctor.

On politics, Ramsey kept running into questions about the effect his party would have on liberal Democrats. "Liberals haven't been that much more helpful to the Mexican Americans. When we say we've got to teach the Anglo politicians a lesson, we mean all their politicians." Still, he found himself in some awkward positions. La Raza's organizers had to gather 22,358 signatures to get on the ballot, and most of these would obviously be at the expense of liberal candidates. As Sissy Farenthold's campaign picked up steam, some of La Raza's people began having doubts, wondering if maybe they shouldn't vote for her instead of signing the petitions, and Muniz, himself, at one point, ordered some television time his group had purchased on a Corpus Christi station to be given to a Spanish language Farenthold-for-governor program. (Looking back, it appears that La Raza's votes probably would not have made the difference in Farenthold's race; many observers think, however, that La Raza probably did cause the defeat of State Senator Joe Bernal, Bexar County Commissioner Albert Pena, Austin legislative candidate Gonzalo Barrientos, and Tom Moore, Jr., the Dirty Thirtian who ran for the senate against Grant Jones.)

It was a long, tough journey for Ramsey, from February to November. But it was all worthwhile, he said. "Raza Unida is not just a party for the Mexicanos—we welcome the Black, the white, Japanese-Americans, Chinese-Americans, poor people, liberals, anybody who wants a change." It would be a weird coalition if he could put it together.

The Democrats: Hiding It Under a Bushel

The story of the 1972 general election for most Texas Democratic candidates was one of running as fast and as far away from presidential candidate George McGovern as possible. Most of them felt that he could only hurt their own efforts and only reluctantly did some of them finally embrace their party's presidential nominee.

It had been a wild year in Texas presidential politics already. A combination of the 1968 Democratic National Convention's reform rules and the existence of three separate grassroot organizations in the state (George Wallace, George McGovern, and Hubert Humphrey) produced a huge change in the makeup of delegations to all convention levels— county, district, state, and national. Old-time party workers who for years had been chosen as delegates through personal influence and the unit rule were either completely left out or allowed in at the indulgence of whichever group controlled their precinct. The state convention, a boisterous 19-hour ordeal, was deeply split and sent a delegation to the national convention with sizable chunks of votes for all three candidates. When their votes were announced on the floor of the convention at Miami Beach, shock must have set in among people all over the country who remembered the rigid control the unit rule had given the Texas Democratic establishment in years past.

Many of the delegates to all convention levels were quite vocal and dedicated to their candidate, and the rifts that were created would be hard to heal. The rifts from the national convention didn't help much, either. For one thing, the two runoff candidates, Dolph Briscoe and Sissy Farenthold, were there as delegates, and their feud was clearly not over. Briscoe was the titular leader of the delegation, and his leadership was not the most decisive the state had ever seen. It must not have been a very enjoyable week for him. The highlight of his leadership came when he cast his vote for the presidential nominee first for George Wallace and then immediately switched it to George McGovern. Thus with one move he alienated two rather large groups of people—the McGovern voters because he voted for Wallace in the first place, and the Wallace voters because he switched his vote to McGovern. That peculiar performance (the "Briscoe flip-flop," Grover called it in his ads later) furnished much ammunition for the "I-told-you-so's" and the "Why, that stupid jerk" remarks. The next night, as his runoff opponent was grabbing national attention with her fight for the vice-presidential nomination, Dolph must have been licking his wounds and wishing he were back in Uvalde.

The Last Election Night

The only mutually hard-fought race in Texas in November was the one between incumbent U.S. Senator John Tower and his Democratic challenger, Harold Barefoot Sanders. Since the Sharpstown Scandal had little, if any, direct effect on either the primary or the general election for this position, scant attention has been paid to their races in this work.

The governor's race was overshadowed by the Senate fight and the presidential battle. Only Grover and Muniz campaigned hard, but no one, it seemed, was paying any attention. Certainly not Dolph Briscoe, who stayed on his Uvalde ranch until the last week or two of the affair. The press was consumed with the Nixon-McGovern contest and the Tower-Sanders battle, and had little time or space for the gubernatorial clash. However, on election night, the biggest surprise of them all turned out to be that neglected governor's race. In Texas, as in the nation, the presidential battle was decided quickly. Tower's victory was clear shortly after that. But the governor's race turned into an all-night thriller.

Henry Grover, struggling almost by himself, had been trying to paint Briscoe as a liberal. He argued that Briscoe and McGovern were birds of a feather, and both deserved to be defeated. Or, he would try to make Dolph appear to be indecisive and incompetent. Footage from Dolph's Miami Beach performance was used to help build the argument, but no one took Henry seriously until his votes started adding up.

Ramsey Muniz had tried to forge his coalition, but had been largely unsuccessful. True, he got the endorsement of some prominent Blacks, including Ralph David Abernathy of the Southern Christian Leadership Conference, Mrs. Coretta King, wife of Dr. Martin Luther King, and Mickey Leland, a Houston Democratic state representative-elect, but the rank and file Blacks did not respond too favorably. The white liberals didn't join La Raza in the numbers Ramsey was hoping for, either. Some were angry with him because he had refused to support McGovern, and some were supporting Grover under the theory that he had a better chance to beat Briscoe. Some of Ramsey's Mexican-American supporters did not want the coalition, anyway, because they feared it might be taken over by the other side, so Ramsey was caught in a squeeze.

As the votes started to come in, Briscoe jumped out into his accustomed lead, but around 9:00, Grover edged by him and took a slim lead. As Grover's lead grew, the Republicans who had contributed to La Raza smiled and said "I told you so." It was not until early Wednesday morning that Dolph's friendly rural areas began coming in, and he regained the lead. Many people who went to bed thinking Grover was now governor woke up to find Briscoe back in the lead. It was a small one, but he never relinquished it. The final percentages were approximately 49% for Briscoe, 45% for Grover, and 6% for Muniz. In the county-by-county figures, Briscoe again walked off with the lion's share, carrying 231 counties. Grover won 20 of them, mostly urban counties or Panhandle counties. Muniz counted three South Texas counties that went for him: Zavala, Jim Hogg, and Brooks.

Briscoe thus backed into the governor's mansion. An angry Grover said if only they'd given him $50,000, he could have won, and announced his candidacy for 1974. Muniz's showing got La Raza a permanent spot on the ballot and he said he was happy.

And lo, the Year of Frank Sharp came to an end.

PART THREE:
THE LEGISLATIVE REACTION

Chapter 8

THE REFORM LEGISLATURE COMES TO TOWN

The New Speaker and His Reform Package

It was January 9, 1973. That huge jury of Texas voters had now three chances to release their frustrations on members of the Legislature, and those who had survived were gathered in Austin along with the replacements for those who had not survived. Reform was heavy in the air around the Capitol. The halls were crowded with friends, relatives and well-wishers who had come to see the swearing-in ceremony, and there was a feeling, or maybe just a hint of a feeling, that this bunch of representatives and senators might really get serious about their house-cleaning job.

In the spotlight this day was the new Speaker of the House, Price Daniel, Jr., the 31-year-old son of former House speaker and governor Price Daniel, Sr. His election had been a certainty for many months, and after speeches on his behalf by a white big-city conservative, a Black female liberal, a Mexican-American liberal, and a white rural Dirty Thirty veteran, he was duly elected without opposition. While the road which had carried Daniel to Gus Mutscher's position of power had been as smooth as an interstate highway for several months, it had in the beginning been as muddy and as treacherous as an East Texas river bottom dirt road after a good rain.

Price, Jr., came to the House from the southeast Texas town of Liberty. He had first been elected back in 1968, and he had been a rather soft-spoken, liberal-leaning representative in his first two terms. After graduating from high school in Austin, he went to Baylor where he acquired a law degree and a reputation as an expert on Texana. His mail-order business in Texas books and documents helped him finance his stay at the Baptist university, but he gave it up after graduation and went back to the family home town of Liberty to begin a law practice. Considering his family's political tradition, it was only natural for him to run for office. In addition to having a political father, his great-great-grandfather, Sam Houston, had also run a few races. His wife, the former

Dianne Ford Wommack, even came from a political family, since her great-grandfather, Thomas Campbell, had been governor of Texas 1907-1911. The pretty Dianne enjoyed politics immensely and was quite a campaigner for her husband.

Price, Jr., says his first two terms in the House left him a bit disillusioned and discouraged because it was so hard to accomplish anything as an individual representative. He was even considering dropping out to return to his law practice before the uproar over Sharpstown gave him some hope that the system might be changed. When some friends approached him during the tumultuous last months of the Mutscher-ruled Sixty-second Legislature with the idea that he should run for speaker, he thought it over for a while, and then, shortly after the session ended, he formally announced his candidacy. He had been on the fringe of the Dirty Thirty movement during the session, winding up with twelve good votes out of nineteen by their reckoning, but he had deserted them on enough key votes to create a bit of distrust among the hard-core Dirty Thirtians. On the other side, among the hard-core Mutscher team members, he could expect little in the way of support. Daniel's formal announcement came on June 21, 1971, and by October, as we have seen, a majority of the members had indicated they were through with Mutscher. The team members and lobbyists who were deserting Mutscher, though, were beginning to line up behind Rayford Price, and he was being considered the front runner for the job.

Then the new year brought in all those federal court decisions in January and the Abilene trial in March. As a result of both, a special session was called in late March, and the speaker's race was evidently settled when Rayford won a 77-65 second ballot vote. The defeated candidate was Representative L. Dewitt Hale of Corpus Christi, a Mutscher man who wound up in the forefront of a stop-Rayford Price movement. Daniel had felt he didn't have the votes to directly challenge Price at this time. Since a loss in a head-on contest would just about settle the issue permanently, Daniel threw his support to Hale, who supposedly would serve only as interim speaker if elected. Hale's defeat left a cloud of despair over the Daniel camp, but within a couple of months, two events brought the sunshine back.

The first and most important was the defeat of Price by Fred Head. Price had returned to Palestine after becoming speaker and found Fred Head messing up his world. Realizing the importance of the coming fight, both sides called in outside reinforcements. A few Dirty Thirtians and even Dianne Daniel went in to help Head, and a couple of Mutscherites joined the fray on Price's side. Head's suprising upset, of course, removed Price from Daniel's road to the speaker's chair.

The second event that helped Daniel was the election of all those new freshmen. Since he had been running for speaker on a reform platform for over a year, he would be a natural choice for these reform-minded freshmen. The road ahead began to straighten out for him. While the stunned team members were trying to regroup he went all over the state gathering commitments from old and new members alike. His gains quickly made it apparent that he had the race won, and early in August, his last remaining opponent, Representative Frank Calhoun of Abilene, officially withdrew. At the time, Daniel was claiming 111 commitments, far over the 76 needed to win.

Late in 1972, Daniel threw his campaign juggernaut, which was by then roaring down the smooth interstate highway, into cruise while he began working on the final details of his reform plans. The rough outlines had been known for quite some time. All along he had promised to be a one-term speaker, and had called for a strong new ethics code for state officials. He also wanted a new lobby control law and a new campaign finance disclosure law in place of the unworkable and unenforceable laws then on the books. His plans called for the creation of a State Ethics Commission to administer and oversee these laws. An access-to-government records act was also in the works, along with a strong law prohibiting closed meeting of public bodies. In the area of legislative procedural reforms, he espoused laws limiting the speaker to a single two-year term; limiting legislative conference committees to adjusting the difference in House- and Senate-passed bills; requiring candidates for speaker to file contribution and expense reports; and prohibiting threats, promises, and bribes in the speaker contest. Slowly, these bills were thought out, drafted, and redrafted so they would be ready to go when the session began. Daniel picked out sponsoring teams, including both veteran and freshman legislators for each piece of legislation, and then had the first nine House Bill numbers reserved for the measures to signify their importance.

The entire package of bills as they were introduced would have gone a long, long way toward turning that private government that Sissy Farenthold cried about in her campaign into public government. Texas voters would have been able to know much more than they had ever dreamed about the financial workings behind governmental actions and decisions. The sponsors and major provisions of House Bills 1-9:

HB 1, the ethics bill, was sponsored by Representative James Nugent of Kerrville and Representative Larry Bales of Austin. The veteran Nugent had for years sponsored an ethics bill, but only in 1971 had he been able to get it passed, and, as we have seen, that ill-fated measure lost its life to an attorney-general's opinion in January of 1972. This year Nugent's name was attached to a bill that (along with HB 2 and HB 4) carried the very heart of Daniel's package: the proposed State Ethics Commission. It would be a twelve member body with two members each to be appointed by the governor, the lieutenant-governor, the speaker of the house, the attorney-general, the chief justice of the supreme court, and the presiding judge of the court of criminal appeals. They would have the power to investigate alleged violations of the proposed laws, to subpoena witnesses for these investigations, and to issue written reports of their findings. All state officers, all state employees earning more than $15,000 per year, all persons appointed to jobs which required Senate confirmation, and all candidates for elective offices would have to file sworn financial statements with the commission. The statement would contain a complete accounting of the financial activity of the officer or employee, his spouse, and his dependent children. A listing would be required of occupational income; interest, dividend, royalty, and rental income. Stocks, bonds, notes, real estate, and business entities held, bought, or sold during the year would have to be disclosed, and gains or losses from any sales would have to be reported. Dollar figures would be given not in actual amounts, but in categories of amounts: (1) under $1000, (2) $1000-$5000, (3) $5000-$10,000, and (4) over $10,000. The ownership of stocks would also be reported by category instead of dollar amounts: (1) under 100 shares, (2) 100-500 shares, (3) 500-2000 shares, (4) 2000-10,000 shares, (5) 10,000-50,000 shares, and (6) over 50,000 shares.

All state officers and employees owning a substantial interest in a business licensed by the State would also have to file an affidavit with the commission disclosing their relationship. Other provisions of the act provided criminal penalties for violations, set the venue for court proceedings in Travis County, and provided penalties for persons who file false complaints to harass individual state officers and employees.

The second bill in the package dealt with a rather sore subject for reformers—lobby regulation and control. The only law on the books was one passed back in a 1957 special session called in response to another juicy political scandal. The law unfortunately had no enforcement teeth in it, and was almost certainly unconstitutional in part. Since few people took it seriously, there were never any prosecution attempts under it. It was, in fact, unworkable, unenforceable, and usually ignored. Daniel chose Representative John Bigham of Belton, a veteran Dirty Thirtian, and Representative Arthur (Buddy) Temple III of Diboll to carry HB 2.

It was a far-reaching bill that required anyone who communicated directly with members of the legislative or executive branch to influence legislation or administrative action to register as a lobbyist with the Ethics Commission (unless they were contacting their own legislator). One who had another to act in his behalf would also have to register. Communicating was defined as "contact in person or by telephone, telegraph, or letter"; legislation was defined as "any matter which must be acted upon by one or both Houses of the Legislature to become effective"; and legislative and executive branches were defined to include state officers and legislators, officers-elect, and legislators-elect, candidates for these positions, and their employees, and employees of agencies in the executive branch. Monthly reports during legislative sessions and quarterly reports thereafter would have to be filed by the registrants, and these reports, along with the initial registration statements, would make public the amount of money spent on lobbying activities, the names of the legislators to whom loans or gifts were given, and the names of persons who gave over $500 to organized lobby groups such as trade associations and chambers of commerce. Other provisions provided criminal penalties for violations of the act, and charged the Ethics Commission with administering the act.

The third bill which created the Ethics Commission and relied on its watchful eye for its enforcement was the campaign finance reporting measure, HB 4. Sponsored by Representative Ben Bynum of Amarillo and Representative Chris Miller of Fort Worth, it, too, would replace an unworkable, unenforceable law. Texas had such a law on its books, but candidates who "forgot" to file reports of campaign expenses and contributions had found out that nothing at all happened to them. And those who turned in reports that were confusing, misleading, or incomplete also found that nothing much would happen to them.

This would all be changed under HB 4, though. Candidates *and* political committees would have to appoint a political treasurer under this bill before they could spend or receive a single penny. This treasurer would be responsible for keeping detailed accounts and making full financial reports to the Ethics Commission. The reports would have to show the full names and addresses of anyone who gave or received over $25 in campaign funds. These reports would be due one month before, one week before, and one month after the election. Candidates who had deficits or surpluses at the time of that last report would then have to file reports every 60 days thereafter until the deficit or surplus was cleared up. Candidates could not accept contributions over $100 from out-of-state political committees unless the money was accompanied by the identification of each person who provided over $25 of the money.

Since these provisions applied both to candidates *and* political committees, the bill would have closed one of the largest loopholes in the old law—the committee that could gather and dispense thousands of dollars without ever having to account for a penny.

Another provision in the bill would apply the financial reporting requirements to campaigns for or against issues or propositions such as constitutional amendments and bond issues.

Corporations, already prohibited from giving money to candidates, would also have been forbidden to make contributions in other ways, such as lending a corporate airplane to a candidate, or allowing its employees to work on company time for candidates.

Criminal penalties were provided in the act, and a section was included that would have allowed the name of a candidate who violated the act to be taken off the ballot. The Ethics Commission was again given enforcement duties.

Two additional bills in the reform package, HB 3 and HB 6, were aimed at opening for public scrutiny the meetings and records of governing bodies.

The open meetings bill, HB 3, was principally sponsored by Port Arthur Representative Carl Parker. It would require all governmental bodies from the Legislature on down to local school boards to conduct their business in public meetings with advance notice being given. A few exceptions, such as discussion of the location of real estate purchases, were made in the act. The definition of meetings as "any deliberation between members of a governmental body at which any public business or public policy is discussed or considered," and the inclusion of criminal penalties for officials who try to get around the act both made it one of the toughest such measures in the country.

Representative Lane Denton of Waco, Representative Camm Lary of Burnet, and Representative Hawkins Menefee of Houston were picked to sponsor HB 6, the open records bill. It would be a historic first attempt at legislating in a sort of never-never land, for most governmental bodies and agencies in the past had just developed their own rules about making their records public. These rules were often quite arbitrary, and their enforcement could be sporadic and selective. HB 3, though, emphatically stated that, with only a few exceptions, "all information collected, assembled, or maintained by governmental bodies is public information." It should be available for inspection during normal business hours, and copies should be available at ten cents per page, too, the bill said. And "the provisions of this act shall be liberally construed so the people can retain control over the instruments they have created."

Some of the exceptions to this act included information made confidential by law, personnel and medical files, state and county attorneys' files on forthcoming legal actions, figures on government contracts obtained by competitive bidding, and records in private legislative offices.

The other four bills in the package were all aimed at needed procedural reforms in the legislature. HB 5, sponsored by Representative Fred Head of Troup, would have limited House-Senate conference committees appointed to adjust the difference in appropriations bills to doing just that. They would not be able to change amounts already agreed upon by both houses. In the past this had been one of the biggest eyesores in the entire legislative process, as the ten members on the committee "wheeled and dealed" each other. Literally millions of dollars that neither house had voted on had been capriciously added to the State's spending bill this way, and occasionally vindictive committee members had been known to inflict punishments on their fellow lawmakers by arbitrarily reducing the funding for their pet projects.

The last three bills were an attempt to clean up one of the wildest political contests in Texas, the race for speaker. Presently, it was a wide-open, no-holds-barred contest with absolutely no rules or laws governing the campaigning.

House Bill 7, sponsored by Representative Neil Caldwell of Alvin and Representative Bill Hollowell of Grand Saline, would limit the speaker to a single term by law. For decades this had been a tradition in Texas politics, but in recent years, speakers had turned to the blatant use of power to perpetuate their reigns.

House Bill 8, sponsored primarily by Baytown Representative Joe Allen, required speaker candidates to report campaign contributions and expenditures just like any other candidate. According to an educated guess, a successful speaker's race could wind up costing upward of $60,000, and, without these reporting requirements, the public would know little about where a candidate might obtain this money, or what obligations it might leave him under.

The last of the bills, House Bill 9, sponsored by Representative Bob Hendricks of McKinney, would prohibit the use of threats and promises of rewards in the speaker's race. Such actions would be felonies carrying prison terms of two to five years as penalties. It would prohibit the promising of choice committee assignments or special treatment for a legislator in return for a favorable vote for a particular candidate for speaker.

Joining Daniel in the planning for this reform package was Randall "Buck" Wood, who was, of all things, a lobbyist. Wood, a 28-year-old lawyer, represented Common Cause of Texas, a unique offshoot of the nation-wide "citizens lobby" organization Common Cause. Founded by former Secretary of Health, Education, and Welfare John W. Gardner, the group dedicated itself to exposing corruption in government and returning that government to "the will of the people."

When the national organization decided to set up some statewide groups, Texas was chosen as the first target because, the directors thought, the recent Sharpstown Scandal had intensified the average Texan's desire to set things straight. Thus, the time would be right for a one-state project, and they hired Wood and Milton Tobian, a former cotton seed products dealer at the Dallas Cotton Exchange, to head up the effort. Wood had served as chief elections officer under Secretary of State Bob Bullock, and knew his way around the Capitol. Wood set as the organization's number one goal, a new ethics code. "We rank pretty low among the states in attitude and in the atmosphere in which legislation is made," he told the *Austin American-Statesman*'s Rick Fish. "Gus Mutscher to this day doesn't believe he did anything wrong, not because he is unwilling to accept reality, but because in his reality, such things were standard practice."

In addition to the ethics bill, Wood set as his priorities the lobby control bill, the open meeting and open records legislation, and the campaign finance disclosure bill. He and Tobian began planning their strategy and organizing their "telephone chains," and they were ready for business.

It was evident from the very first day in the new House that things would be different this session than they were back under Gus Mutscher. While Speaker Daniel had committed himself to throwing the weight of his office behind the nine reform bills, he had also stated that he would have no other legislative program as speaker. He was planning to preside fairly and impartially, and House members could cast their votes without fear of retribution by the speaker. In view of the dictatorial "team" tactics of the past several speakers, this declaration was viewed somewhat skeptically. The doubts quickly disappeared, however, as Daniel presided with a fairness that astonished even his enemies, and the representatives soon began praising the "openness" and the "new day" in their letters back home.

The "openness" necessitated some long work hours during the session and this House went down as one of the hardest working groups in Texas legislative history. The members got a glimpse of what the session held in store for them on the very first day when they stayed in session beyond 6 p.m. putting the finishing touches on their new rules. These rules required a five-day public notice of all committee meetings, and tape recording of all committee meetings and House sessions. Record votes were necessary on bills in committees, and closed meetings, or meetings on the floor while the House was in session, were prohibited. Fiscal notes estimating the cost of all bills were called for, thus giving the members the opportunity, for the first time, to see the "price tag" on each bill before they voted on it.

The New Lieutenant-Governor
And The Senate

While the new speaker and his reform package captured the headlines in the first week of the new legislative session, the spotlights shifted their attention across the rotunda as the second week began. On Tuesday, January 16, William P. Hobby, Jr., was sworn in as the new presiding officer in the Senate, elected on a promise to make Texans "a good lieutenant-governor. Honestly."

The betting around the Capitol that week was that any reform bills would have a harder time getting through the Senate than they would the House, not because of the new lieutenant-governor, but because of the makeup of the new Senate. As mentioned before, 15 of the 31 senators would be there for the first time, but eight of these 15 were former representatives who had been known as Mutscherites during the previous session. Their election plus the strength that the previous Senate's power structure had retained through Hobby's committee assignments made many people think the upper house would be extremely status-quo minded during the session.

A conflict over the rules highlighted the first week of the session with Hobby attempting to restore some of the power that had been stripped from the lieutenant-governor in a post-Sharpstown special session. The area of concern was his power to make committee assignments, and Hobby won the fight while evidently agreeing to preserve the existing lines of power. Senator William T. Moore of Bryan, for example, retained his chairmanship of the powerful State Affairs Committee, and Senator A.M. Aikin of Paris stayed on as chairman of the Finance Committee.

There were a few procedural reforms installed early in the session such as a fiscal note for all bills and a 24-hour notice rule for taking up bills out of order, but on the whole, Hobby maintained a tight control and the body operated much as it had in previous sessions—by the two-thirds vote rule. As bills come out of committee in the Senate they are placed in numerical order on the calendar, where they must be acted upon in the same order. A senator who has on the calendar a rather unimportant bill with a low number can thus block more important bills by refusing to bring his bill up for debate. The only way around such a roadblock is a motion to bring up a bill out of its regular order, which requires recognition by the lieutenant-governor and then a two-thirds vote. This tradition has increased the power of the presiding officer and has necessitated a lot of head counting before such motions are made, since eleven senators can block it.

The Fight for Reform

And so it began. The eyes of Texas were watching as the legislators got down to business. In their 140 days, they would have the opportunity to restore public confidence in the governing process. If they needed any reminder of the job ahead they got it the week after the inauguration festivities when a jury in Amarillo found John Osorio guilty of conspiracy and embezzlement charges which grew out of the Sharpstown investigation. Osorio, who later received a three-year prison sentence for the conviction, told the *Associated Press* in an exclusive interview that the government's main target had really been Ben Barnes. The indictments had been returned only after he refused to say he "bought off Barnes," he claims.

Action on the reform bills opened in the House of course. They were duly referred to committees, where they were all reported out favorably, and floor action on the bills began in late January.

House Bill 5, the conference committee limitation bill, was the first to come up for a vote, and it was overwhelmingly passed to the Senate on

January 29. House Bill 3, the open meetings bill, had been on the calendar earlier, but action on it had been postponed as some legislators began to hear concern from elected officials back home about the bill's definition of "meeting". Afraid that a conversation over a cup of coffee with another official might subject them to criminal penalties, they argued for a change in the definition. The bill's principal sponsor, Representative Carl Parker, attempted to meet these objections by accepting an amendment providing that such conversations would be all right, so long as a quorum of the body was not taking part. Some other amendments were attached over Parker's objections that they would severely cripple the bill, though. One sponsored by Representative Tom Uher of Bay City, and approved by a 78-67 vote, exempted all meetings for the hiring and firing of personnel from provisions of the new law. Representative Ray Hutchison of Dallas offered another amendment which provided criminal penalties for anyone who intentionally filed a false complaint under the proposed law. Parker argued this could be used to intimidate citizens, but the House went along with Hutchison by a 72-71 vote.

With these amendments, the bill sailed through the House on a 132-13 vote on January 30.

The first major controversy of the session arose in early February, and as might be expected, the center of the storm was reform. On February 7, Lieutenant-Governor Hobby announced his plans to invite 150 Texans, one from each House district, to a Citizens' Conference on Ethics in State Government to be held in Austin on March 20-21. This conference would provide some "citizen input" on the reform bills, said Hobby, so he saw no reason for Senate action on those bills until after the conference.

Daniel visited with Hobby the next day to express his concern over "any unnecessary delay" in the passage of those bills. Pointing out that Texans had shown their desire for "immediate reform" in last year's elections, Daniel said he felt the responsibility for those reforms should be on the elected officials in Austin. The lieutenant-governor replied that he foresaw no delay for the reform bills because of the ethics conference. Until the 60th day of the session, which was March 9, it would take a four-fifths rules suspension vote to pass any legislation because of a constitutional limitation, he reminded Daniel.

On February 12, freshman Representative Arthur E. (Buddy) Temple III blasted Hobby in a personal privilege speech on the House floor. The attempt to delay the passage of these bills, said Temple, was an "affront" to the House and to the "intelligence of the people of this state." It is presumptuous "for the lieutenant-governor to assume that he can unilaterally select 150 Texans who are more representative of this state's population than those selected by the people themselves," he continued. Many of the House members gave Temple a standing ovation as he concluded, but Hobby had no comment and went on with plans for the conference. The relations between the two houses and their presiding officers deteriorated during the month of February. Three more of the reform bills were passed by the House during February and sent to the Senate.

Action was completed in the House on February 8 on House Bill 2, the lobby control bill, and Speaker Daniel called the bill as it was sent to the Senate "the best lobby regulation bill ever passed by a legislative body in this nation." Both committee and floor action produced some changes, but the sponsors of the bill were able to fight off amendments that would weaken the bill. Anyone who spent more than $150 per quarter to communicate with state officials (except his own representative or senator) would have to register, and those who gave over $250 yearly to lobbying organizations would now have to be identified. An amendment removing the State Ethics Commission was killed by a 96-47 vote, and an amendment by Representative DeWitt Hale exempting from the registration provisions citizens who lobbied their own senator or representative, or the governor or lieutenant-governor was defeated by a 72-72 tie, with the speaker casting the tie-making vote.

On February 13, the House passed House Bill 6, the open records bill, and sent it across the rotunda to the Senate. Sponsors of the measure lost only a few votes on amendments, but won the major fight when they defeated Representative E.L. Short's efforts to make provisions of the bill optional.

House Bill 8, requiring financial reporting in the speaker's race, got its stamp of approval from the House on February 22. Its sponsors, Representative Joe Allen of Baytown and Representative John Wilson of La Grange, successfully fought off major changes in the bill's provisions, but lost some votes on a few minor amendments. An attempt by Representative Hilary Doran of Del Rio to completely remove a $25 limit on unreported spending by individuals in behalf of speaker candidates was killed by a 75-66 vote. Amendments were added which apparently prohibited labor unions and officials in the legislative and executive branches from making contributions to candidates.

March proved to be one of the most tumultuous months of the session, at least where the reform bills were concerned. And again, lest the legislators forget their roots, there were daily warnings emanating (in the form of wire service reports) from Dallas where another Sharpstown-related trial was in progress. It began in early March, this time with Osorio, Waggoner Carr, and Joseph P. Novotny as co-defendants on mail and wire fraud charges. Novotny entered a plea of guilty shortly after the trial began, leaving Carr and Osorio to share the headlines. Carr himself arose in the last day of the trial to deliver an impassioned plea for his freedom, and was overjoyed when the jury returned with "Not guilty" verdicts for both himself and Osorio.

The legislative action stole the show from the judicial process, though, when the House began what turned out to be a bitter, three-day-long floor fight over House Bill 1, the ethics bill. The two sponsors, Representative Jim Nugent and Representative Larry Bales, split the blanket before the fight ended, with Bales calling for the defeat of the amended bill.

It began on Wednesday, March 7, but the real fireworks didn't come until Thursday. Two amendments proposed and passed that day left a bitterly divided and angry group of legislators. One, sponsored by Representative Bill Sullivant of Gainesville and adopted by a 74-62 vote, changed the method of selecting members of the Ethics Commission. Instead of having the governor, lieutenant-governor, speaker of the house, attorney-general, chief justice of the supreme court, and the presiding judge of the court of criminal appeals each select two members, the Sullivant amendment would have the twelve members selected by random drawing from names submitted by the state's district judges. Since a bill containing the first method had already passed to the Senate (House Bill 2) it created an extremely confusing situation (and provided much grist for the senators' chuckle mill later).

The furor, though, came over an amendment offered by Representative Fred Agnich, a Dallas Republican, and the possessor of first-rate Dirty Thirty credentials. His amendment, which over the next few weeks drew more editorial criticism than perhaps any other piece of legislation during the entire session, turned the bill's public financial disclosure requirements into a secret process. Public officials responsible for filing such statements under the bill would file them in sealed envelopes, and the Ethics Commission then could not open them unless it found probable cause to do so, either in response to a complaint, or from an investigation on its own. Action on the floor was hot and furious before the vote, and the amendment slipped by on a 71-70 vote.

Those who had voted with Nugent and Bales against the amendment immediately hurled charges that Agnich had damaged the bill possibly beyond repair. "We were willing to put strict controls on the lobby," the disgusted Bales told his fellow members, but "reform as it relates to us proved to be too bitter a pill to swallow." Houston Representative Hawkins Menefee called the actions "a crippling blow to the reform movement." Speaker Daniel, who voted against the amendment, said "I'm very, very, disappointed. I don't think the House acted in accordance with the mandate of the people as expressed in last year's election."

Daniel, Nugent and others worked frantically overnight hoping to come up with some way to undo the Agnich damage, but they had to have a two-thirds vote to make any changes on a bill's third reading and they could not muster the votes. After the crippled bill was finally approved on Friday night by a 101-21 vote, the weary speaker told a reporter he thought that a lack of communication might have been one of the reasons it passed. "I had 12-15 House members come to me today to say they had no idea the Agnich amendment did what it did. If they had, they said they would not have voted for it . . . . The conclusion I draw is perhaps even Mr. Agnich didn't know what his bill did." Buck Wood, the Common Cause lobbyist, blasted the bill as "little more than a bad joke," and Representative Carlos Truan of Corpus Christi, like Agnich a member of last session's Dirty Thirty, called the bill an "unethics bill . . . special interest legislation for those who want the kind of secrecy and deceit in Austin that led to the Sharpstown scandal."

Reaction from around the state was quick to come in, and it was almost 100% against the action the House took. The lawmakers seemed to ignore the fact that "the recent Texas election demonstrated vast public concern over Austin ethics," complained the *Corpus Christi Caller*. "What the House did to the ethics bill was rape, pure and simple," opined Sam Kinch, Jr. in *The Dallas Morning News*. Lynn Ashby's column in the *Houston Post* noted that all but one or two of the Republican representatives from Houston had voted to gut the ethics bill. He warned them: "Perhaps our good Republicans get 'reform' and 'liberal' mixed up. But they had best get that straightened out in a hurry, for it is clear that Texans of all political stripes have had their fill of the old ways . . . ." Even the executive board of the Baptist General Convention of Texas got into the act, passing a resolution calling for "full and open financial disclosure."

Representative Agnich in the meantime, was overwhelmed by these criticisms. Other than a few ineffective statements by fellow Republicans decrying the liberals' attempt to "McGovernize" the reform bills, he had few defenders. In April he sent a newsletter explaining his position to voters in his district. The concern which led him to offer the amendment stemmed from these factors, he said: (1) the inclusion of thousands of state employees under the act; (2) the selection process for members of the Ethics Commission; (3) the too-detailed disclosure requirements; and (4) the unwillingness of the bill's proponents to compromise any of these points.

With reverberations of the bitter ethics fight still rumbling over the legislative landscape, the second week in March found a third high state official entering the battlefield. Attorney-General John Hill had been given the House-passed lobby control bill by the Senate Jurisprudence Committee Chairman Charles Herring of Austin. Herring asked Hill for an opinion as to the bill's constitutionality, and on March 13, Hill returned it with a notation that portions of it should be rewritten to remove possible problems. Portions of it were vague, portions of it were too discriminatory, and portions of it tried to impose criminal penalties selectively, he said. Members of the Senate, angry at Daniel by now over his remarks about their reform posture, used the ruling to poke fun at the speaker. Daniel was pleased with the ruling, though, noting that it upheld most of the bill, and that the problems Hill mentioned could be solved rather easily.

Another of the reform bills, House Bill 9, the legislative bribery bill, received overwhelming approval in the House on March 15. Not a single member of the House voted against the bill. Less than a week later, House Bill 7, the measure limiting speakers to a single term was passed over a few objections. This left only two of the reform bills still in the House, and put more pressure on Hobby and the Senate.

Hobby's concerns at the moment were elsewhere, though, for his long-awaited Citizens' Conference on Ethics in State Government was about to get underway. He chose former State Senator Jack Strong to chair the conference (Strong had been the original Senate sponsor of the infamous Sharpstown bills), and picked Madelin Olds of Corpus Christi, a Del Mar College government instructor and former aide to Sissy Farenthold, as vice-chairman. Almost all of the delegates showed up for what was billed as a "totally open" session to get their input on the matter of ethics.

The participants worked diligently through general sessions, and committee and subcommittee meetings, and on March 21 released their conclusions. The "citizen input" immediately proved to be rather embarrassing for Hobby, because their recommendations were much stronger than he was willing to support. They came out strongly for a State Ethics Commission with extensive investigatory powers, tough public financial disclosure statements, and standards of conduct for public officials, lobbyist registration and reporting requirements that were stronger than the tough, already-passed House Bill 2, stronger laws governing the area of campaign finance reporting, and adequate salaries for members of the Legislature. Their proposals were just as tough as, and even tougher in some areas than the speaker's reform package.

Meanwhile, back in the Senate, on the same day the conference finished its work and issued its report, the first of the reform bills to come up for a vote on the floor was killed by a decisive 21-10 vote. It was House Bill 5, the conference committee limitation bill, and it had been considered by many to be the least controversial of all the reform bills. On this day, the Senate gleefully buried it beneath a flood of derisive comments. Senator A.R. Schwartz of Galveston proclaimed it to be an unconstitutional bill that would restrict the appropriations process. The strong editorial support for the measure, he said, only shows that "editorial writers who don't know what they're talking about . . . must be writing in the same pubs."

Over in the House, Daniel called the defeat a "stunning blow." He presided the same day over the passage of House Bill 7, the bill limiting speakers to a single term, but he told reporters that "if this is any sign of things to come from the Senate . . . 'the late reform program' might be an accurate characterization."

A few days later Hobby jumped back into the headlines when he disclosed that he would not support the Ethics Commission concept proposed by Daniel and urged by his own ethics conference. While he supported most of the group's proposals, he said, he just had reservations about the desirability of an ethics commission. Governor Briscoe had earlier come out against such a commission, and, with their opposition, clouds of gloom began to roll over the proposal. Tempers all over the Capitol were getting short, now. The heat in the press had been transferred from the ethics bill fight in the House to the action, or lack thereof, in the Senate. Several senators angrily denounced the press collectively in speeches on the Senate floor, arguing that they were more concerned about the content of the bills than the speed with which they were passed.

The month of April brought with it a slight respite in the battle of words between the two houses. Late in March the Senate had passed its version of House Bill 3, the open meetings bill, and on April 4, Representative Carl Parker persuaded his fellow House members to go along with the changes the Senate had made. The bill was a big improvement over existing law, and the upper house had "shown good faith in sending us back a true open meetings law." The Senate struck the once-controversial Hutchison amendment completely out of the bill, and added an amendment exempting meetings of public officials at social functions or workshops from the provisions of the bill. Mindful of the criticism it had received, the Senate collectively congratulated itself on its work. "We've been criticized in the press for being anti-reform," Senator Ron Clower remarked, "but we're just trying to make sure we do the right thing."

The House action in concurring with the Senate amendments sent the open meetings bill on to the governor for his signature. They also completed action on the same day on House Bill 4, the campaign finance disclosure bill. This was the last of the bills to be acted on in the House, and the fate of the package now rested with the Senate. The senators quickly passed out two more of the bills, House Bill 8 and House Bill 9, and the scene now temporarily shifted to the governor's office. Mr. Briscoe responded with action, signing House Bill 3 into law on April 11, and House Bills 8 and 9 on April 18. Later in April final action of a sort came on another bill, when Attorney-General Hill ruled House Bill 7 unconstitutional in response to a query from Senator Bill Moore, chairman of the State Affairs Committee. It was the only one of the bills to lose its life to such an opinion, and Daniel felt that it might have accomplished its purpose anyway. The overwhelming legislative support it received would cause future House members to "think long and hard" before re-electing a speaker.

The box score as the legislative session entered its last month showed that three bills had become law, two had been killed, and four were still in the Senate. All of the remaining bills finally wound up on the governor's desk, but three of them made it there by the hair of their chinny-chin-chins in the last hours of the session. The fourth, House Bill 6, the open records bill, passed the Senate in revised form on May 17. Representative Denton, the House sponsor, looked over the changes, decided the Senate version was actually tougher than the House-passed measure, and convinced the other representatives to concur in the changes. This sent the bill on to the governor for his action. Buck Wood, the Common Cause lobbyist, estimated later that over half the original bill was his own handiwork; the version that passed, he said, was one of the best in the land. Daniel used the occasion to offer an olive branch to the Senate, issuing a statement praising two senators, Charles Herring and Bill Meier, for their "leadership in helping to improve" the House-passed bill.

With less than two weeks left in the session, which would automatically end at midnight on Monday, May 28, the Senate finally got around to voting on the first of the remaining three bills. It was the ethics bill, House Bill 1, which had come out of Senator Herring's Jurisprudence Committee in substantially different form. His viewpoint was that elected officials are honest, said Herring, "and should not be presumed to be dishonest." Thus the Herring substitute watered down many of the provisions of the House-passed version. His rewrite would apply only to major state office-holders, members of the Legislature, judges from the district level up, and candidates for those offices. It did require an annual public filing of a financial statement, but only sources (not amounts or even categories of amounts) were called for. Those statements would cover only the financial affairs of the office holders, and not those of spouses or dependent children. The Ethics Commission concept was removed, also. Dallas Senator Oscar Mauzy offered several floor amendments aimed at strengthening the bill, but he was voted down on every one. One which would have provided a financial statement with amounts included was defeated 21-10. Lieutenant Governor Hobby called the bill a "strict, workable ethics measure," but Mauzy derided it as a shame . . . "nothing but a piece of paper that says 'ethics.'"

When word of the passage of Herring's substitute for House Bill 1 crossed the rotunda, Representative Nugent rose to ask the House members to reject the Senate-passed version and send the bill to a conference committee. The representatives cheered and stomped as the furious Nugent denounced the measure. "What the Senate has sent us is a mewling pussycat pet of a bill—just a whimpering echo of an ethics bill," he roared. They want us "to feed pablum to the public instead of the meat and potatoes of information and openness to help the public put an end to backroom secrecy and special-interest deals." Nugent's motion carried and Daniel appointed Nugent, Bales, Temple, James Kaster of El Paso, and Bill Blythe of Houston as the House conferees. Hobby's conference committee appointments included Mauzy, Herring, H.J. Blanchard of Lubbock, Meier, and Tati Santiesteban of El Paso.

Attempting to get all of the conferees together for their first meeting on this important bill proved to be a frustrating job—particularly for the House conferees. The first two meetings were set for Thursday, May 17, and on both occasions all five of the Nugent-led group showed up to find themselves being boycotted by four of the five Senate conferees. Only Senator Mauzy appeared at the meetings, and the four absentees explained later that they stayed away from the first meeting at Hobby's request and personal conflicts prevented them all from showing up for the second meeting. On Friday, the angry House members marched across the rotunda to look for the senators, and finally cornered four of them in a noon meeting of Herring's Jurisprudence Committee. They sat patiently as the committee disposed of its business, and then got the senators to agree to a get-down-to-business meeting on the following morning.

The senators were late the next morning (as they were for almost all of the meetings, and since three members from each side had to be present for votes to be taken, the House members spent many hours sitting and waiting over the next few days), but when the deliberations finally began, they quickly jumped at one of the key points of disagreement: whether appointed officials should be treated separately as far as financial disclosure requirements are concerned. The Senate had treated them separately, passing Senate Bill 883 which required only a conflict-of-interest type statement from them. Representative Temple popped the question for the House members, "Why shouldn't appointed officials be treated the same as elected officials? I've never had it adequately explained to me why they shouldn't," he stated. Senator Herring was the first to reply, saying that good, qualified people won't serve in appointive offices if a thorough financial statement has to be filed. "They are not going to put with that type of harassment," he continued. "I'm not as concerned about the problem," countered Temple. "I think our governor can find someone [willing to serve]." Nugent pointed out that these appointed officers and state employees handle 80-90% of the State's revenue without any type of legislative appropriation, and he wanted them to be included in the bill's coverage. The senators reluctantly gave in after more discussion, but it took several more meetings to finally agree on exactly which state officials and employees would be covered. Another major issue to surface here was whether to create an Ethics Commission. The senators quickly told the representatives that the Senate unanimously opposed any such body, and they were not prepared to compromise on that point. Nugent then indicated his desire to postpone that conflict to the very end, so the House conferees could get a clear picture of the worked-out bill before they considered giving up the commission. The senators agreed to this, and the committee then took the rest of the weekend off.

The weary solons began the last full week of the session on Monday, May 21. The ethics bill conference committee found itself sharing the spotlight with an increased concern in the House over the fate of those other two reform bills. Both were still in committee, and the ever-present last minute legislative log jam heightened the possibility that they might not pass before pumpkin time at midnight on May 28. House Bill 2, the lobby control bill, had passed the House way back on February 8, and had spent most of the time since then languishing in a subcommittee of Senator Herring's Jurisprudence Committee. The proposed legislation had already created some hard feelings and tense press releases. Attorney-General Hill's ruling that parts of it were in need of rewriting gave the senators good excuse to rewrite the bill. Herring put it in the hands of Dallas Republican O.H. "Ike" Harris, and he came forth with a version in mid-April that left Daniel and the House sponsors aghast. Representative Bigham said the bill "completely aborted our efforts for reform"; Daniel called it a "step backward," and Buck Wood termed it a "joke." The torrents of criticism put pressure on Hobby and the Senate, and, within a week, a bristling Harris gave in to coercion from the lieutenant-governor and withdrew the substitute. Hobby didn't like all the criticism, however, and he used the occasion to fire off a strongly-worded release accusing Daniel of "childish bickering" and "petty criticism."

Harris and his subcommittee held more hearings on the subject, and, with Hobby's staff taking a large role in drafting, finally came forth with another proposal. Criticism of this version was almost as violent as it had been about the first substitute, but it was approved for floor debate. On Tuesday of this last week, it gained final passage after the Senate rejected a series of attempts by Senator Mauzy to strengthen the bill. Hobby congratulated the senators for their "calm deliberation" on the bill, and announced that, though some would call it weaker than the House version, he figured it was stronger because it removed the objections that Attorney-General Hill had raised. That's not all that was removed, shot back Daniel. The Ethics Commission was taken out, as well as requirements for expense reporting while the Legislature is not in session. Only paid lobbyists would be required to register, and anyone else could spend any amount of money to influence legislation without having to register. Buck Wood told reporters, "It's not a good bill . . . I'm not even sure it is any significant improvement over our present law."

Bigham and Daniel hoped to persuade the House to reject the Senate version and thus send this bill also to a conference committee. They faced a formidable floor fight, though, for a number of lobbyists were placing a lot of pressure on the House members to agree with the Senate changes. Daniel charged that "ruthless, selfish conspirators" were trying to tell House members that if they didn't go along with the Senate version they would get no bill at all, and the blame would fall on them. All of the lobby pressure began taking effect, and a worried Daniel called dozens of members into his office to ask for their help. He was able to turn the tide, and the vote to send the bill to conference was 106-37. Daniel later called it "the toughest fight of my political career." The strong lobby pressure caused one astonished freshman legislator to remark that he could have financed his entire next race on that one vote alone. Appointed as House conferees were Bigham, Temple, Lynn Nabers of Brownwood, Ben Munson of Denison, and Felix McDonald of Edinburg. The Senate conferees were Harris, Herring, Mauzy, Jack Ogg of Houston, and Peyton McKnight of Tyler.

The remaining bill, House Bill 4, also went to a conference committee late in the last week of the session. As the week began, however, it appeared that it just might be dead forever, for it was locked deep in a subcommittee of Senator Moore's State Affairs Committee. Moore had been growling and grumbling all session long about those reform bills, and he had plainly meant to kill House Bill 4 when he put it in the subcommittee. For a long time he even refused to appoint members of the subcommittee, and in the last week he gavelled his last planned committee meeting to a close without allowing the subcommittee to report the bill back. Buck Wood had tried without success during the session to get Moore to allow the bill out. He now tried another tack—going to Hobby's people to get them to work on Moore. Hobby had recently admitted raising some $300,000 in campaign funds since the election, and Wood told his staff he'd begin yelling that Hobby was trying to keep the bill from passing so he could escape any reporting requirements. The message evidently got through to Moore, because another meeting was quickly set. At the Wednesday meeting an obviously-miffed Moore told the bill's Senate sponsor, Senator Meier, "It's a horrible bill, but I've been coerced." When Meier said he'd be glad to look at any amendments Moore might have, the angry Moore snapped back, "I don't have any amendments because I don't plan to vote for this bill or to read it."

As the bill came out of this committee, it was very close to the House version. Floor action on the legislation came the next day, and two damaging amendments were attached by Senator H.J. Blanchard of Lubbock. One exempted unopposed candidates from the bill's reporting requirements, and the other eliminated the requirements for continuous post-election reporting until the deficits or surpluses were cleared up. Blanchard's amendment required only one final report 90 days after the election. House sponsor Ben Bynum examined what the Senate had wrought, and on Friday got the House to reject the bill so a conference committee could be appointed. He indicated that there were not any major problems with the bill, and he felt the conference committee could work out the differences without too much trouble. Bynum, Miller, Tom Craddick of Midland, Camm Lary, Jr., of Burnet, and George Preston of Paris were appointed to speak for the House, while Hobby selected Meier, Schwartz, Chet Brooks of Pasadena, Nelson Wolff of San Antonio, and W.E. Snelson of Midland to work for the Senate.

And so, as the legislators went into the last weekend of the session, the fate of three of the major reform bills, ethics, lobby control, and campaign contributions, was still up in the air around the crowded Capitol building. The scene in the big, pink granite edifice had taken on a madhouse aura now. In addition to the usual session crowd of legislators, lobbyists, newsmen, and employees, the Capitol was being inundated with people who had come to see the last-day-of-the-session show. Relatives of the legislators, constituents hoping to bring last-minute pressure for or against particular bills, television crews from stations in the state's larger cities (there was even a crew from the ABC-TV network news program), and tourists just hoping to find some excitement were making it difficult to get around in the Capitol building.

Adding to the confusion was the fact that, in addition to the three reform bill conference committees, similar groups were at work on a number of other major pieces of legislation. With the approaching Monday midnight deadline, these committees worked through the weekend. Not only did they have to resolve the differences in the bills, but also they had to contend with the logistical problems of getting their final versions signed by at least three conferees from each house, typed and printed, distributed to the members' desks, and brought up for a vote before the bewitching hour.

Predictably, the first of the reform bill conference committees to get its problems settled was the one working on the campaign contribution measure. Representative Bynum, the House sponsor, came away with praise for Senator Meier, who had carried the bill through the hostile Senate. Their report kept a number of major provisions of the House-passed bill, though the Ethics Commission, which was removed by the Senate, was not restored. Instead, it created a state Elections Commission, composed of several judicial and political party officials, and county Elections Commissions, composed of the chairmen of the two major political parties in each county, and a district judge from each of the counties. These commissions were empowered to investigate complaints and to inform the proper county or district attorney of any violations they discover. All candidates *and* political committees would have to appoint campaign managers to be responsible for receiving and spending funds and making the proper reports. A compromise between the schedule of required reports in the House version and Senator Blanchard's amendment wound up with candidates having to file one report yearly until post-campaign surpluses or deficits were cleared up. The pre- and post-campaign reports would have to include the full names and addresses of contributors, and those who received over $10 from the treasure chest. Blanchard's amendment freeing unopposed candidates from these reporting requirements was retained, as was the prohibition against contributions from labor unions. Contributions of over $500 from out-of-state political committees were prohibited unless accompanied by the identity of each person supplying over $100 of the contribution. The signed conference committee report went off to the print shop, and Bynum lauded Meier as a man who was "really dedicated to the concept" of campaign financial disclosure.

Meanwhile, in the ethics conference committee, things were about the same at the end of the last week as they had been at the beginning, in spite of an arduous series of meetings. Part of the problem was the high rate of absenteeism on the part of the Senate conferees, and an inability on the part of the conferees to come up with an acceptable compromise in the major areas of disagreement complicated matters even more.

The importance of the deliberations was highlighted by the occasional visits paid the conferees by Speaker Daniel and Lieutenant-Governor Hobby. Attorney-General Hill, at Daniel's request, had also assigned one of his attorneys, Elizabeth Levatino, to work with the group.

As the week began, twice-daily meetings, one in the morning and one in the afternoon, were scheduled. The Tuesday afternoon session was cancelled however, so some of the Senate conferees could fly to Corpus Christi for the wedding of Senator Mike McKinnon. On Wednesday afternoon, the House group showed up at the appointed time and then sat and twiddled their thumbs for over one and a half hours before the senators arrived. A longer-than-usual Senate session, and a special meeting of Herring's committee delayed them, they explained upon their arrival. The House members had grumbled angrily during their wait, but a majority of them remained present. "I have infinite patience, up to a point," Nugent told reporters.

His patience wore out the next morning, however, when all but one of the senators failed to show up for a 9:00 meeting. At 9:45 the embittered Representative Kaster declared senators to be an "endangered species like the whooping crane," and the representatives stalked out in a huff. Nugent took to the House floor to give a sarcastic attendance report, and requested the sergeant-at-arms to bring some cots in so they could meet "day or night" with the senators.

The headlines all week long had them on the "brink" of agreement, but as the last week turned into the weekend, the big problems remained unsolved. The senators had given up on leaving appointed officials completely out of the bill, but the questions of which appointed officials to cover, and how much financial information they should disclose had been kicked around all week without any sort of satisfactory answer being found.

Saturday morning brought the worst temper flare-up yet, and for a while, it began to appear that the conferees might be at an impasse. The session began at 8:00 a.m.; when a quorum of senators had showed up at 8:35, Nugent began pushing the meeting along, hoping to come to some final decisions. Shortly after 9:00, the senators began drifting off to attend other meetings, and Nugent complained that further delays could result in no bill at all. A sharp remark by a senator then really set him off.

Glowering at the remaining senators, he thundered, "Maybe I'm just a wee bit suspicious that this is an attempt to kill the bill."

"That's an irresponsible statement," snapped Senator Herring.

"You think ethics is irresponsible, Senator."

"Well, I start out with a feeling people are basically honest, but you think people are dishonest."

"I don't need a senator to tell me what I think," fumed Nugent. "I'm perfectly capable of stating my position."

"I wouldn't want to vote on that," Herring countered.

This exchange left both sides angry and tense. "Just tell us what you've got to have to come off that commission," Senator Blanchard told the House members, and the meeting ended with them promising to deliver to the senators a complete take-it-or-leave-it draft by 5:00 p.m. Saturday.

During the afternoon, the conferees gathered again, this time in Governor Briscoe's office. After listening to the governor urging them to come up with a bill, they broke up again, and agreed to resume their haggling on Sunday morning. This would give the senators an overnight break to study the take-it-or-leave-it bill given them by Nugent's group.

A speech on the Senate floor by Senator Moore later that afternoon did little to settle the angry feelings between the houses. A session-long enemy of the reform bills, Moore had told a reporter who, earlier in the week, had asked him what he thought of reform, "I'm not for none of that shit, and you can quote me." This day, he rose to denounce reform again. "Reform is a bunch of hogwash . . . this has been the worst legislative session in history because of the weak leadership in the House," he said. He complained that the Senate had "been flooded" by bills passed on the consent calendar, and continued his tirade with another swipe at Daniel: "Gus Mutscher had ten times as much honor as the current Speaker of the House." To a colleague who asked what suggestions he had, he shouted "Let's reform the reformers," using the derisive "ree-form" pronunciation then in use by the legislators dissatisfied with the reform bills.

On Sunday, the senators took the offensive, walking into an 11:00 a.m. meeting with a complete take-it-or-leave-it draft of their own. The surprised representatives took it, spent a couple of hours looking at it, and found that the financial disclosure for appointed officials was not as complete as the statement required of elected officials, and it seemed that they were back where they had been in the first meeting. When the senators returned, Nugent told them, "I just think the public has a right to know the financial activities of one who makes decisions involving these huge amounts of money. Maybe they won't like [some action of the official] and will raise a clamor. We've got to get the public more involved in our government or else we face questions about the viability of the system."

"I'm not interested in viability any more," said the exasperated

Senator Blanchard, "I'm just interested in midnight tomorrow coming."

Finally, the House conferees offered to accept the Senate's language in another trouble spot (the degree of disclosure of retainer income by lawyer-legislators) if the senators would accept the House members' desires to put appointed officials under the more complete financial reporting requirements. The senators mulled it over, then accepted the deal, and for the first time, it began to appear that Texas would get an ethics bill.

With the deal made, the tone of the meeting grew lighter for the first time in many days. The only disagreement left came over the issue of including members of college boards of regents under the stricter filing requirements. Representatives Bales, Temple, and Blythe were all for including them, but the senators were not. "I just have to assume that most people are honest," said Blanchard, " . . . the best code of ethics is when you raise your hand and say 'so help me God.'"

Reluctantly, to keep from killing the bill, Bales and Temple gave in, and the regents were left out.

About all that had to be done now was compile a list of the appointed officials to face the stiffer requirements, and the conferees turned to this problem almost gleefully. "Let's add this board . . . . don't forget that one . . . which board takes care of? . . . add the officers of Common Cause [as Buck Wood stepped in] . . . are any of you mad at any particular board? . . ."

At about 11:00 p.m. Sunday night, the last of the minor problems had been resolved. The bill was sent out to the print shop for a final report to be printed, and the weary conferees went home to bed.

Their final version called for all elected state officials from the level of district judge up, all salaried appointed officials, executive heads of state agencies, and members of the State's major boards and commissions to file annual statements detailing the financial activity of themselves and their spouses and dependent children. These reports would include a list of professional and occupational income, trust income, and interest, dividend, royalty, and rental income; a list of stocks, bonds, notes, and real estate held, bought, or sold (and the gain or loss from the sale); a list of notes over $1000 owed to others; a list of gifts received worth over $250; a list of corporations controlled by the person; and a list of memberships in corporate boards of directors. Categories of amounts (under $1000; $1000-5000; over $5000) would be used in the reports instead of actual dollar amounts. Other state officers would have to file reports showing any possible conflict of interest they may have because of their position. With the removal of the Ethics Commission from the bill, the secretary of state was designated to receive and maintain the reports.

After reading over the final printing Monday morning, nine of the ten conferees signed it, making it official. (Herring was the holdout, telling the *Austin American*'s Rick Fish that he didn't sign it "because of my philosophy . . . I believe people are basically honest and decent and we don't need a bunch of laws about it.") Attention then turned back to the floor of each house, where the conference committee report still faced one more vote of approval.

At this point in time, on Monday morning of the last day of the session, the lobby control bill conference committee was still having its problems. It was the last of the three major bills to gain a conference committee settlement, and it took most of the day for this to come about. On Sunday the House conferees had given their take-it-or-leave it version to the senators, and Monday morning found three of the senators not yet ready to take it. These senators, O.H. "Ike" Harris, Peyton McKnight, and Jack Ogg, indicated they didn't want to kill the bill, but they sure weren't ready to vote on it as it was. "I've not found much interest in my district for any kind of a lobby control bill," Harris remarked, and McKnight nodded his head in agreement. The House conferees obviously felt they had given up as much as they could, and it began to appear that the two groups were at "loggerheads," as Ogg put it. The House members, in their last offer, had given up on the Ethics Commission, and had taken out the language requiring the disclosure of lobbyists' employers. Also removed was the requirement that the lobbyists report the recipients of their largesse.

As the day went on, it became increasingly clear that the House conferees would have to give up a little more if they wanted to get a bill. The senators remained intransigient, and the lobbyists watching the deliberations kept smiling. At one point, one of the Capitol's premier lobbyists summoned one of the senators out of the meeting, sent him back to fetch a copy of the bill, and then walked off down the hall with him, pointing at some provision of the bill and talking rapidly. Finally at a late afternoon meeting, the impasse broke when the House conferees agreed to some more pulling of the bill's teeth. All reference to "administrative practices" was removed, meaning that any lobbying activities before state agencies did not have to be reported. The clause requiring anyone spending $150 per quarter to register was raised to $200, and the requirement that the identity of those giving $250 yearly to organizations that lobby be reported had its figure raised to $500. At 9:00 p.m., with three hours to go, the necessary signatures were placed on the conference committee report. It's not what we wanted, Representative Bigham sadly noted, but "it is stronger than present law . . . it begins to tell us who is paying the lobby and how it is used."

Provisions of the conference committee report require that anyone who communicates directly with a member of the legislative or executive branch (and candidates for, members-elect, and employees of these branches) to influence legislation must register as a lobbyist if (1) they spend over $200 in a calendar quarter on such communication (except for their own food, travel, and lodging); or (2) they act for someone else and receive compensation; or (3) they act as a part of their regular employment whether or not additional salary is received. "Legislation" as defined includes matters which are before or may come before either house. The registrants must file expense reports monthly during legislative sessions, and quarterly thereafter, showing an itemized breakdown of their spending. Those who contribute over $500 annually to organizations which lobby will have to be identified. Knowingly using false statements to lobby is prohibited, and the hiring of a lobbyist with his compensation to be contingent upon his success in killing or passing a bill is also prohibited. The required reports will be filed with the secretary of state and violations of the bill carry penalties of one year in jail and/or $1000 fine.

All three of the bills passed with only hours left in the session. Floor action on the ethics bill and the campaign contributions bill came quickly and was rather anti-climactic. The lobby control bill, though, took some rather unusual parliamentary maneuvering to, get through. With the compromise coming as late as it did, a filibuster of sorts (by Senator Ogg) was going on in the Senate, and it took some quick-gaveling by Lieutenant-Governor Hobby to break the filibuster long enough for the bill to be brought up. Over in the House, the printed conference committee reports did not arrive until after 10:00 p.m. Since they had a rule requiring material to be on the members' desks two hours before it could be voted on, it would take a two-thirds vote to suspend the rule in order for the report to be approved. Daniel explained the situation to the members, and at 11:00 recognized Bigham for the motion. It carried, the bill passed, and the last of the remaining reform bills went to the governor's desk for his signature.

Chapter 9

A LOOK BACKWARD AND A LOOK FORWARD

It is midsummer, 1973, at this writing. Over two years have passed since those headlines screaming about Sharpstown began appearing in January of 1971. Clearly, there has been a lot of change since those days. The voters have voted, the legislators have legislated, and the reporters have reported. By any measure, the biennium produced some sharp breaks in Texas' political continuity. Ben Barnes's downward plunge, Sissy Farenthold's rise to fame, the housecleaning in the executive branch, the large legislative turnover, and the resulting emphasis on reform all point to the possibility of much political change.

It's quite difficult at this time, though, to get a grasp on all this. What did all those new faces in Austin accomplish? Will the new reform laws actually allow the public to get the necessary information to make intelligent election decisions? Will the changes bring an end to that private government that Sissy Farenthold tried so hard to call to the voter's attention? Did Sharpstown really bring about substantive change in the way things were being done, or did it only bring about a change in the people who are doing it? These are all related questions, of course, and since they are political questions, the answers are likely to vary from observer to observer. The answers to some of the questions, too, depend largely on future happenings.

Without a doubt, some of those new faces came to Austin and carved out old-style voting records. Whether they will get away with this depends on the 1974 elections. If they do, then Dick Reed's fear that the voters might be satisfied with a change in personnel will have been well taken. The memory of voters is sometimes short-lived, and the people who took office because of Sharpstown may not face the same degree of scrutiny that their predecessors did. (In fact, there were those in 1972 who thought that the voters extracted their pound of flesh with such force in May and June that they were both exhausted and embarrassed by it, and by the end of the year were only wanting to get back to their normal pursuits.)

Whether the reform laws actually passed by the 63rd Legislature help bring an end to the private government Sissy talked about depends primarily on how well they are administered, obeyed, and enforced in the future. During the fights over the bills, a lot of rhetoric spewed forth from both sides, either praising the bills as a panacea, or damning them as unneeded and immoral. Both were exaggerations, and both obscured the problem they were all aimed at: How much should the public know about its government?

Senator Herring's protestations during the ethics bill conference committee deliberations are an example. People are basically honest and decent, he said over and over. That's a reasonable statement, and no one would have seriously argued with him over it, but it had nothing to do with the reasoning behind the ethics bill. Those who make the rules for a democratic society (or those who determine where to place new schools, or which tax to increase, or which industry to get tough with over pollution) should not be afraid to let that society see how those rules are made. If they are, and if they keep those citizens away from the rule-making process, then the disrespect and distrust those rule-makers create by their actions will damage the foundation of that society. It may be only a slight crack, and the citizens may learn to live with it, but that foundation will not be as sturdy as it once had been.

That ethics bill was never meant to be a challenge to the honesty of the officials it would require to file financial statements. It was only meant to allow the citizens to be aware of any possible problems or conflicts of interest these officials might have.

Those seven reform bills that passed provide the citizens of Texas a much greater opportunity to know about their government's workings than they ever had before. They are a major improvement over the few existing laws in this area, and the 63rd Legislature can, indeed, take a bow for its actions on these bills. For just a little bit more, though, they could have been much, much better. And while the 63rd Legislature will go down in history as the one that finally did pass what appears to be a workable lobby control bill, and finally did require financial reports from office-holders, and finally did declare public meetings and records to be open for public inspection, it will also go down as the one that failed to answer all of those "yes-but" questions:

1. *Yes*, they passed all those good reform laws, *but* why didn't they create an Ethics Commission? This question would have to be addressed primarily to the senators, since they were the ones so strongly opposed to it. The reports and statements required in the new laws will go to the secretary of state, a largely administrative office, held by a political appointee, usually considered the governor's man. There is certainly no criticism meant of the present secretary of state by these remarks; it's just that past secretaries of state, with a few notable exceptions, have allowed persons filing similar reports to get away with many irregular, misleading, and confusing statements. Too, this office does not have the investigation and subpoena powers that were in the original ethics bill. This will hamper any sort of inquiry into questionable financial reports.

2. *Yes*, they passed a better campaign finance disclosure bill, *but* why did they free unopposed candidates from its provisions? It's not unusual for powerful lawmakers to run unopposed, and it's not unusual, either for these individuals to gather contributions during these non-campaigns. This loophole should not have been created, and a future Legislature should eliminate it.

3. *Yes*, they required lobbyists to register and to report their expenses, *but* why didn't they require the reports to name the recipients of their gifts? After all, the people should be able to know who gets lobbied, as well as who does the lobbying.

4. *Yes*, they passed a bill requiring financial disclosure on the part of many state officials, *but* why did they leave out so many others, such as members of college and university boards of regents? These individuals make just as many important and controversial decisions as some of the officials included. Why, also, didn't they include county and local officials in these statements? County government, especially, is one of the last unredeemed strongholds of bossism, favoritism, and the spoils system in the country. Representative Nugent's worries about the viability of the system are well worth repeating here, and a future session of the Legislature surely must face up to this problem.

5. *Yes*, they passed a lot of good reform legislation, *but* why was it fought so hard, especially in the Senate? Why was it finally cast by many as a liberal-conservative issue? Surely, it shouldn't be, for both well-meaning liberals and conservatives should be interested in restoring the confidence of the people in their government.

We could go on, perhaps, but the biggest of these "yes-but" questions should be directed toward the voters, not the Legislature: *Yes*, the voters did once rise up and throw the rascals out, *but* will they keep paying attention long enough to determine how many other rascals slipped in, and will they hold the new rascals as accountable as they did the old? The answer to this question will, of course, determine the course of future legislatures. If the voters answer affirmatively, then some of the other questions above will be dealt with by future legislatures, and the laws passed by this session will be strenghthened. If they say "no," then those future sessions may well remove some more teeth from this one's reform dentures. (See Appendix C for a look at what the author thinks to be important votes on reform bills during the 63rd Legislature.)

This is not meant to be a section on political predictions, for the agents of political change and the whims of the voter make prognostication a hazardous venture. It is, instead, meant to be a glimpse at some of those agents of political change and the personalities likely to be affected by them in the forseeable future.

In 1972, the change occurred could be attributed to three main agents: the Sharpstown Scandal, single-member legislative districts, and the Democratic Party's new reform rules. The big one, Sharpstown, will not be around anymore, at least not to the extent that it affected the 1972 election. Corruption in government may still be an issue because of the still-unfolding Watergate Scandal on the national level, but that's far and distant and not likely to become an issue in Texas political races.

Single-member legislative districts will be on the scene from now on, and their important consequences in Houston, Dallas, and Bexar counties have been duly noted. At this writing it appears that they may come slowly, if at all, for the rest of the state's metropolitan areas, because the 63rd Legislature failed to carve them out, and a United States Supreme Court decision has temporarily taken some of the heat off.

The third agent of change had very little effect on the average Texan unless he happened to attend a Democratic precinct convention. If he did, he probably saw more democracy in the Democratic Party than anyone had ever seen before. In fact, it was almost more democracy than the Democratic Party could stand. The rules made for interminable conventions, they were cussed by Democrats both before and after the McGovern Disaster, and they were ridiculed by the unbelieving Republicans. Yet that Texas delegation to the Democratic National Convention probably more accurately represented the wishes of rank and file Texas Democrats than any other similar group in years.

It was a traumatic experience for the old-time party leaders, and great numbers of them lost their accustomed places. They may not get them back, either, for the two factions who gained the most from the new rules, the McGovernites and the Wallacites, have evidently found victory to their liking. Some bugs will, no doubt, have to be worked out of the rules, but that battleground will be far removed from Texas. Whatever happens there will be of great import to Texas Democrats, and their attention will surely be on the battle. The average Texan, though, probably will care little about it.

While we're on the subject of political parties, a mention of the Republicans is in order. One might think that they'd be at last on the verge of making Texas into a true two-party state after all the good things that happened to them in 1972. After all, Nixon thoroughly stomped McGovern all over Texas. Senator Tower was re-elected over a formidable Democratic challenger, and former Governor John B. Connally led an illustrious group of Texans into Nixon's camp. But the Texas Republicans, with their usual flair, seem at this point to have blown it again. Nixon's win, it appears, was as much due to anti-McGovern feelings as it was to pro-Nixon thinking. Tower won, but it was more a personal victory and a coat-tail ride than it was an outburst of Republicanism. And by Mid-1973, those coat-tails had turned into sand bags as Nixon sank deeper into the Watergate mess.

On May 2, 1973, Connally formalized all his work for Nixon by publicly switching to the Republican Party. That wave of Texans that was supposed to follow him over to the other side failed to materialize, though. Not a single current office-holder followed Connally, and when ex-House Speaker Rayford Price made the switch, it was in a little-noticed news conference. Silver-haired John went back to Washington to seek his fame and fortune while helping Nixon out of the Watergate jam, but reports at this time indicate that is not working as Connally had hoped.

Republicans in the Legislature didn't bring the party much credit, either. They had a golden opportunity to gain some more respectability in the voters' eyes by helping bring about some of the Sharpstown-spawned reform legislation, but most of them wound up as enemies of the reform movement. And one, Fred Agnich, even sponsored one of the session's most controversial anti-reform amendments. Most of their gains, in terms of numbers in the 63rd Legislature, was due to the single-member districts, and they'll probably keep those gains. Their collective track record in this session, though, did little to win them new friends and voters.

Going from agents of change to personalities, one finds that two of the names that figured most prominently in Texas politics in 1972, Barnes and Farenthold, are hardly mentioned any more, at least as potential statewide candidates.

Ben Barnes went off to Brownwood after his term expired, and he's been applying his trememdous energy to the business ventures of Herman Bennett. He's kept an extremely low (non-existent) political profile there, and if he's not enjoying Brownwood, he's not telling many people about it.

Sissy Farenthold has remained in politics, but her directions are toward Washington and away from Texas. She campaigned actively for the McGovern-Shriver ticket in the fall of 1972, and the following February she was elected Chairwoman of the National Women's Political Caucus. Her friends will probably be after her to run for governor again in 1974, and though she still thinks Briscoe is a bowl of pablum, her work for McGovern and her time spent away from Texas would certainly make it a difficult race. That's assuming Briscoe runs, of course, an assumption just about everyone is making at this time.

The man from Uvalde has remained almost as puzzling as he was during his race. He provided little in the way of leadership to the Legislature. He did make them live up to his "no-new-taxes" promise but it took a federal revenue-sharing windfall and a two-year delay of any meaningful solution to the school financing problem to bring it off. Still, it was brought off, and for that, prayers of thanks and disbelief are probably still winging skyward from the voters. The absence of major mistakes, the strong two-term tradition, and his own campaign financing capabilities all would make it very difficult to mount a serious challenge against him in 1974.

Lieutenant-Governor Bill Hobby came away from the legislative session marked as a heavy because of the reaction to reform from the senators he presided over. He got a tremendous amount of bad press during the session, and more than one person on both ends of the political spectrum came away wondering about his actions. All those reform bills did slip through on the last night, though, and it would be difficult to use reform as a campaign issue against him. His own financial capabilities, too, would help him in any serious political fight in 1974.

Speaker Daniel is the one most often mentioned as a potential challenger of Hobby. Their session-long feud continued after the session, and has led to much speculation that Price, Jr., might try to defeat Hobby instead of retiring to his law practice in Liberty. Daniel's one-term pledge has left him in a move-up-or-out position, but there's nowhere to move without a hard fight. Those hard fights cost money, and Daniel almost certainly would not be able to match Hobby in the campaign spending race.

The only other name accounting for much political talk in Austin is Attorney-General John Hill. He, you'll remember, has already tried for governor once, and talking about running for it again is his favorite pastime, according to his friends. His actions so far in the consumer protection and pollution control areas have not been too far away from his campaign promises, but he, like Daniel, would be at a campaign money disadvantage in a death struggle with Briscoe in 1974.

As Gus Mutscher might say, a lot of things can happen. There's almost a year to go before the primaries, and most of the principals mentioned above will be involved in a historic constitutional convention beginning in January, 1974. Thus it's probably best to leave this discussion with that reminder from Chapter One that the only thing constant about politics is change itself.

NOTES AND APPENDICES

Appendix A
Election Returns for the
1972 Governor's Race

This appendix gives the final election results in the governor's race in each of the nine geographic regions of Texas. These nine regions are: the Gulf Coast, Southwest Texas, South Texas, the German Hill Country, East Texas, North Texas, the Panhandle, Central Texas and West Texas. Any attempt to split Texas up in this manner will almost certainly create some difference of opinion over which counties to use as the boundary lines. The author's choices are shown in the map on page 219; the counties in each region are listed below. (Persons interested in regionalism in Texas politics should read D.W. Meinig's delightful book, *Imperial Texas*, a cultural essay on Texas geography.)

1. the Gulf Coast counties—Orange, Hardin, Jefferson, Liberty, Chambers, Harris, Galveston, Fort Bend, Brazoria, Wharton, Matagorda, Jackson, Victoria, Calhoun, Refugio, Aransas, San Patricio, Nueces

2. the Southwest Texas counties—El Paso, Hudspeth, Culbertson, Reeves, Jeff Davis, Presidio, Brewster, Pecos, Terrell, Crockett, Val Verde, Schleicher, Sutton, Edwards, Kimble, Real, Bandera

3. the South Texas counties—Bexar, Medina, Uvalde, Kinney, Maverick, Zavala, Frio, Atascosa, Dimmit, LaSalle, McMullen, Live Oak, Webb, Duval, Jim Wells, Kleberg, Zapata, Jim Hogg, Brooks, Kenedy, Starr, Hidalgo, Willacy, Cameron

4. the German Hill Country counties—Mason, Gillespie, Kerr, Kendall, Comal, Guadalupe

5. the East Texas counties—Lamar, Red River, Bowie, Delta, Hopkins, Franklin, Titus, Camp, Morris, Cass, Rains, Wood, Upshur, Marion, Van Zandt, Smith, Gregg, Harrison, Henderson, Rusk, Panola, Anderson, Cherokee, Shelby, Nacogdoches, Leon, Houston, Angelina, San Augustine, Sabine, Madison, Trinity, Polk, Tyler, Jasper, Newton, Grimes, Walker, San Jacinto, Montgomery

6. the North Texas counties—Cooke, Grayson, Fannin, Denton, Collin, Hunt, Tarrant, Dallas, Rockwall, Kaufman

7. the Panhandle counties—Dallam, Sherman, Hansford, Ochiltree, Lipscomb, Hartley, Moore, Hutchinson, Roberts, Hemphill, Oldham, Potter, Carson, Gray, Wheeler, Deaf Smith, Randall, Armstrong, Donley, Collingsworth

8. the Central Texas counties—Johnson, Ellis, Somervell, Bosque, Hill, Navarro, Coryell, McLennan, Limestone, Freestone, Bell, Falls, Robertson, Burnet, Williamson, Milam, Brazos, Blanco, Travis, Lee, Burleson, Washington, Hays, Bastrop, Fayette, Austin, Waller, Caldwell, Gonzales, Lavaca, Colorado, Wilson, Karnes, DeWitt, Goliad, Bee

9. the West Texas counties—Parmer, Castro, Swisher, Briscoe, Hall, Childress, Bailey, Lamb, Hale, Floyd, Motley, Cottle, Hardeman, Foard, Wilbarger, Wichita, Clay, Montague, Archer, Baylor, Knox, King, Dickens, Crosby, Lubbock, Hockley, Cochran, Yoakum, Terry, Lynn, Garza, Kent, Stonewall, Haskell, Throckmorton, Young, Jack Wise, Gaines, Dawson, Borden, Scurry, Fisher, Jones, Shackelford, Stephens, Palo Pinto, Parker, Hood, Erath, Eastland, Callahan, Taylor, Nolan, Mitchell, Howard, Martin, Andrews, Loving, Winkler, Ector, Midland, Glasscock, Sterling Coke, Runnels, Coleman, Brown, Comanche, Hamilton, Mills, Lampasas, San Saba, Llano, McCulloch, Concho, Tom Green, Menard, Irion, Reagan, Upton, Crane, Ward

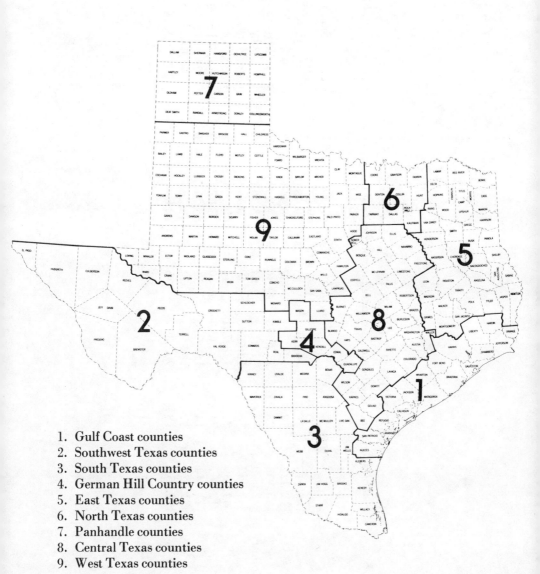

1. Gulf Coast counties
2. Southwest Texas counties
3. South Texas counties
4. German Hill Country counties
5. East Texas counties
6. North Texas counties
7. Panhandle counties
8. Central Texas counties
9. West Texas counties

FIRST PRIMARY RESULTS—MAY 6, 1972
(votes for minor candidates eliminated for purposes of this table)

Area	Barnes		Briscoe		Farenthold		Smith	
	votes	percent	votes	percent	votes	percent	votes	percent
Gulf Coast	85,215	16%	190,724	35%	230,054	42%	36,135	7%
Southwest Texas	12,322	18	25,701	37	20,964	31	9,593	14
South Texas	55,463	23	112,575	46	61,850	25	13,610	6
German Hill Country	2,540	13	12,719	64	3,265	17	1,233	6
East Texas	47,052	18	126,302	48	50,141	19	38,218	15
North Texas	84,730	24	148,781	41	105,198	29	20,052	6
Panhandle	12,167	24	25,634	50	7,074	14	5,981	12
Central Texas	41,844	14	156,716	51	85,241	28	24,071	7
West Texas	51,023	17	164,245	54	48,264	16	41,816	13
Totals	392,356	18%	963,397	45%	612,051	28%	190,709	9%

GENERAL ELECTION RESULTS—NOVEMBER 7, 1972

Area	Briscoe		Grover		Muniz	
	votes	percent	votes	percent	votes	percent
Gulf Coast	420,388	47%	450,995	49%	39,545	4%
Southwest Texas	50,520	48	39,429	37	16,775	15
South Texas	185,786	49	123,129	33	69,818	18
German Hill Country	18,643	52	15,889	44	1,738	4
East Texas	172,469	57	123,620	42	1,657	1
North Texas	307,832	41	411,222	55	32,752	4
Panhandle	39,548	41	56,136	58	1,429	1
Central Texas	212,518	55	137,214	36	35,480	9
West Texas	225,789	54	176,361	43	14,924	3
Totals	1,633,493	49%	1,533,986	45%	214,118	6%

RUNOFF PRIMARY RESULTS—JUNE 3, 1972

Area	Briscoe		Farenthold	
	votes	percent	votes	percent
Gulf Coast	223,432	42%	305,923	58%
Southwest Texas	30,724	47	33,982	53
South Texas	144,628	57	110,740	43
German Hill Country	11,302	71	4,564	29
East Texas	141,599	64	81,091	36
North Texas	185,897	56	148,899	44
Panhandle	25,070	59	14,260	41
Central Texas	170,525	61	110,775	39
West Texas	161,991	69	74,360	31
Totals	1,095,168	55%	884,594	45%

Appendix B
The Dirty Thirty's Reform
Voting Analysis of the 62nd Legislature

This appendix consists of the Dirty Thirty's Reform Voting Analysis of the Sixty-second Legislature. The nineteen votes they considered the most important are listed first, followed by the voting records of the individual representative:

1. Motion to table Representative Neil Caldwell's motion to instruct Committee on House Administration to report House Simple Resolution 89 (Ethics) within 7 days. (Feb. 16, 1971)
    Vote: 110 to 35, 4 not voting.

2. Representative Frances Farenthold moved, as a matter of privilege, to take up and consider House Concurrent Resolution 87 (Ethics). The speaker did not recognize Farenthold on the motion stating that the resolution was not privileged. This vote is against sustaining the chair's ruling. (March 15, 1971)
    Vote: 118 to 30, 2 not voting.

3. House Simple Resolution 89: Motion to table Representative Tom Bass's amendment to require the speaker to appoint members of the General Investigating Committee within 10 days. (March 29, 1971)
    Vote: 110-35, 4 not voting.

4. House Simple Resolution 89. Motion to table Representative Tom Bass's amendment to instruct General Investigating Committee to investigate passage of House Bill 72 and House Bill 73, Banking Bills passed during the called session in 1969. (March 29, 1971)
    Vote: 108 to 35, 6 not voting.

5. House Simple Resolution 89: Motion to table Representative Edmund Jones's amendment requiring the General Investigating Committee to investigate the Sharpstown Bank incident. (March 29, 1971)
    Vote: 110 to 28, 11 not voting.

6. House Simple Resolution 89: Motion to table Representative Will Lee's amendment requiring members or employees of the Texas Legislature who purchased stock in National Bankers Life to testify before the General Investigating Committee. (March 29, 1971)
    Vote: 111 to 30, 8 not voting.

7. House Simple Resolution 9: Adoption of Representative Jim Nugent's substitute for Representative John Hannah's amendment limiting House conference committees. The Nugent substitute lessened the restrictions placed upon conference committees from those provided in the Hannah version. (Jan. 20, 1971)
    Vote: 102 to 38, 9 not voting.

8. House Simple Resolution 9: Motion to table Representative Jim

Earthman's amendment requiring financial disclosure by all members of the House to be filed annually and to be public record. (Jan. 20, 1971)

Vote: 118 to 24, 7 not voting.

9. House Simple Resolution 9: Motion to table Representative John Bigham's amendment to institute limited seniority of House members on committees. (January 20, 1971)

Vote: 115 to 28, 6 not voting.

10. House Simple Resolution 9: Motion to table Representative Farenthold's amendment to allow witnesses before committees of the House to be taped and to allow for distribution of such testimony in written form to any member of the House or Senate. (January 20, 1971)

Vote: 119 to 26, 4 not voting.

11. House Simple Resolution 9: Adoption of the permanent Rules of the House of Representatives. (Jan. 20, 1971)

Vote: 125 to 15.

12. House Joint Resolution 18: Motion to table Representative Tom Moore, Jr.'s amendment providing commission to set up procedures for requiring all elected and appointed state officials to fully disclose all their financial holdings and sources of income to the Secretary of State. (Feb. 1, 1971)

Vote: 83 to 59, 7 not voting.

13. Final Passage of House Bill 783, House Redistricting. (May 29, 1971)

Vote: 88 to 51, 12 not voting.

14. Senate Bill 11, Appropriations: Motion to table Representative Tom Bass's amendment not to allow expending of funds on any defense of redistricting except for single member districts. (April 22, 1971)

Vote: 101 to 37, 11 not voting.

15. Senate Bill 11, Appropriations: Motion to table Representative Carlos Truan's amendment to cut appropriations to the L.B.J. State Park from one million dollars to the amount requested by Parks and Wildlife Department, one hundred thousand dollars. (April 22, 1971)

Vote: 93 to 48, 8 not voting.

16. Final Passage of Senate Bill 11, Appropriations. (April 22, 1971)

Vote: 113 to 24, 13 not voting.

17. Motion to table Representative Farenthold's motion to instruct House Conferees on Appropriations Bill to: (1) Any item included in both reports must be included in conference report; (2) If amount of item in both bills is identical, the amount cannot be changed in final report; (3) If amounts vary, the amount of the item in the final report can be no larger or no smaller than amounts in the two versions; (4) If an item is in one version of the bill, it may be

included at the discretion of the committee but the amount may not be larger than that in the version containing the item; (5) If an item is in neither House or Senate bill it cannot be included in the conference report unless approved by both Houses; (6) If the conference committee wants to take action in violation of the above instructions it must be approved by the House specifying: (a) exact nature of matters to be considered, (b) specific limitations being suspended, (c) specific action contemplated, and (d) reason why suspension is being requested. (May 10, 1971)

Vote: 100 to 38, 11 not voting.

18. Adoption of the Conference Committee Report on Senate Bill 11, Appropriations. (May 31, 1971)
    Vote: 104 to 43, 3 not voting.

19. Also considered, those members who filed financial disclosure statements. (Record available in the office of the Secretary of State.)

VOTING RECORDS OF INDIVIDUAL MEMBERS

RV = Reform Vote
NRV = Non-Reform Vote
NV = Not Voting

	RV	NRV	NV
Bill Blythe, Houston	19	0	0
Frances Farenthold, Corpus Christi	19	0	0
Edmund Jones, Houston	19	0	0
R.C. "Nick" Nichols, Houston	19	0	0
Rex Braun, Houston	18	0	1
Jim Earthman, Houston	18	0	1
Dick Reed, Dallas	18	0	1
Dave Allred, Wichita Falls	18	1	0
Walter Mengden, Jr., Houston	18	1	0
Tom Moore, Jr., Waco	18	1	0
John Bigham, Temple	17	0	2
Ed Harris, Galveston	17	1	1
Paul Moreno, El Paso	17	1	1
Lindsey Rodriguez, Hidalgo	17	1	1
A.S. "Sid" Bowers, Houston	17	2	0
Lane Denton, Waco	17	2	0
Carlos Truan, Corpus Christi	17	2	0
Maurice Angly, Jr., Austin	16	2	1
Fred Head, Henderson	16	3	0
Zan Holmes, Jr., Dallas	15	1	3
Neil Caldwell, Alvin	15	2	2
Bill Bass, Ben Wheeler	15	4	0
Charles Patterson, Taylor	14	3	2
Tom Bass, Houston	14	5	0
Ben Grant, Marshall	14	5	0
Will Lee, Houston	14	5	0

	RV	NRV	NV
Fred Agnich, Dallas	13	6	0
Tom Craddick, Midland	13	6	0
Curtis Graves, Houston	12	2	5
John Hannah, Lufkin	12	2	5
Price Daniel, Jr., Liberty	12	6	1
Dan Kubiak, Rockdale	12	7	0
R.L. "Bob" Vale, San Antonio	11	8	0
Robert Gammage, Houston	10	9	0
Vernon Beckham, Denison	8	11	0
Jack Hawkins, Groesbeck	8	11	0
Ed Howard, Texarkana	8	11	0
Joe Allen, Baytown	7	8	4
Bill Finck, San Antonio	7	12	0
Tom Christian, Claude	5	12	1
Johnny Nelms, Houston	5	13	1
A.L. "Tony" Dramberger, San Antonio	4	15	0
Jim Clark, Houston	4	15	0
Guy Floyd, San Antonio	4	15	0
Rayford Price, Palestine	4	15	0
Joe Salem, Corpus Christi	4	15	0
Vernon Stewart, Wichita Falls	3	14	2
A.C. Atwood, Edinburg	3	16	0
Lauro Cruz, Houston	3	16	0
Bob Hendricks, McKinney	3	16	0
Bryan Poff, Jr., Amarillo	3	16	0
Leroy Wieting, Portland	3	16	0
Nelson Wolff, San Antonio	3	16	0
W.C. "Bud" Sherman, Fort Worth	2	14	3
Joe Hanna, Breckinridge	2	15	2
James Stroud, Dallas	2	15	2
John Allen, Longview	2	17	0
Frank Calhoun, Abilene	2	17	0
Sam Coats, Dallas	2	17	0
James Cole, Greenville	2	17	0
Harold Davis, Austin	2	17	0
Jake Johnson, San Antonio	2	17	0
James Kaster, El Paso	2	17	0
Wayland Simmons, San Antonio	2	17	0
Lindon Williams, Houston	2	17	0
Will Smith, Beaumont	1	12	6
Honore Ligarde, Laredo	1	13	5
Fred Orr, DeSoto	1	15	3
John Traeger, Seguin	1	15	3
Dave Finney, Ft. Worth	1	16	2
Grant Jones, Abilene	1	16	2
Gibson Lewis, Ft. Worth	1	16	2
L. DeWitt Hale, Corpus Christi	1	17	1
Carl Parker, Port Arthur	1	17	1

	RV	NRV	NV
Henry Sanchez, Jr., Brownsville	1	17	1
Ben Atwell, Dallas	1	18	0
George Baker, Fort Stockton	1	18	0
Phil Cates, Pampa	1	18	0
Bill Clayton, Springlake	1	18	0
Terry Doyle, Port Arthur	1	18	0
Wilson Foreman, Austin	1	18	0
Clyde Haynes, Jr., Vidor	1	18	0
Rufus Kilpatrick, Beaumont	1	18	0
James Lovell, Crockett	1	18	0
Franklin Ace Pickens, Odessa	1	18	0
Renal Rosson, Snyder	1	18	0
Bob Salter, Gatesville	1	18	0
H. Tati Santiesteban, El Paso	1	18	0
Chris Semos, Dallas	1	18	0
Paul Silber, San Antonio	1	18	0
D.R. "Tom" Uher, Bay City	1	18	0
J.E. Ward, Glen Rose	1	18	0
Tom Niland, El Paso	1	18	0
Dean Cobb, Dumas	0	13	6
Neal Solomon, Mount Vernon	0	14	5
Oscar Carillo, Benavides	0	15	4
Gayle Ingram, Quitman	0	15	4
Tommy Shannon, Fort Worth	0	15	4
Griffith Moore, Dallas	0	16	3
Ralph Wayne, Plainview	0	11	8
Jack Blanton, Carrollton	0	18	1
Ben Bynum, Amarillo	0	18	1
Dee Jon Davis, Big Spring	0	18	1
Forrest Harding, San Angelo	0	18	1
W.S. "Bill" Heatly, Jr., Paducah	0	18	1
Cordell Hull, Fort Worth	0	18	1
Dick McKissack, Dallas	0	18	1
Menton Murray, Jr., Harlingen	0	18	1
Richard Slack, Pecos	0	18	1
Billy Williamson, Tyler	0	18	1
Joe Wyatt, Bloomington	0	18	1
Dean Neugent, Dickinson	0	16	3
Don Adams, Jasper	0	19	0
John Boyle, Jr., Irving	0	19	0
Bill Braecklein, Dallas	0	19	0
Steve Burgess, Nacogdoches	0	19	0
Don Cavness, Austin	0	19	0
Hilary Doran, Jr., Del Rio	0	19	0
Charles Finnell, Holliday	0	19	0
J.A. Garcia, Jr., Raymondville	0	19	0
Joe Golman, Dallas	0	19	0
Joe Hawn, Dallas	0	19	0

	RV	NRV	NV
Bill Hilliard, Fort Worth	0	19	0
Tom Holmes, Granbury	0	19	0
Joe Hubenak, Rosenberg	0	19	0
Delwin Jones, Lubbock	0	19	0
Charles Jungmichel, LaGrange	0	19	0
Lou Kost, Jr., San Antonio	0	19	0
Ray Lemmon, Houston	0	19	0
Frank Lombardino, San Antonio	0	19	0
Raul Longoria, Edinburg	0	19	0
R.B. McAlister, Lubbock	0	19	0
Mike Moncrief, Fort Worth	0	19	0
Aubry Moore, Hillsboro	0	19	0
Jon P. Newton, Beeville	0	19	0
John Poerner, Hondo	0	19	0
Bill Presnal, Bryan	0	19	0
Gerhardt Schulle, Jr., San Marcos	0	19	0
E.L. Short, Tahoka	0	19	0
James Slider, Naples	0	19	0
Bill Swanson, Houston	0	19	0
Elmer Tarbox, Lubbock	0	19	0
Charles Tupper, Jr., El Paso	0	19	0
Tim Von Dohlen, Goliad	0	19	0
Joe Spurlock II, Fort Worth	0	19	0
Lynn Nabers, Brownwood	0	19	0

Appendix C
Reform Voting Analysis
of the 63rd Legislature

This appendix will show the voting record of all members of the Sixty-third Legislature on what the author considers to be the most important reform votes of the session. Fourteen roll call votes have been selected for this reform voting analysis, eight from the House of Representatives, and six from the Senate. A list of these votes follows, along with an explanation of their significance. The author's opinion about what is a "reform" vote and a "non-reform" vote is also stated; (a "reform" vote is one *for* meaningful reform of Texas government; a "non-reform" vote is one *against* meaningful reform of Texas government).

ROLL CALL VOTES IN THE
HOUSE OF REPRESENTATIVES:

1. This is the now-famous amendment offered by Representative Fred Agnich to House Bill 1, the ethics bill. The Agnich amendment, as it became known editorially, allowed the financial statements called for under the bill to be filed in sealed envelopes. Thus, they would not be available for public inspection. The Ethics Commission could not open those envelopes unless it found probable cause to do so, either in response to a complaint or from its own investigation. The amendment carried by one vote, seventy-one to seventy, with the Speaker voting against it. A "no" vote is a "reform" vote; a "yes" vote is a "non-reform" vote. (March 8, 1973)

2. This vote was on an amendment attempting to undo the damage done to House Bill 1 by the Agnich amendment. It was offered by Representatives Gene Jones, Fred Head, and Carlos Truan on the day after the Agnich amendment was adopted. It would have made the financial statements public records open to public examination. Since this amendment was offered when the bill was up for final passage, it required a two/thirds rather than a simple majority to pass. Thus, the seventy-five to fifty-three vote in its favor was not enough to win passage. A "yes" vote is a "reform" vote; a "no" vote is a "non-reform" vote. (March 9, 1973)

3. This vote came on a motion to table an amendment to House Bill 2, the lobby control bill, by Representative Wayne Peveto. The amendment would have killed the Ethics Commission and given its duties to the Secretary of State's office. The motion to table carried by ninety-six to forty-seven. A "yes" vote is a "reform" vote; a "no" vote is a "non-reform" vote. (February 7, 1973)

4. This vote was on Representative L. De Witt Hale's attempt to

amend House Bill 2, the lobby control bill. The amendment would allowed anyone to spend any amount of money in lobbying his own representative or senator, or the governor or lieutenant-governor without having to register as a lobbyist or make reports of lobbying expenditures. The amendment lost on a seventy-two to seventy-two tie vote, with the Speaker casting the tie-making vote. A "no" vote is a "reform" vote; a "yes" vote is a "non-reform" vote. (February 7, 1973)

5. This vote was on a motion to table Representative Terry Doyle's amendment to House Bill 2. The amendment would have removed a requirement that anyone spending over $150 per quarter on lobbying activities should register as a lobbyist. The motion to table prevailed by an eighty-three to fifty-five vote. A "yes" vote is a "reform" vote; a "no" vote is a "non-reform" vote. (February 7, 1973)

6. This vote, one of the most publicized of the session, was on a motion to reject the changes the Senate had made in House Bill 2, the lobby bill, and send the measure to a conference committee. The Senate action had weakened the bill considerably, and there was a lot of pressure on the representatives from lobbyists who wanted them to go along with the changes. The motion passed by a one hundred-six to thirty-seven vote. A "yes" vote is a "reform" vote; a "no" vote is a "non-reform" vote. (May 24, 1973)

7. This vote was on the adoption of Representative D.R. "Tom" Uher's amendment to House Bill 3, the open meetings bill. The amendment exempted meetings of governmental bodies for personnel matters from all provisions of the bill. Thus, the notice for such meetings would not even have to be posted. It was adopted by a seventy-eight to sixty-seven vote. A "no" vote is a "reform" vote; a "yes" vote is a "non-reform vote. (January 29, 1973)

8. This vote was on a motion to table Representative Hilary Doran, Jr.'s amendment to House Bill 8, the speaker's race financial reporting bill. The bill as written allowed an individual to spend up to $25 on behalf of a speaker candidate without having to report it. Doran's amendment would have removed that $25 figure, thus allowing any amount of unreported spending by the friends and supporters of the various speaker candidates. This amendment would have seriously weakened the bill. It was tabled by a seventy-five to sixty-six vote. A "yes" vote is a "reform" vote; a "no" vote is a "non-reform" vote. (February 21, 1973)

INDIVIDUAL VOTING RECORDS

R = Reform Vote
N = Non-Reform Vote
P = Present, Not Voting
A = Absent

Member	#1	2	3	4	5	6	7	8	Total		
Adams, Herman, Jr.; Silsbee	R	R	N	N	N	R	N	R	4R	4N	
Agnich, Fred; Dallas	N	N	N	N	N	N	N	N		8N	
Allen, Joe; Baytown	R	R	R	R	R	R	R	R	8R		
Allen, John; Longview	R	R	R	N	N	R	R	R	6R	2N	
Allred, Dave; Wichita Falls	R	R	R	R	R	R	N	R	7R	1N	
Atwell, Ben; Dallas	N	A	N	N	A	R	N	N	1R	5N	2A
Bailey, Kay; Houston	N	N	N	N	R	R	N	N	2R	6N	
Baker, Andrew; Galveston	R	R	R	R	R	R	R	R	8R		
Bales, Larry; Austin	R	R	R	R	R	R	R	R	8R		
Barnhart, Ray; Pasadena	N	N	N	R	A	R	N	N	2R	5N	1A
Bigham, John; Temple	R	R	R	R	R	R	R	R	8R		
Bird, Ronald; San Antonio	R	R	R	R	R	R	R	R	8R		
Blake, Roy; Nacogdoches	N	N	R	R	R	R	N	A	4R	3N	1A
Blythe, Bill; Houston	R	R	R	R	R	R	N	R	7R	1N	
Bock, Bennie II; New Braunfels	N	N	N	N	N	R	N	N	1R	7N	
Boone, Latham III; Navasota	N	N	N	N	R	N	N	N	3R	5N	
Bowers, A.S. "Sid"; Houston	N	N	N	N	N	R	N	N	1R	7N	
Bynum, Ben; Amarillo	N	R	R	R	R	R	R	R	7R	1N	
Caldwell, Neil; Alvin	R	R	R	R	R	R	R	R	8R		
Calhoun, Frank; Abilene	N	N	N	N	N	N	N	N		8N	
Canales, Terry; Premont	N	R	A	A	A	N	N	A	1R	3N	4A
Cates, Phil; Pampa	R	R	R	N	R	R	N	N	5R	3N	
Cavness, Don; Austin	N	N	N	N	N	N	N	N		8N	
Clark, Jim; Houston	R	R	R	R	R	R	R	R	8R		
Clayton, Bill; Springlake	N	N	N	N	R	N	N	N	1R	7N	
Cobb, Dean; Dumas	N	N	N	N	N	N	N	N		8N	
Cole, James; Greenville	R	R	N	N	R	N	R	N	5R	3N	
Coleman, Ronald; El Paso	R	R	R	R	R	R	R	R	8R		
Coody, W.G.; Weatherford	R	R	R	R	R	R	R	N	7R	1N	
Cooke, C.C. III; Cleburne	R	R	R	R	R	R	R	N	7R	1N	
Craddick, Tom; Midland	N	N	N	N	N	R	N	N	1R	7N	
Daniel, Price, Jr.; Liberty	R	P	R	R	P	P	R	P	4R		4P
Davis, Robert; Irving	N	N	R	N	R	N	N	N	2R	6N	
Denson, Woody; Houston	R	R	R	R	R	A	R	R	7R		1A
Denton, Lane; Waco	R	R	R	R	A	R	N	R	6R	1N	1A
Donaldson, Jerry; Gatesville	N	N	N	N	N	N	N	N		8N	
Doran, Hilary Jr.; Del Rio	A	A	N	N	N	N	N	N		6N	2A
Doyle, Terry; Port Arthur	R	N	A	N	N	N	R	R	3R	4N	1A
Dramberger, A.L. "Tony"; San Antonio	N	N	A	N	A	N	N	N		6N	2A
Edwards, J.C. III; Conroe	R	R	R	R	R	A	R	R	7R		1A
Evans, Charles; Hurst	N	N	R	R	R	N	R	N	4R	4N	
Finnell, Charles; Holliday	R	R	N	N	N	R	N	N	3R	5N	

	#1	2	3	4	5	6	7	8	Total
Finney, Dave; Fort Worth	N	A	R	R	A	R	R	R	5R 1N 2A
Foreman, Wilson; Austin	R	R	R	R	R	N	R	N	6R 2N
Fox, Milton E.; Houston	N	N	N	N	N	R	N	N	1R 7N
Garcia, Matt; San Antonio	R	R	R	R	R	R	R	R	8R
Gaston, Frank; Dallas	N	N	N	N	N	N	N	N	8N
Geiger, Richard S.; Dallas	N	A	N	N	N	R	N	N	1R 6N 1A
Grant, Ben Z.; Marshall	R	R	R	R	R	N	R	R	7R 1N
Green, Forest; Corsicana	N	R	R	R	R	R	N	N	5R 3N
Green, R.E.; Houston	R	R	R	R	R	R	R	R	8R
Hale, L. DeWitt; Corpus Christi	R	R	R	N	N	N	A	N	3R 4N 1A
Hall, Anthony; Houston	R	R	R	R	R	R	R	R	8R
Hall, W.M. Jr.; Laredo	R	R	R	N	R	R	R	R	7R 1N
Hanna, Joe C.; Breckinridge	N	N	N	N	N	R	N	N	1R 7N
Harris, Ed; Galveston	N	N	R	R	R	R	R	R	6R 2N
Hawn, Joe; Dallas	N	N	N	N	N	R	A	N	1R 6N 1A
Head, Fred; Troup	R	R	R	R	R	R	R	R	8R
Heatly, W.S. Jr.; Paducah	N	A	A	A	A	R	N	N	1R 3N 4A
Henderson, Don; Houston	N	A	N	N	N	R	N	N	1R 6N 1A
Hendricks, Bob; McKinney	N	N	R	R	R	R	N	R	5R 3N
Hernandez, Joe; San Antonio	A	A	R	R	R	R	R	R	6R 2A
Hilliard, Bill; Fort Worth	N	N	R	N	N	N	R	N	3R 5N
Hoestenbach, John; Odessa	N	N	R	R	R	R	R	R	5R 3N
Hollowell, Bill; Grand Saline	R	R	R	R	R	R	R	R	8R
Howard, Ed; Texarkana	N	N	N	N	N	R	N	N	1R 7N
Hubenak, Joe; Rosenberg	R	R	R	N	N	R	N	N	4R 4N
Hudson, Sam III; Dallas	R	R	R	R	R	R	R	R	8R
Hutchison, Ray; Dallas	N	N	N	N	N	N	N	N	8N
Johnson, Ms. Eddie B.; Dallas	R	R	R	R	R	R	R	R	8R
Jones, Gene; Houston	R	R	R	R	R	R	R	R	8R
Jones, Luther; El Paso	R	R	R	R	R	R	R	R	8R
Kaster, James; El Paso	N	R	R	R	R	N	N	R	5R 3N
Korioth, A.J.; Farmers Branch	N	N	N	N	N	N	N	N	8N
Kubiak, Dan; Rockdale	R	R	R	R	R	R	R	R	8R
Laney, James; Hale Center	N	N	N	N	N	N	N	N	8N
Lary, Camm Jr.; Burnet	R	R	R	R	R	N	R	R	7R 1N
Lee, Doyce; Naples	N	N	N	N	R	N	N	N	1R 7N
Leland, Mickey; Houston	A	A	R	R	R	R	R	R	6R 2A
Lewis, Gibson; Fort Worth	N	R	R	R	R	R	R	N	6R 2N
Lombardino, Frank; San Antonio	R	R	R	R	N	N	R	R	6R 2N
McAlister, R.B.; Lubbock	R	N	R	R	R	R	R	N	6R 2N
McDonald, Felix; Edinburg	N	A	N	N	N	R	N	N	1R 6N 1A
McDonald, T.H. Sr.; Mesquite	N	N	N	N	R	N	A	R	2R 5N 1A
Madla, Frank; San Antonio	R	R	R	R	R	R	R	R	8R
Maloney, Robert; Dallas	R	N	N	N	N	N	N	N	1R 7N
Martin, Elmer; Colorado City	N	N	R	A	N	R	N	N	2R 5N 1A
Massey, Tom; San Angelo	N	N	N	N	N	R	N	N	1R 7N
Mattox, Jim; Dallas	R	R	R	R	R	R	R	R	8R
Menefee, Hawkins; Houston	R	R	R	R	R	R	R	R	8R

	#1	2	3	4	5	6	7	8	Total		
Miller, Ms. Chris; Fort Worth	A	A	R	R	R	R	R	R	6R		2A
Montoya, Greg; Elsa	R	R	R	R	R	N	R	R	7R	1N	
Munson, Ben; Denison	N	N	N	R	R	R	N	N	3R	5N	
Murray, Menton Jr.; Harlingen	N	A	R	N	N	R	N	A	2R	4N	2A
Nabers, Lynn; Brownwood	N	N	R	N	N	N	N	N	1R	7N	
Newton, Jon; Beeville	N	N	R	N	N	R	N	N	3R	5N	
Nichols, R.C.; Houston	R	R	R	R	R	R	R	R	8R		
Nowlin, James; San Antonio	N	R	N	N	N	N	N	N	1R	7N	
Nugent, James; Kerrville	R	R	R	N	N	N	N	N	3R	5N	
Olson, Lyndon Jr.; Waco	N	N	R	R	R	R	N	N	4R	4N	
Parker, Carl; Port Arthur	R	R	R	R	R	R	R	A	7R		1A
Parker, Walt; Denton	N	A	R	N	A	R	R	N	3R	3N	2A
Pentony, Joseph; Houston	R	R	R	R	R	R	R	R	8R		
Peveto, Wayne; Orange	R	A	N	N	N	R	N	N	2R	5N	1A
Poerner, John; Hondo	R	R	R	N	N	A	N	N	3R	4N	1A
Poff, Bryan Jr.; Amarillo	N	R	R	R	R	N	N	N	4R	4N	
Powers, Pike; Beaumont	R	R	N	N	N	R	N	R	4R	4N	
Presnal, Bill; Bryan	N	N	N	N	N	R	N	N	1R	7N	
Preston, George; Paris	R	R	R	R	R	R	R	R	8R		
Ragsdale, Paul; Dallas	R	R	R	R	R	R	R	R	8R		
Reyes, Ben; Houston	R	R	R	R	R	R	R	R	8R		
Reynolds, Richard; Richardson	N	N	N	N	R	N	N	N	1R	7N	
Rodriguez, Lindsey, Hidalgo	N	R	R	R	R	R	R	R	7R	1N	
Rosson, Renal; Snyder	N	N	N	N	N	R	N	N	1R	7N	
Russell, Jerry; Garland	N	A	N	N	N	R	N	N	1R	6N	1A
Sage, Joseph; San Antonio	N	N	R	N	N	R	N	N	2R	6N	
Salem, Joe; Corpus Christi	R	A	R	N	R	N	R	R	5R	2N	1A
Sanchez, Henry; Brownsville	N	N	R	N	R	R	N	R	4R	4N	
Schieffer, Tom; Fort Worth	N	N	R	N	R	R	R	R	5R	3N	
Scoggins, Ralph; El Paso	A	A	A	N	N	N	N	A		4N	4A
Semos, Chris; Dallas	R	R	R	N	R	R	N	R	6R	2N	
Sherman, W.C. "Bud"; Fort Worth	P	R	R	N	R	N	N	R	4R	3N	1P
Short, E.L.; Tahoka	N	N	N	N	N	N	N	N		8N	
Simmons, Wayland, San Antonio	N	N	N	N	N	N	R	N	1R	7N	
Slack, Richard; Pecos	N	A	R	N	A	A	N	N	1R	4N	3A
Spurlock, Joe II; Fort Worth	A	A	A	A	A	R	A	A	1R		7A
Sullivant, Bill; Gainesville	N	N	N	N	R	R	N	R	3R	5N	
Sutton, G.J.; San Antonio	R	R	R	R	R	R	R	R	8R		
Tarbox, Elmer; Lubbock	A	A	R	R	N	A	N	N	2R	3N	3A
Temple, Arthur III; Diboll	R	R	R	R	R	R	R	R	8R		
Thompson, Ms. Senfronia; Houston	R	R	R	R	R	R	A	R	7R		1A
Truan, Carlos; Corpus Christi	R	R	R	R	R	R	R	R	8R		
Tupper, Charles Jr.; El Paso	R	R	A	A	A	R	R	R	5R		3A
Uher, D.R. "Tom"; Bay City	N	N	N	N	N	N	N	N		8N	
Vale, R.L. "Bob"; San Antonio	R	R	R	R	R	R	R	R	8R		
Vecchio, James; Arlington	R	R	R	R	R	R	R	R	8R		
Vick, Larry; Houston	A	A	N	N	N	R	A	R	2R	3N	3A
Von Dohlen, Tim; Goliad	R	N	R	N	N	R	N	R	4R	4N	

	#1	2	3	4	5	6	7	8	Total		
Washington, Craig; Houston	R	R	R	R	R	A	R	A	6R	2A	
Waters, Ron; Houston	R	R	R	R	R	R	R	R	8R		
Watson, Ed; Deer Park	R	R	R	R	R	R	R	R	8R		
Weddington, Ms. Sarah; Austin	R	R	R	A	R	R	N	R	6R	1N	1A
Whitehead, Emmet; Rusk	N	R	R	R	R	A	R	R	6R	1N	1A
Whitmire, John; Houston	N	N	R	N	R	R	R	R	5R	3N	
Wieting, Leroy; Portland	N	R	R	N	R	N	R	N	4R	4N	
Williams, Lindon; Houston	R	R	R	R	R	R	N	R	7R	1N	
Williamson, Billy; Tyler	N	N	N	N	N	N	N	N	8N		
Willis, Doyle; Fort Worth	N	A	R	R	R	N	N	R	5R	2N	1A
Wilson, John; La Grange	N	N	N	N	N	R	N	R	2R	6N	
Wyatt, Joe; Victoria	N	R	N	N	N	N	R	N	2R	6N	

ROLL CALL VOTES IN THE SENATE:

9. This vote was on an amendment offered by Senator Oscar Mauzy to House Bill 2, the lobby control bill. Action taken on the bill while it was in the Senate Jurisprudence Committee weakened it considerably, and Mauzy offered a series of amendments aimed at strengthening the bill when it came up for debate on the Senate floor. The Jurisprudence Committee removed the language creating the State Ethics Commission from the bill, and this amendment would have restored it. It failed by a ten to twenty-one vote. A "yes" vote is a "reform" vote; a "no" vote is a "non-reform" vote. (May 22, 1973)

10. This vote was on another of the amendments to House Bill 2, the lobby control bill, offered by Senator Mauzy on the Senate floor. It would have required lobbyists to report the names of legislators and other officials upon whom they spent more than $50 in a filing period. It was defeated by a fourteen to seventeen vote. A "yes" vote is a "reform" vote; a "no" vote is a "non-reform" vote. (May 22, 1973)

11. This vote was on an amendment offered by Senator Mauzy to House Bill 1, the ethics bill. Like the lobby control bill the ethics bill was weakened by action taken in the Senate Jurisprudence Committee. Senator Mauzy then offered a series of amendments on the floor of the Senate when the bill was debated. This amendment, which lost by a thirteen to sixteen vote, would have added some standards of conduct for public officials. A "yes" vote is a "reform" vote; a "no" vote is a "non-reform" vote. (May 15, 1973)

12. This vote was on another of the amendments Senator Mauzy offered in an attempt to strengthen House Bill 1, the ethics bill. It would require annual financial statements showing amounts and sources of income to be filed by all state and local officeholders. State employees making over $12,000 per year would also have been required to file these statements. The amendment was killed by a ten to twenty-one vote. A "yes" vote is a "reform" vote; a "no" vote is a "non-reform" vote. (May 14, 1973)

13. This vote was on an amendment offered by Senator H.J. "Doc" Blanchard to House Bill 4, the campaign finance reporting bill. His amendment, adopted by a sixteen to fifteen vote on the Senate floor, removed a requirement for all candidates to file campaign finance reports for as long as they have either deficits or surpluses in their campaign funds. His amendment would require only one final report to be filed sixty days after the election. A "no" vote is a "reform" vote; a "yes" vote is a "non-reform" vote. (May 24, 1973)

14. This vote was on the passage of House Bill 5, the conference committee limitations bill. The measure would limit conference committees, groups of legislators appointed to iron out the differences

in bills passed by both houses, to adjusting the differences in such bills. Provisions agreed on by both houses could not be changed, and items not found in either bill could not be added. Some conference committees in the past have been pretty free-wheeling, and have either changed items agreed on by both houses, or indiscriminately added items not voted on by either house. The bill was killed by a ten to twenty-one vote. A "yes" vote is a "reform" vote; a "no" vote is a "non-reform" vote. (March 21, 1973)

INDIVIDUAL VOTING RECORDS
R = Reform Vote
N = Non-Reform Vote
A = Absent

Member	9	10	11	12	13	14	Total	
Adams, Don; Jasper	N	N	R	N	R	R	3R	3N
Aikin, A.M. Jr.; Paris	N	N	N	N	N	N	6N	
Andujar, Ms. Betty; Fort Worth	N	N	N	N	R	R	2R	4N
Blanchard, H.J.; Lubbock	N	N	A	N	N	N	5N	1A
Braecklin, Bill; Dallas	R	R	R	N	R	R	5R	1N
Brooks, Chet; Pasadena	R	R	R	R	N	R	5R	1N
Clower, Ron; Garland	R	R	R	R	R	N	5R	1N
Creighton,Tom; Mineral Wells	N	N	N	N	N	N	6N	
Gammage, Robert; Houston	R	R	A	R	R	R	5R	1A
Harrington, Roy; Port Arthur	R	R	R	R	R	R	6R	
Harris, O.H.; Dallas	N	N	N	N	N	N	6N	
Herring, Charles; Austin	N	N	N	N	N	N	6N	
Hightower, Jack; Vernon	R	R	R	N	N	N	3R	3N
Jones, Grant; Abilene	N	N	N	N	N	R	1R	5N
Kothmann, Glenn; San Antonio	R	R	R	R	R	N	5R	1N
Longoria, Raul; Edinburg	N	R	R	R	R	N	4R	2N
Mauzy, Oscar; Dallas	R	R	R	R	R	R	R	6R
McKinnon, Mike; Corpus Christi	N	N	N	N	N	N	6N	
McKnight, Peyton; Tyler	N	N	N	N	N	N		6N
Meier, Bill; Euless	N	N	N	N	R	N	1R	5N
Mengden, Walter, Jr.; Houston	N	N	N	N	N	R	1R	5N
Moore, W.T.; Bryan	N	N	N	N	N	N	6N	
Ogg, Jack; Houston	N	N	N	N	N	N	6N	
Patman, William; Ganado	R	R	R	R	R	N	5R	1N
Santiesteban, H. Tati, El Paso	N	N	N	N	N	N	6N	
Schwartz, A.R.; Galveston	N	R	N	N	R	N	2R	4N
Sherman, Max; Amarillo	N	N	N	N	N	N	6N	
Snelson, W.E.; Midland	N	R	R	R	R	N	4R	2N
Traeger, John; Seguin	N	R	R	N	N	R	3R	3N
Wallace, Jim; Houston	N	N	N	N	R	N	1R	5N
Wolff, Nelson; San Antonio	R	R	R	R	R	N	5R	1N

A Note On Sources

There are few books on recent Texas politics. General background information can be found in a number of textbooks and readings books:

Anderson, James; Murray, Richard; and Farley, Edward. *Texas Politics: An Introduction.* New York: Harper and Row, 1971.

Benton, Wilbourn E. *Texas: Its Government and Politics,* (3rd edition). Englewood Cliffs, N.J.: Prentice Hall, Inc., 1972.

Gantt, Fred, Jr.; Dawson, Irving O.; and Hagard, Luther G., Jr., eds. *Governing Texas: Documents and Readings* (2nd edition). New York: Thomas Y. Crowell, 1970.

Jones, Eugene W.; Ericson, Joe E.; Brown, Lyle C.; and Trotter, Robert S., Jr. *Practicing Texas Politics.* New York: Houghton Mifflin, 1971.

Kraemer, Richard H.; and Barnes, Philip W. *Texas: Readings in Politics, Government, and Public Policy.* San Francisco: Chandler Publishing Co., 1971.

MacCorkle, Stuart A.; and Smith, Dick. *Texas Government* (6th edition). New York: McGraw-Hill, 1968.

McClesky, Clifton. *The Government and Politics of Texas* (4th edition). Boston: Little, Brown and Co., 1972.

Nimmo, Dan; and Oden, William. *The Texas Political System.* Englewood Cliffs, N.J.: Prentice-Hall, Inc., 1971.

Books other than textbooks and reading books:

Banks, Jimmy. *Money, Marbles, and Chalk: The Wondrous World of Texas Politics.* Austin: Texas Publishing Co., Inc., 1971.

Conn, Jerry Douglas. *Preston Smith: The Making of a Texas Governor.* Austin and New York: Jenkins Book Publishing Co., Inc., 1972.

Katz, Harvey. *Shadow on the Alamo.* Garden City, N.Y.: Doubleday & Co. Inc., 1972.

Kinch, Sam, Jr.; and Procter, Ben. *Texas Under a Cloud.* Austin and New York: Jenkins Book Publishing Co. Inc., 1972.

Meinig, D.W. *Imperial Texas.* Austin and London: University of Texas Press, 1969.

Peirce, Neal R. *The Megastates of America.* New York: W.W. Norton & Co. Inc., 1972.

Sources other than books:

Newspapers are an invaluable source for anyone studying current Texas politics. Issues of the following papers were examined regularly:

Austin American-Statesman	*Houston Chronicle*
Corpus Christi Caller-Times	*The Houston Post*
The Dallas Morning News	*San Antonio Express-News*
Dallas Times-Herald	*The San Antonio Light*
Fort Worth Star-Telegram	*Texas Observer*

INDEX